Elizabeth Durack

Art & Life

Elizabeth Durack
Art & Life

Selected Writings

Edited by Perpetua Durack Clancy

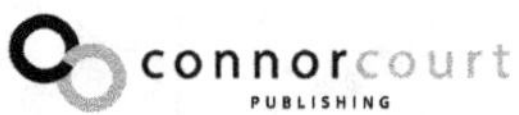

Published in 2016 by Connor Court Publishing Pty Ltd

Connor Court Publishing Pty Ltd
PO Box 7257
Redland Bay QLD 4165
sales@connorcourt.com
www.connorcourt.com
Phone 0497 900 685

ISBN: 978-1-925501-09-4

Cover design: Rosalie Tanner, Graphic Design

Cover Elizabeth Durack at the Athenaeum Gallery, Melbourne, 1961

Photo © courtesy John Cato

Printed in Australia

Art is the solution to a problem
that does not exist until it is solved.

Kimberley Michael Durack

Contents

Prologue

Consciousness comes slowly
slowly swelled by the stealthy streams of our senses –
more than five of them.

A net-work of rivulets interlace
rising almost imperceptibly
in high and hidden places
to ribbon down in cascades
here and there hither and yon.

Some peter out
some gather strength
others cut clear channels.
Some lose their way
and form ox-bows that neither come nor go
over the map –
the great, dry, sprawling map of a life-time –
the while, tributaries converge, gather momentum
peak to flood level, subside.

Then
heavy with mud, lees, detritus, sludge –
fan out in a delta at the very edge of the sea.

But of all the streams that contribute to form
the river
which is the most seminal?

The hungry eye?
the eager ear?
tell-tale nose?
testing tongue or tactile finger?

And what of that
un-nominated, un-mappable extra –
separate, yet part of the whole,
bestowed at birth
gratis
by who knows whose
fun-loving fairy god-mother?

Elizabeth Durack
Perth, October 1987

Introduction

"And what of that un-nominated, un-mappable extra?" – *the impulse that drives certain people to pursue what they must, no matter the cost? While the 'extra' is intangible it can be defined, perhaps, as a gift.*

It was a bountiful gift that Elizabeth Durack received. It combined energy, insight, a sense of proportion and hands that could place, on any surface of her choosing, what she perceived through her eyes, mind and heart. From an early age Elizabeth grasped and ran with her gift. At times she treated it carelessly, even ruthlessly, at other times with great reverence and seriousness.

Early on Elizabeth claimed the Kimberley landscape and the people who were part of it as her own 'corner of nature'.[1] And for years she was known for depicting her corner with empathy and detachment. That corner however was not static – nor was her development as an artist. Over the years, as winds of change swept through the country, movement, turbulence, disquiet became ever stronger features of her work.

Better known as a painter than writer, Elizabeth Durack enjoyed writing. She experimented with several genres although published little. Sorting her estate my brother, Michael, and I saw how extensive were her written works. In addition to uncountable letters (and that's without all those dispersed far and wide over eight decades) the archive contains diaries, essays, travelogues, a memoir, fiction and poetry.

Initially the aim for this book was to present some examples of the different genres that Mother had tackled and hope that, from them, a portrait or profile of the artist would emerge. Then it was suggested that the excerpts could be linked with a brief introduction at the start of each decade. That's how *Art & Life* proceeded and how it has turned out to be a bit of a hybrid – nine-tenths *auto*biography, the rest *bio*graphy – albeit but a fraction of the whole.

Towards the end of her life, as Elizabeth's own river began to 'fan out in a delta at the very edge of the sea', as 'fumes of fancy and fact emerged above and below the horizon' and as 'a result of the [Mabo] verdict national schism, legal polemic and public bewilderment ensued', she distilled a lifetime of learning, of observation and of contemplation into a series of paintings that embodied a new Australian vision.

In a daring leap of imagination and rapprochement, Elizabeth handed over this work to compatriot, Eddie Burrup. He – independent and unencumbered – could express better than she the distress of Australia's old people about the way they themselves, along with traditional customs, were ignored in ill-fated, if well-intentioned, efforts to remedy past and present tragedies. The Durack/Burrup gesture was variously interpreted. The loudest voices denounced Elizabeth claiming she had appropriated Aboriginal culture.

The selections in this book, from the life and the loneliness of a long-distance artist, reveal a story somewhat more complex.

Perpetua Durack Clancy
Djumpakine, Easter 2016

A note on the text

Extracts have been chosen from written works by Elizabeth Durack that span the 1930s through to the year 2000. They include a memoir of the 1920s written in 1987. Most of the selections are manuscripts – in hand-written, typed or digital form held by the estate. Published works are noted in the Chronology. Spelling errors have been corrected, with a few idiosyncratic exceptions. The inconsistent use of upper or lower case for common nouns has been retained – as have pre and post-metric measurements, distances, currency. Cuts within extracts are indicated by ellipses (…). Chapter headings, apart from the 1970s and the year 2000, are lines by Elizabeth Durack from sources recorded in the Endnotes.

Acknowledgements

For most constructive suggestions in bringing *Art & Life* to fruition the largest debt is owed to Michael Clancy and Michael Connor.

I have been fortunate also in receiving support and comment from Margaret Parker, Maureen Smith, Joyce Lebra, Anne Durack Barker, John Durack, Kylie Jennings, Rosalie Tanner, John McDonald and Tom Stephens. I also acknowledge assistance from the staff members of the State Library of Western Australia and the agreement of several private collectors to reproduce their paintings in this book.

Connor Court Publishing responded affirmatively – and within a week! – to my proposal to publish excerpts from mother's writings. The project was off to a good start. It has continued so throughout, for which I thank Anthony Cappello and CCP staff.

Art & Life
is dedicated to my mother and father and uncle Kim

Images

1920s

The Amber Decade

Give or take a year this side or that of it my amber decade is the whole of the 1920s. So it is that everything within that time frame is preserved for me forever intact. It has only to be turned this way or that and I can see all its imprisoned contents with total clarity.

Sometimes two images from different quarters come together and mirror one another. From various angles they will touch off the same auditory response. As the needle falls into the same groove the self-same tune issues forth from Sonora.[2]

Memoir[3]

By the time my memory starts to function consecutively in contrast to scattered points of recall, we are all living – my sister Mary and my four brothers[4] – in our old house '263' at the corner of Victoria Avenue and Adelaide Terrace. And there we stayed all together throughout the whole of the 1920s – a tightly locked, self-relating family group, a closed circuit within the general mechanism of a small isolated city.

The proximity of Christian Brothers College across the road and Loreto Convent just two doors away further ensured our immurement. The children who travelled to school by tram from other parts of the city, let alone those from South Perth who took a ferry were, by comparison with us, globe-trotters …

Our childhood was punctuated by our father's annual migration to the Kimberleys. The biggest events on our family calendar were the day of his departure and that of his return. Our whole ménage, like the bird world, was adjusted to this pattern. Whether Dad was in Perth or not family talk was predominately of the north, of the seasons, the cattle, the country, markets and the blacks.

Thus it is that everything in time and place, that lies within that amber decade is preserved for me forever intact … Ensuing decades disclose themselves with less facility, scattered, dispersed and unconfined they sprawl far and wide over the map of the world, over the width and breadth of the time of our lives …

~

When we first went to school there were no tennis courts. The Convent block, which sloped steeply, ran parallel to ours – and to the Miss Parkers' and the Hayes' and the Quinlans' on the other side. Three flights of wooden steps ran through three terraces that were overgrown with coarse buffalo grass. The gravel playground, shaded with a huge Moreton Bay fig tree, was on a level with Adelaide Terrace.

The Convent, like its neighbours, had once been a private house. In 1897 it was acquired as the first Loreto premises in Western Australia and then the original building was added to and adapted for its new role in life.

A large two-storey classroom wing ran off at right angles to the main building. This contained the big General Assembly room and from it other smaller rooms, both upstairs and down, spread about in various directions. The whole layout of the place was rambling and almost completely anti-architectural – this was part of its charm.

The original old balcony of the house and the verandah beneath it were both enclosed with narrow windows. The lower section was known as 'The Glass Passage'. This was a utilities area. On long tables the nuns polished the silver candlesticks and arranged the flowers for the chapel. Here too a lunch – jugs of weak tea, bread and jam and biscuits – was served for girls who hadn't brought their own. Mary and I went home for lunch and only brought lunch at such time as when the big Spring-clean operation was in progress prior to Dad's return from the north.

The floor of The Glass Passage was covered with undulating lino that rolled around like the sea when a wild wind blew under the door and rattled the window panes in winter time.

Perth can be windy at any time of the year quite apart from the actual wind tunnels that we have created in St George's Terrace after Palace Court and its companions came down and the high risers wedged in their ugly bulks.

Windy in the Spring when the wisteria, which has waited to fall open until it feels safe from winter, sometimes lasts only a few days before being blown to smithereens.

Windy in early summer when the native trees divest themselves in preparation for the deep, deep heat.

Windy in high summer when the little boats tip and flounder in the stiff sou'westerlies on the blue river and the board sailors come to grief in Matilda Bay.

Windy, windy in the winter time when the great surf pounds the beaches and the river sprays high over its retaining wall.

Only in autumn does the wind let up. It is then that the heavenly days of our Indian summer stretch out sometimes till the end of May before the first storm is heralded with the screech of cockatoos and hail stones as big as plums that crack the tiles on our roofs …

The Chapel was situated at the other end of The Glass Passage. This was a large oval room with bay windows that caught the afternoon sun and into which the altar was recessed. Other smaller altars stood on either side – one for Our Lady, one for St Joseph – guardian of the Saviour Child – and one for the Sacred Heart.

Coarse coir matting down the aisle muted alike the patter of small feet or clodhoppers. For those of us unable to gain a *prie-dieu*, it left deep indentations on bare knees the discomfit of which we offered up to the suffering souls in Purgatory.

Mother Dominica's music room also led off from the Glass Passage and this, in turn, went through to the front entrance hall with St Joseph's parlour on one side and a larger reception room on the other. In this chill room, redolent with the smell of floor-polish, the annual music exams were held …

~

The installation of tennis courts – in an old neglected garden beyond the terraces – was a daring project and a major financial step for the

Convent. For years the proceeds from the annual Fete and innumerable raffles were devoted to defraying the cost. Eventually construction of the new tennis courts commenced and soon a wide expanse of gravel was taking on its final shape. Then the river flooded – the biggest flood ever recorded and the rising water threatened the whole undertaking.

We watched the watery encroachment – over the retaining wall, over the Esplanade. Our own back yard was awash but the sandy soil there and the deep hollows left from the recent removal of [pioneer aviator] Major Brearley's hangar helped the water to soak in. But with the newly impacted gravel it was another matter. Crisis loomed.

"Pray," said the nuns. "Pray." So we slipped in and out of the Chapel all day. The girls from South Perth were marooned. The ferries had ceased to run.

When everything appeared lost and the water continued to rise Mother Colombanus was inspired to act. We were just breaking up for the mid-morning recess when we saw her mount a chair in the Assembly room and take down from the wall the picture of Our Lady of Perpetual Succour. Holding it like a shield in front of her and praying aloud she strode outside across the playground and descended the terrace steps. We watched her from underneath the Moreton Bay fig tree. Then we saw her walk through the mud and fling the holy image as far as she could into the water. At first it appeared to float, the wooden frame supporting it like a boat. Then, gradually, it came to rest in one spot and we noticed that the grey water turned a light yellow colour. The flood was subsiding! As from that moment! The very moment that Mother Colombanus threw down the picture – the tennis courts were saved!

Even for a natural sceptic like myself it was impressive evidence of the power of prayer.

(Might this, then, prove to be the ultimate bonus of those eleven years of my Convent immurement – the vague but persisting reassurance that somewhere out there, just beyond the rim of despair, lies always a latent and potential source of hope and help?)

~

Sister Ita told the story at Christian Doctrine time. It was during the Reformation – "the so-called Reformation," said Sister Ita – that a newly established Loreto Convent in the north of England was besieged by a hoard of wicked men who threatened to seize the Tabernacle and destroy the Blessed Sacrament.

They were about to storm the gates and pour into the Convent grounds when suddenly Saint Michael stood before them – a dazzling figure clad in shining armour and brandishing a sword. At the sight of him the blasphemous crowd became terrified and fled in all directions, and any who hesitated were struck blind by the light that blazed from Saint Michael's eyes.

Ever since, on the anniversary of his Feast Day in September, the littlest girl in every Loreto Convent throughout the world carries a picture of the Archangel triumphing over Satan and places it before the altar at evening Benediction.

As I was not only the littlest girl at the Convent in Adelaide Terrace but also the handiest, this joyful commemorative responsibility fell to me.

Mother Dominica opened the big front door. As she did so the wind caught her habit and sent it streaming behind her. She raised her hand to secure her veil.

"Quickly, Bett-bett dear," she said. "We are all waiting for you." In the chapel the nuns were in their *prie-dieux*, the priest stood with his back to them and the light caught the gold-embroidered cross on his chasuble.

The wind bent the flames of the candles and the wax was running down one side. Breathing in the smell of incense, I took up the picture (it was quite heavy) and walked down the aisle as Sister Ignatius played the harmonium.

Tantum ergo Sacramentum
Veneremur cernui,
Et antiquum documentum
Novo cedat ritui …

Afterwards the nuns gathered round and Mother Dominica took me through to the Glass Passage and gave me a sweet red drink. I really didn't want it. I only wanted to get back home. It was nearly dark and the wind was blowing …

~

Sister Ita's infant classroom was on the ground floor at the far end of the big two-storey classroom block. It must once have been part of the outhouses of the original dwelling as it was made of stone while the new wing was brick with wooden verandahs and stairways. We had our own shoe-room. This was also of stone and was some distance from the Big girls' shoe-room further along the verandah …

There were always a few little boys as well as girls in Sister Ita's class. They stayed until they made their First Communion.

Father McMahon is coming to examine us before we make our First Confession. If we pass we will go on to make our First Communion on All Saint's Day on November 1st.

"Mary, hear my Catechism. No, not Chapter 1, I know that. Chapter 2."

"How can we know God on earth?"

"We can know God on earth by seeing the wonderful things he has made …"

"Go on!"

"I can't – I'm stuck."

"… and by learning the truths he has taught."

"Oh dear, I know I shall fail."

But we all passed and Father McMahon told Sister Ita we were exceptionally good and better than the class of boys he had examined the previous day. On asking one of them what was the first thing Moses did after crossing the Red Sea the reply had been: "He dried himself."

1930s

No one knows there's a moon in London[5]

All through her schooling, until matriculation in Perth, Elizabeth lived vicariously in the north. When in 1933, at the age of 17, she went to live on Argyle Downs – the head station of the extensive Kimberley lease held by Connor Doherty & Durack (CD&D) since the 1880s – Elizabeth felt she had reached a long-awaited promised land. Her father Michael Patrick, brother Reg and sister Mary were there along with a large cattle station community. The Depression had peaked and although its effects remained widespread the times were stimulating and productive.

The sisters collaborated on articles and books about life on the stations that were published in The Western Mail *and* The Bulletin. *In May 1936 they sailed for London. From there they travelled widely through England, Ireland, France and Italy. By mid-1937 they were back in Perth.*

Though keen to return, Elizabeth was soon very restless. She was in a quandary about Tom Naughton – a fraught relationship that had started soon after her arrival at Argyle. There was no outlet for her talent in Perth and even had an art school existed then, brief experience at London's Chelsea Polytechnic had left her disenchanted with the academy. So she returned to Argyle – only to find no solution there either.

Desperate about what to do next and short of cash, Elizabeth applied to the Chief Medical Officer of the Northern Territory for a job. Within weeks she was accepted as a trainee nurse at the Darwin Hospital.

PDC

Diary: 29 September 1937, Nurses' quarters, Government Hospital, Darwin

One of these days I'll lie down still
Still and get everything straight.
But just for the present
It will all have to wait.

One of these days I'll stop so quiet
Quiet as a stone
But then I must be far from here
And I must be alone.

I'll lie on the leaves that have left their tree
Or the sand by the rim of the sea.

Diary: 1 November 1937

Free until 1.30 again – went to Rapid Creek last night with Tom Wells after I came off at seven. A place about seven miles from Darwin, very lovely, a salt water stream that joins the ocean. Rather too dark last night because there was no moon but as the tide was out it was good for catching crabs on the rocks with the aid of a torch. Hundreds of them, crab catching is one of my accomplishments and I got several and put them in our handkerchiefs and will draw them this morning if there is time. Should be writing out a General Nursing Lecture but somehow have got that 'simply can't' feeling about doing anything in that line.

10pm: Have never yet felt so completely and utterly disinclined for nursing than I did this afternoon. Became terribly enthusiastic about crabs, would like to go in for them in a big way. "Nurse, old Butler's toe nails and fingernails are half an inch long. You must cut them."

Old Butler had just come in this morning, very old, bearded and partially paralysed with no control over his bladder. The second ward is just a chamber of horrors. Madam Tussaud's is nothing to it. Old Lee in one corner, Anastas in the other, old Sell and now Butler. Old Finn and Delany are alright because they can move around.

Diary: 2 November 1937

Quite an uneventful day but terribly busy. 6.00am – 1.00pm is just a horror particularly the early part, before the day is properly there. The place seems full of the most repulsive, filthy old derelicts one could possibly imagine. They come in from the bush and from Chinatown and from Frog Gully. There are eighteen men in here now and five of them are completely helpless and I really wonder how much longer I can bear to put penises (is that the plural?) into the mouths of bottles for the filthy old creatures that have never had anything touching them except gins. All the same it is better to do this than to change the whole bed. Poor old Butler is one of them. His right leg is stiff and huge and red and oozing. I asked him how he felt. He told me through his enormous growth of beard in his weird high-pitched voice: "I feel .. I feel .. I don't know how I feel .. I can't describe how I feel .. I feel .. rotten."

Skipped lunch so I could come over to my crabs and anyway having seen food around all the morning one's inclination to partake of any oneself completely evaporates.

Diary: 4 *November 1937*

The tide is far out and it's hot as hot with the crickets singing all the time on the one note and Bertha's cloths flap-flapping on the lines.

Arrived over to lunch quite bright and spry and had a whole bucket of cold water thrown over me by Matron [Ashburner]. I had arranged with NW [another Probationer] to take her 1.30 –9.30pm shift if she took my 6.00-1.00 and 5.00-7.00am which she was quite agreeable about. It appears though that Probationers may not thus arbitrarily take time-tables into their own hands as was made quite clear to me in just so many words, and a few more, by Matron. I felt quite put out for exactly half an hour but by the time I had given out the mixtures the old a-plumb [sic] had returned and I saw how funny the whole situation was and would have loved my brother [Reg] to have been there during the dressing-down period. He would have endorsed most heartily all that Matron had to say to me …

I am not working at all well now. The old willingness is going out of the feet and hands and all my fingers do all the time is itch to get at pencil and paper. If only I could wander around at peace and under a cloak of invisibility I would indeed be happy, but all these scribblings that I've got here are done under the utmost difficulties. I keep my sketch book in my pocket and have to shove it away every time I hear professional footsteps approaching and if I do get seen with pencil and paper I just assume an expression of grave concentration and make a show of counting the patients and jotting down who is on a full diet and who on a light etc. These quarters are in deadly silence now all the Sisters are in bed and the sound of my pen seems like a big noise. There's no getting out of the 5.30 turnout in the morning so I guess it's time I went to bed.

Letter: Elizabeth Durack in Darwin to Reg Durack in Sydney, 6 November 1937

Darling Brother

I have just been standing out in the pouring rain so if there are big blobs on this page you will know they are not caused from 'sorrow, crown of sorrow remembering happier days …' because really the smell of this wet ground and the sound on the roof and the way the gutters are running with a loud trickling noise when the down-pour eases off for a few moments, brings old Ivanhoe [Station, East Kimberley] so poignantly back to me that I feel I want to yell to all the good nurses and give off a bit of what's going on inside me. I just hate to think what it'll be like at 70, because at 22 what I want to say a 100 times is: "do you remember …?" But I'll skip it because of course you do anyway and the three of us [Reg, Mary and Elizabeth] know that what ever else becomes dim with time those days of ours together at Ivanhoe will always stand out clear and sharp.

Before I started this I debated with myself whether it were better to write you a good long letter when I was really in the letter-writing mood or a short quite imperfect one as I feel this will be as it is written with half a mind (I am sorry to say) on getting flat out on the old toil-wracked back. But I thought me that if ever you felt similarly I know what I should like to get, viz. the short and imperfect letter in place of a delayed good one.

When your letter arrived I should have saved it till I got back to the quiet of my room, which would have been about an hour or so later (as I was off at seven that day), but my impatience got the better of me. So while I was waiting for the cook to prepare two light diets I ducked round behind the kitchen on the cement verandah affair where the washing-up goes on (and on and on), and which commands quite the most glorious view in Darwin, and tore open your envelope (Q 1, parse and analyse – "I ducked round behind the kitchen" – principal sentence …). I am glad, dear, that your parsing and analysing of yourself still goes on.

This must eventually lead you to the work you will really settle on. No, I don't think it's 'blind optimism' on your part at all. There must be, and is, something in you that causes this festering and that will in the end come to some definite head (what a horrible sentence. It is like something twice as horrible I saw this morning being cut out).

I was most interested to hear of your half-mapped idea of the medical profession as a foundation and want to know any more, even trivial details, of how you might be able to work this. I am glad you said 'as a foundation' because just to be a doctor is about quarter as bad as just to be a nurse.

I am more than ever at sea about myself and wonder whether I am just an insincere hypocrite or a good actress. Darling brother, you would laugh to see me. I am *so* docile, *so* obedient, *so* eager (on duty), but oh I do hate this work. I'm not a scrap interested in what goes on inside the body or the various messes that come out of it, but its outline, against the light, that's another matter. Spent a couple of weeks plunged in utter gloom, from which I have now emerged, to find myself making sketches all round the hospital of the terrible, ugly, but utterly fascinating old atrocities I have to nurse. I had a few spare moments just when all the dinners were given out and was doing a three-quarters length of an old boy, who is paralysed, when along comes Matron: "What ever are you doing nurse?" She sounded and looked too surprised at my pencil and sketchbook to be cross but all the same I must be more watchful in future. These rubber-soled shoes the Sisters and Matron wear (and of course ourselves, but the nurses don't count) are a curse to me at present. I have a nerve in my right eye that won't stop jumping from listening because of course when on duty we are on duty and the idea of doing anything else for those eight hours is utterly out of the question. But get them I must, and will, and anyway what could be more utterly blissful than to get the sack.

I had a letter from dear old Mary the other day. She sounds very happy and utterly a-plumb [sic] with life as usual. It's only you and I who are the mugs, Bids [family name for Reg], and get ourselves into such uncomfortable states of mind and body for no real or tangible reason.

Doris passed her exams. I haven't seen her since she was here in hospital with a badly burnt hand for a few days. She is awfully pretty. She and Dr Cook [CE (Mick) Cook, Chief Medical Officer] are still very close friends. It really is rather a remarkable affair. As Doll so aptly put it: "If he had have dropped Doris, Darwin would have received her with open arms and said 'poor Doris' but the fact that she's held him all this time, that's the part Darwin can't get over."

Dear I loved the photo, thank you! It doesn't flatter but still it's Bids, dear, dearer, dearest old Bids and looking so nice and natty too and who's your companion? or doesn't he count? I have it on my dressing table and the maid was very interested the other morning when she was sweeping out my room and wanted to know if it was my boyfriend. "Better than all your boy-friends," I assured her. "My brother!"

Good-bye dearest, can you hear the thunder? It's just running all over the sky – north, south, east and west. A sort of continuous angry grumbling. Yes, dear, of course I remember the weather at the time of Flo's wedding, those are the things we remember, aren't they?

love from Elizabeth

Old Mr Ronan told me to send you his kind regards and appreciated very much that letter you wrote him before you left about his son. He is a dear old boy and is always picking out interesting articles and giving them to me and I always have to give them back unread because I never have time but he doesn't know so it matters less. Have you heard anything of Tom [Naughton]? Where he is, why or for how long?

Telegram to Elizabeth Durack in Darwin, 20 November 1937, sent from Melbourne Stock Exchange Post Office

REGRET TO INFORM YOU TOM HAD CAR ACCIDENT PASSED AWAY LAST NIGHT PRIVATE BURIAL MONDAY – FRANK NAUGHTON

Interview: Film Australia 1997, Elizabeth Durack and Robin Hughes[6]

Elizabeth Durack: *Touching on another aspect of my life, which I won't go into deeply, I – and it's almost a cliché – but I had a desperately unhappy love affair, early, in the north. And I think it sort of shattered me to a large extent, so that everything else was irrelevant to a large extent, you know.*

But you know, that was what made me perhaps dislike London and being abroad so much, was that I really didn't want to go away. But I was committed to it by that time, I was committed to it.

I can remember the boat pulling out from the Wyndham jetty, and looking at my tears dropping down into the muddy waters of the Gulf. But I thought I'd come back. I thought I'd come back, and that, you know, that everything would work out. But I never saw him again. He was killed.

Robin Hughes: *How?*

Elizabeth Durack: *It was a motor car accident. He was a wild boy, a very wild boy. But wonderful charm, and wonderful.*

Robin Hughes: *How did it affect the way you looked at things?*

Elizabeth Durack: *Perhaps the whole of my life is the answer to that. The whole of my life since then is the answer to that. Including marriage and lovers and friends …*

Diary: 27 November 1937

Better to have waited till today before I picked this up again. It came on Monday afternoon.

Thank God for my nursing and the filthy old men and the impossibly bad patients that nearly exhaust me with their demands and thank God for the people all around me. Thank God that my hands are busy because when I stop … Enough now – sometime I shall start from when I first heard that voice coming round the verandah at Argyle with Reg. I was in Mary's room and I remember thinking, "That's not a local voice …"

Diary: 3 February 1938, Myrtle Fawcett's home, Fannie Bay, Darwin

Well, off to Tenimbar [Island] in the morning with Eric Foxton and Myrtle Fawcett in the *Aroetta.* Oh I hated having to tell the Matron I was leaving. Told her on Monday morning. Went round to her office and, swallowing hard, said: "I came to tell you Matron that I am thinking of leaving." She was quite surprisingly nice about it.

I told her that I had been offered this other job in the Library (this diary's so behind that I haven't said anything about this but it's all fixed up for the end of the month) and that I was wanting to go on this lugger trip with Eric and Myrtle. She thought the notice rather short. However, things have moved rapidly since then. Spent the afternoon rushing all round Darwin. First to the Customs where Myrtle and I signed on as crew among about 30 Malays, such fun, and then I showed my passport and then round to Jolly's where I bought a bigger suitcase. Then went round and saw the Wells. They lent me a couple of books to read.

Diary: 4 February 1938, on the Arafura Sea

On board the *Aroetta* ! tossing about on the pale green sea with little bits of spray flying up on either side. Left Darwin at five minutes to ten, the jetty lined with the friends of the Malays we have on board. We climbed down a little perpendicular ladder on to the boat. It's swaying round a lot, I think, but Eric says it's calm so it must be.

Diary: 5 February 1938

It's today but I'll go on about yesterday otherwise I'll get all mixed up. Well, Myrtle and I spent most of the day in a more or less drugged state on our deck chairs not daring to move for fear of the worst while

Eric sprang all round the ship, up the rigging and along the splashed decks and kept exclaiming how lucky we were to have it so calm though of course we were bound to strike "a bit of weather" sooner or later. Myrtle made a gallant effort now and again and picked up her [fishing] line for a while but had to drop back very soon.

We sighted Bathurst Island about two in the afternoon and by four were running along parallel to the coast and then down Apsley Channel which separates Bathurst from Melville Island. I had no idea the islands were so close. The Channel is only a little wider than Suez. Four natives came out in a long boat, their strong black bodies sharp against the still lead grey of the water and the sky. They were smoking pipes made from crabs' claws and bailed the water out of their boat with a big shell.

As *Aroetta* drew close there were shouts and yells of delight from the dozens of little red-saronged black figures who raced along the beach. One tiny little mite who couldn't keep up with the bigger ones flopped down on his little fat bottom and yelled.

Father [McGrath][7] and Brother [Smith] were working on the *St Francis* and they helped us out of the dinghy and welcomed us to Bathurst Island. We had rather thought we might go on that evening but one glimpse of the place decided us to stay. The beach is lined with native humpies under the coconut palms and behind are the mission buildings, the priests' house, the nuns' quarters, the chapel etc. I have never seen so many beautiful trees – mango trees & limes & frangipani & mandarin & bushes of snow-white gardenias & poincianas.

We had a shower. Myrtle and I debated whether or not to wear our kimonos on the walk from our house, where we were to sleep, to the shower room, quite a little distance along the path by the sweet potato garden carefully barbed-wired in. "We live in no fool's paradise about the blacks," said Father McGrath.

There is an elongated pump handle, a pipe which runs up with a showerhead in the bathroom. A couple of lubras swing on to it and the water gushes out. Marvellous cool soft water. We had our dinner with the priest and the two brothers. There was the usual little scuffle over Grace. Potato soup and salmon patties; mashed potato and tinned spaghetti; rice milk pudding and stewed peaches & tea.

It was the first Friday of the month so there was Benediction in the little wooden chapel. And there was St Joseph & the Virgin & The Little Flower taken all this way and planted in this strange remote place. The *Oh Salutaris* burst forth in positively deafening volley of sound. We sat in the back row and it must have been agony for the little black kids not being able to stare at us but they had obviously been told that they must not do this as when one would twist her head and look at us with her enormous black eyes she was promptly twisted round by one of her companions who, in the twisting round process, would manage to get in a look at us herself.

We sat on deck chairs in the open with the stars brilliant above and two big coconut palms, one a little bigger than the other, a semi-circle of a hundred little girls in four rows dressed in red turkey-twill skirts. The light from the lamps arranged at either end made their eyes glow and glitter and little brown bodies shine. And they *sang for us*. Every conceivable song from *Who Killed Cock-Robin* to *Daisy Bell* and back again to *Fideste*.

Letter: Elizabeth Durack, Fannie Bay, Darwin to Reg Durack on Auvergne Station, 24 May 1939

Darling Brother

I have just been enquiring about the time *Maroubra* sails and they tell me Saturday morning so I shall have this ready to go thereby. As you see I am still in Darwin and will be until the end of the month. I am staying with Myrtle [and Jim Fawcett] and have been since I arrived on the 6th. If we had been able to get a radio to you we were going to send you this wire: Definitely *not* small boat, concentrate on push-bike, caravan or perambulator.

love Marabetic – from which you can gather.

Yes, but the river was a dream of beauty Reg – that evening when we left you waving from the top of the truck. Perhaps it was the sadness of parting that added an extra poignancy to the beauty and mystery of the scene, the scene as unreal yet alive as a fairy tale, purple hills and crimson earth, fluttering white wings and glass-clear water, the warm golden reds of sunset and the cool amethyst depths of the sky around the full moon. You saw it too and I've seen it a thousand times but from the loft of the *Maroubra* I felt like a stranger viewing it all for the first time.

The next afternoon we were some hours on the lifeless silt at the bottom of the Victoria River and then after mooning around, paddling in a few little puddles, taking a few snaps and just beginning to get a bit bored, we heard a roar. And far in the distance we saw the water racing towards us like a brown wall. In about ten minutes we were afloat again and all the unevenness of the riverbed was made even again. The tide was so strong it sometimes swung the boat right round, by this time the river had broadened out enormously, a great stretch of water, vaster than the Cambridge Gulf, with the same low craggy red sandstone bordering the edges. We sat on the deck late that night though everything had not quite the same sting as the night before. I wrote a long song in the moonlight –

I'm glad the awning is hiding the moon
Because it is so bright –
I know it's round and yellow
I know its light is white
The ash of a thousand smokes
The dregs of a thousand beers
The urge of a thousand kisses
The salt of a thousand tears …

It is endless – goes on with a similar verse and chorus alternating a thousand times.

The next two days were what gave us the inspiration for the wire we intended sending you. Miss Underwood, who we soon called Olive, was terribly sick. Mary and I were sick but not bad. Darwin Harbour was a welcome haven. Myrtle gave us a great welcome when we arrived up here on Saturday morning. Horry was not here but there were numerous telegrams from him, he had been waiting in Wyndham. Naturally Mary was very anxious to get to him. [Mary had married pioneer aviator HC Miller in December 1938.] After several delays she eventually got away on (I think it was) Thursday 11th. I have had a couple of wires from her since her arrival in Perth. She is well except for a cold and is getting some clothes made to fill the need. Also she says (in her letter to Myrtle) that all family and friends are alarmed at the rapid development and thinks twins imminent (?) but she has not seen a doctor yet. I got one scrappy letter from Kim which I will enclose.

On my arrival here I got an urgent wire from Dad asking me to wait and help him entertain the Gowries [Governor-General, Lady Gowrie, and party] when they go through Argyle in July. I was far from keen on the idea but eventually wired him saying I would wait here till the end of the month and see him. He should be around on Wednesday, if he does as I ask him.

This may be the first news you get about Frank Clancy [a journalist whom Reg had known in Sydney and suggested Elizabeth contact when she was there] and me who are going to get married. Frank sent me an article the other day to forward to you which I will be, if I can find it. He says: 'It is excellent in analysis even though Mr Trotsky's remedy is only another brand of Fascism.'

Don't ask me how all this happened because I'm not too sure myself. There were a couple of letters here from Frank when I arrived. We sent a couple of wires and he wired: "*When and where do you want Grace said – Sydney, Melbourne or Perth?*" And last week he wrote to Mother and Dad asking if we could get engaged. So far I have not heard from Dad but am hoping for a wire or a letter shortly. If I get one before this mail closes I'll tell you. Just where Grace is going to be said is rather vague at the moment. Frank says: "All these things are in your hands, of course." But heavens, I don't know how to go about planning a thing like a marriage, so I'll write and tell him that unethical though it is, he'd better do the planning and I'll do the falling in.

He tells me Abbey [his older sister] leaves for America in June and also said he would like her to be there. I said in my last letter that as I'd be at Argyle until well into July I thought that probably after Abbey's return in six month's time and after Pettigrew's arrival would be the best time but I don't know. Anyway, it'll all work out, I suppose.

You must now spring to pen and paper and write Frank a letter just explaining implicitly that I'm a Bad Lot and to steer clear of me before it's too late. He'll be expecting such a letter from you and I have warned him to, at least I think I warned him in my last letter, I meant to, if I didn't.

To tell you the truth, Reg, the events of the last couple of weeks remind me somewhat of [head stockman] Sid Byers' comment on our doings of Xmas Day: "None of us knew what the hell we were doing."

I am writing this after lunch and the cross-outs mean that I'm beginning to miss my siesta. Myrtle is asleep. She sends you fond love. Speaks often of you and hopes you are well and wishes you were here too. The Abbotts [Darwin Administrator] are away. Aubrey comes back tomorrow. Darwin is more unbelievable than ever. In fact, if it wasn't for Frank it would be unbearable – God what people! But strange, the District Naval Officer, Walker, I nearly died when he said last night: "Lord, have I got to spout lies to the little bastards in the morning about the glory of the British Empire etc." I got him aside and discover he is almost one of us. I am going round at 5 this evening to have a talk to him and his wife.

Pam and little Jimmy have been asking each other for the past week: "Pam, do you know your three things?" Pam: "I love my country the British Empire, I will serve her King, King George the 6th, I will obey her laws for the glory of the Empire."

This morning all the kids, white, black and brindle, were presented with a bag of lollies by the Government under the auspices of the Victoria League and given a holiday having made the town (the welkin?) ring to the strains of the song: "Three cheers for the Red, White and Blue."

Last night I went with the Matron of the compound Mrs Gribbon (Myrtle's sister) to see *Snow White* with 60 half-caste kids. The tiny ones went to sleep; the bigger ones went nearly mad with excitement. The last time I saw it was in Sydney with Frank and his girlfriend. I only saw Frank twice without her.

Frank has finished his book and is getting it published. He writes: "When I mentioned *the Job* I meant *book*, Elizabeth. I don't like calling it a book until it is published. It was a job to me, it was a gaol, out of which I had to escape. I don't know whether you will like it or not. I don't know whether anyone will like it. Its ending has annoyed the publisher but to alter it would be to shatter its unity. However, that is all right, as he thinks there is money in it – which I doubt." I would like to send you his letters only I want them myself. I will show them to you if I see you at Argyle when I'm there. Hell, have I got to go back to Argyle? …

This is a nice paragraph so I'll quote it to you. I had told him that I didn't warm up to Villon's poetry: "It's a poor translation of Villon, Elizabeth, although I liked some of the ballads and a few scattered lines in the testaments. Swinburne and Henley both made better jobs of the sections they did but probably you would not care for their versions either. I use poetry as a kind of opium and my opinions on it are biased by that fact. For instance, I dislike the polished and perfect verse of AE Housman because he gives you his images in compact form, to be taken or rejected, as correct and as external as a draughtsman's sketch. Villon, like Thompson and Blake, evokes no series of fixed images, but invites one into a world of horror and beauty and squalidness, but a world in which one obtains a harmony with Being itself. Transitory and subjective, the harmony is exquisite at the moment, and in moments of remembrance. Such lines of Thompson's as:

Come you living or dead to me, out of the silt of the Past,
With the sweet of the piteous first, and the shame of the shameful last?
Come with your dear and dreadful face through the passes of Sleep,
The terrible mask, and the face it masks – the face you did not keep?

Or Keats':

Magic casements, opening on the foam of perilous seas, in faery lands forlorn.

Goodbye for the present, dearest Brother. I am having 'a good time' in Darwin – have some lambs fresh from Duntroon to amuse myself with. I'll leave this open.

Ever your loving,
Elizabeth

Letter continues, 8.00am: Friday 26 May

Must finish this off this morn, dear boy. Myrtle is sending you a few papers. I looked for something to send you but found nothing so I forward you this *Vogue* – the magazine for *Mesdames Les Bourgeoisie.* It is very interesting and very beautiful. Read the article on page 32. The last paragraph is interesting, such complacency is a little pathetic. My impulse is to pack up all these beautiful things and beautiful creatures and unpack them again when the mess is cleaned up, but it would only be cruel. It is that precious hedged in feeling of their privileged state that gives them their a-plumb [sic], without it they would be lost. What a shame, Reg, we'll never live to see the new *Vogue.* You and I will only see the face of tomorrow which is going to be nothing like as lovely as these here today. There is no news I can give you. I know considerably less about world affairs than I did at Argyle listening in to the various news with old Pal [Tom Naughton] and laughing over them and reconstructing the bla. To the people of Darwin, Darwin is the world and the universe, *c'est tout.* My God, what a collection of people, I have them all in my mind. I may make use of them someday – it is so interesting but oh, it is so depressing.

I'll send you a couple of photos of me. I took a lot to send to Frank. Frank sent me a lot of him and Abbey and of course, Clancy fashion, sister Pat too and numerous friends for good measure.

I am waiting for a wire from Dad. He got bruised, don't panic, when he fell down the other day. A car knocked him down in the Terrace. I don't think he can be too bad as Mother wrote me a page and a half before she mentioned it. I hope he's alright. I don't know yet whether he'll be coming round here or whether I'll meet him in Wyndham next Thursday. I can't read all this over. Did I tell you Myrtle is coming to Argyle to help me with the Gowries. As soon as they go I will probably be off to Sydney. Mother says "come home", but no, I hate Perth. It is an insufferable place. I just go rotten in Perth. No more news from Kim on Wednesday. Myrtle and I go to another dance tomorrow night. I have been trying to make my blue voile wearable by sewing a lot of velvet flowers round the neck but I don't think it's any good. I can't worry too much though as I am easily the best looking girl here so I always have 'a reeeeel good time' at dances. Goodbye, darling. This is a very unimaginative letter, no mention or questions of yourself, dear. How are you, and Auvergne and the men and the blacks. You know what I want to hear. It all has become suddenly a bit misty only very temporarily though. My heart is in the north because it is such a hateful place. Darwin is a silly place. I can't stand it. God what a collection of people. Hope I see you in July.

love from your always loving sister,

Elizabeth

PS Myrtle sends love again. Hopes to see you when she flies over in July. Gowries due Wyndham 9th July. Dad arranges motor transport to Argyle and they stay till Wednesday. Kim has some comments on this ...

How is the bullock muster going? Remember me to Sid and Scotty and old Jack. I wonder is there anything I have forgotten to tell you. Letters are terrible things. Saw Geoff Towers. He didn't know who was going to inspect your 'drome.

Cheerio dearest – love,
Elizabeth

Letter: Elizabeth Durack on Ivanhoe to Frank Clancy in Sydney, 16 June 1939

Dear Frank

It is no use trying to write with so much talk going on around me but the lights are getting dimmer and if I don't write tonight I will miss the plane in the morning. The talkers are Daddy and Reg and Kim and a drover and the manager here and Dr Steinberg [Isaac Steinberg, leader of the Jewish Territorialist Movement] and a dreadfully scientific young man from the WA University and of course every now and again I have to have something to say too. Dr Steinberg is up here to see if the north would do for Jewish refugees. He is a m . . . no, not marvellous – that's hats and Gary Cooper – I think he is a wonderful old boy. He was Minister for Justice in Lenin's government and knows a terrible lot. He thinks what you think about Trotsky. I think he is an anarchist and is very upset about what happened to them in Spain. Oh well, you'll be glad to know I'm nothing, only I suppose even if one's nothing one's something, it's very difficult. Anyway, whatever it is, I'm not it.

Your letter came this morning – dear, it was wonderful. I was dying to know something about you – you were a long time telling me. I am thrilled with your brief autobiography and the news of your book. I am longing to read it. You must be feeling pleased with yourself. I am glad you are vain. I hope you always remain so because so long as you are vain I shan't feel sorry for you. Once I feel sorry for anyone it's terrible. I let Daddy read your letter – you don't mind? – he was very impressed about the book. He takes a lot of notice about other people's opinions. He also said: "humm – he doesn't send you his love." He thought this a little unethical. Am sure he would have liked to see a few extravagant phrases, he would have thought them fitting.

Oh golly, Frank, the Doctor has started writing beside me in Hebrew(?). He starts from the right and goes to the left. I saw one of his notebooks lying round yesterday and thought I'd just glance through it but it was hieliogriphics [sic]. I told Kim and he said no it wasn't, it was German. I thought Kim was above a thing like that but it was Hebrew because I just asked him. He is a vegetarian and is slowly starving to death in this country where beef is eaten three times a day and meat sandwiches for morning and afternoon tea. His tie fell into some tomato sauce and I said I'd fix it for him. It was a nice pale grey and when I ironed it, it went an ugly brown and I don't know what to do because I'm not game to give it back to him. What would you do in a case like that? Perhaps he's forgotten all about it. I hope so.

I very much wish I could talk to you. What I should do is wait until everyone goes to bed and then write you a long letter but looks like everyone's here for the night. Reg is getting a bad time in an argument at the moment. In ordinary conversation you'd think the old Doctor could hardly speak English but the moment he starts an argument he comes into his own. I'm glad Reg is being beaten; he gets too much of his own way. It is rather funny. I just winked at the earnest young scientist but as he didn't wink back I feel rebuked.

Frank, I like the idea of living near Sydney, but out of it, very much. I asked Reg what that would mean and he said "chickens" – but it wouldn't, would it? When I leave here I shall go and see Mother in Perth but I have an idea that Daddy likes someone to say "Great Living Scott" to several times a day so I may wait and go down with him in August.

Myrtle is coming to Argyle in July and will probably stay till the end of the month. She wants a picnic so we will be doing some travelling round, I suppose. I have had a good few picnics lately so am feeling rather blasé about them but it will be nice having her here.

I was interested to hear about Lochaver and Greenvale. I suppose Pat is sorry to leave the former. Greenvale sounds lovely. What about Kurrajong, you were talking about going there before, weren't you? Is it a town, or what? I can't see a map around so can't find out.

Mother and Daddy will probably come over with me to Sydney whenever we like. I told Daddy I didn't want to be married in a church and he nearly hit the roof. "But Great Living Scott, my dear girl, you told me Frank was a Catholic. Surely he wants to be married in a church?" I gulped and said something placating as quick as I could. Dam [sic] – it seems to be everyone else's business but our own.

Tomorrow morning we leave for Argyle. We would have left days ago but it rained, most extraordinary for June. The dear old Doctor thinks he is having a terrifying time, the roads leave him speechless. Before he left Wyndham Reg heard him saying to himself: "Courage!" but he would probably think nothing of a few bombs. Reg flies back to Wyndham on the same plane as this letter. He is writing to you but just when, I don't quite know. I started a letter to Abbey but Kim says it wouldn't get to Sydney by the 20th so I'll finish it and send it and it may get there before she sails.

Goodnight, Frank – there was something I was going to say but I've forgotten what it was.

Elizabeth

Oh yes, I'm glad you feel like that about the novel, no, don't get a regular job. We can live on wild honey alone – without the locusts. Kim took a movie of me wading into a pool and eating some wild passion fruit. It was growing all round the edge of the pool in the hills about three miles away. I'll address Abbey's letter c/- The Australia Hotel as I don't know where she will be in Sydney.

1940s

Country so gloriously and naturally endowed[8]

The 1940s, for Elizabeth, was a decade of intense activity in both her personal and professional life. Living in Sydney after marriage to journalist Frank Clancy and corresponding daily with Mary in Perth, Elizabeth illustrated and supervised the publication of several books including the sisters' best known co-production: The Way of the Whirlwind *(Consolidated Press, 1941). I was born in Sydney the year* Whirlwind *came out; Michael in Brisbane in 1943. Children and wartime civilian travel restrictions did not prevent Elizabeth returning north, landing in on her ever-tolerant brothers Reg on Auvergne and Kim and Bill at Carlton Reach, Ivanhoe. For most of the decade Elizabeth lived peripatetically in Sydney, Alice Springs, Hermannsburg, Beagle Bay, Darwin, Brisbane, Melbourne, Broome and on East Kimberley cattle stations. Immediately after the War, with a mixed blessing from Frank and cooperation from Mary and Horry who had a house in Broome, she flew from Melbourne to Broome taking Michael and me with her. Soon after arriving she set to work on long-gestating, ambitious plans to capture in paint the essence of Broome, its past and its present. Subject matter included many of the town's cosmopolitan inhabitants, people she saw (contrary to much contemporary opinion) as the vanguard of a positive, bright future for Australia.*

Time & Tide, *Elizabeth's first solo exhibition, consisted of almost 100 paintings. It opened in Perth in August 1946 and travelled on to Melbourne and Sydney. The work itself and the ideas expressed were both shocking and stimulating for most of those who viewed it. Art historian Bernard Smith, who opened the Sydney exhibition at the David Jones Gallery on 31 January 1947, said: "Miss Durack has produced her own language … and extended our field of vision."*[9]

Earlier the same day a review had appeared in The Sydney Morning Herald *by its art critic, Paul Haefliger. It was a savage review – one that might have prompted a talent with less drive and confidence, to throw away her paints and give up entirely. Yet this review (along with other unhelpful ones over the years) somehow proved a stimulus. Elizabeth's principal inspiration remained the northern landscape, its people and culture and, by the end of her life, she had held over 60 solo exhibitions, participated in many group shows and received significant acknowledgment for her artistic achievements.*

PDC

Letter: Elizabeth Durack in Sydney to Frank Clancy in Melbourne, 1 February 1947

Dearest Frank

I am very glad you rang this morning and on going to the Bank I collected your express letter which was very nice. It must have arrived yesterday but I only called at the Bank once about 9.30am.

Well dear I know you are anxious to know about everything and although not very much in the mood for writing, will try to tell you. Saturday afternoon and the trams roaring hollowly down Pitt Street. Have had a bit of a sleep, as a matter of fact my mind is not on this letter but turning over the best way to tackle everything on Monday.

However – I woke early yesterday morning and went straight round to Wynyard to get the *Herald.* It is hard to describe how I felt on reading that criticism, I think sheer anger was the uppermost sensation. I went weak with anger and then the blood seemed to come pouring back and I could have killed the man if he had have been near me. The unfairness of it, the sheer meanness, the spitefulness and the — heavens.

I couldn't eat any breakfast though tried to reason with myself, take it easy now, what does it matter – you've had a lot of good critics, what harm can one bad one do you? What? So you can't take it? Little girl has to be praised all the time or she gets cross – but no amount of reasoning with myself made any difference. It was not right, the leading paper of NSW was circulating in thousands for people to read that I was hanging 'amateurish' pictures, that I didn't know how to draw, that I was walking before I could crawl – I – me – Elizabeth, who waited 30 years before she dared put a picture in a frame, hang it on a wall, price it with the conviction that the price was only a 10th of what it would be in 50 years time. So my very timidity, my very hesitancy, my modesty and reserve, were being used as tools to wound me, not only wound but utterly annihilate, if this critic had his way. As for the reference of plagiarism of Matisse, I don't so much as make comment.

I looked up the Pink Pages and went to an address in Hunter Street, a solicitor called Maurice McGrath. I told him the story and said I wondered if the artist had any case in such a situation. He was a nice chap (one hand missing, poor fellow). He considered it a while, asking value of pictures hanging etc. Said he would need time to think about it but rang then a barrister friend of his. Gave him the story over the phone (clever how concisely and accurately he stated things in a few sentences). The barrister's reply was he feared the artist in such cases had no standing whatsoever, that unless it could be proved that there was *personal malice* behind the critic, or unless the critic had said the pictures were *not worth the money asked* the artist had no kick coming. Apparently a number of people have tried to get a case against Neville Cardus [British music critic] for similar reasons and have always failed. This seemed to make sense to me and although I was tempted to see another solicitor I have abandoned that idea. I paid Mr McGrath 10/6, thanked him and left – decent fellow – intelligence.

I then got Paul Haefliger's address from *The Herald*. (He has no office there, lives and works at 36 Ocean Avenue Double Bay.) I took a taxi straight out. A quiet, tree-lined street off the main road towards the Harbour. A big house (40 – 45 years old) apparently divided somehow. I was pretty nervous. I asked the taxi to wait. I didn't know what the set-up was at all. Vaguely in the back of my mind I thought he was a bachelor living alone or with his mother. In the back of my mind I seemed to want to hit him, on the head, but I realised it was a bad thing to assault a person in his own home. I knocked at the door. A rather pretty little woman [Jean Bellete] opened it, rather arty in slacks. (I hear she is a Tasmanian, quite a good artist.) Actually there was something nice about her, she acted well, she asked me in, said she would get Paul. She was nervous but was trying to act well and I admired her for it. I sent the taxi away. Paul came in and his wife brought some coffee and withdrew. Two pretty big rooms opening into each other. Bookcase choco-block of books on European art, a bit of sculpture, some paintings. I took him quietly but accused him of not looking at the pictures. I was at the gallery all the time. He came in, made a few remarks (not about my pictures) to Tatlock Miller who was also there (I rather liked him), flounced down the gallery, took off his coat, settled himself comfortably, got out a book of synonyms and did some writing. (This is apparently his method – no doubt because he has no office – to do the stuff in the gallery then types it and hands it in.) He was there a good while, certainly. Of course I did not approach him for fear of being importunate. He did not say a word to me. Picked up a couple of prints from Miss Stell (?) and blew off. He certainly never read the Brochure (he admitted this to me, said he read it that morning only) nor the Catalogue. He tried to be nice to me. Tried to turn the conversation constantly to make a flippancy of it: "Was I too cruel then …? Will they come after me with a pop-gun …?" (some reference to the family). However, overall I got what I wanted: he did not look at the pictures, he did not know there were drawings there, he did not read the Brochure, he had never seen another line I'd drawn, nor ever heard my name. It was like talking to Hector Fuller [manager of Rosewood, East Kimberley] the way he contradicted himself at every turn. Actually by this time I was feeling a bit sorry for him, damn it, and I don't want to. I want to keep feeling wild with him and do my best to kick him out of his job which I intend to this week. He sought to destroy me and I shall not rest until I have injured him in the same way as I consider false and stupid criticism can injure me at the present time. He was of course taken aback when I told him about MacDonald and Turnbull [two Melbourne art critics] and the thought came to me that serious as this whole business is to me it is more serious to these dopes and twerps, they will still be squabbling and spinning, when I'm the hell —

But it was getting late. I had arranged to meet Abbey, Bernard Smith, Mr Greenwich (from UNO – Will Ashton couldn't come) at the Australia [Hotel] at 12.30. By the time Haefliger had accompanied me to the main road, insisted on buying a *Sun* for me (Tatlock Miller's review: "Ah, he was kind to you, I was too cru–el." Silly bastard, as if I want people to be *kind* to me – Jesus) it was 20 to one. I got a taxi. Flew back to this hotel. Rang Abbey waiting outside the dining room, changed and dressed far too hurriedly and got there about quarter past one. Bernard Smith thought it was a terrifically daring thing to do, I hadn't considered such an aspect. Abbey was worked up too and thought the papers should know. Bernard Smith really hates him, or I don't know about hates him but completely disagrees with his whole approach to art criticism.

It was 3 before we got to the gallery. Quite a good crowd. Will Ashton was terribly upset about Haefliger. He said it was serious, a calamity, an insult to himself ("As if David Jones would go to all the trouble of hanging pictures if I did not think them good"). He had been sure that *this* time Haefliger would give an enthusiastic review, for so long he has apparently been attacking competent technicians on their lack of spirit. Ashton was *sure* this show was into his hands. When I told him I'd gone to see Haefliger he said: "Good for you. He is a coward and a bully. I have been speaking with Lloyd Jones and he considers, with me, that the whole matter must be brought before Warwick Fairfax, says you should get someone of note to take you along." I said to Ashton: "No, I shall go along alone and talk to him." Ashton agreed this was a good idea: "your background and as good and better than a Fairfax. You're a fine person, Miss Durack. It's good to deal with someone with two feet on the ground. You can't go wrong but all the same this criticism is a serious thing." After this talk Ashton and Bernard Smith and I went up to the stage where Ashton introduced us both. B Smith spoke quite well – a little bit school teacher-ish but nevertheless good and sensible. (Oh, while I was with Haefliger a wire came for him that read: *Greatest esoteric flap doodle you've ever written, angel boy. (signed) NOT Durack.*)[10] Also on the subject of wires I received yours dear and many thanks, it echoed my own sentiments.

Bernard Smith pointed out that here was a new approach to Art, something that had never before been done in Australia, quite a bit like this. Abbey was taking notes so she may have most of the speech down. Bill and Noni[11] were there, Rudder (his boss) decent cove, Mrs Cowell (the Russian, wants to buy *Dampier*, I think, but hasn't yet made up her mind). Oh yes, Dave Wildy, all dressed up in a bola [sic] hat. Some Chinese from the Consulate, some Americans (Foster?) who were very keen, a girl who used to be at the Darwin Hospital with me (Theresa O'Mahoney), some people from London, Beatrice McGuer, Miss Kelly from *The Bulletin*, oh I can't remember them all, people coming and going, all talking to me. Pat and Bill Davidson there later, some South African friends of Kim's.

A few drawings went and a small oil – Frank, *Why is this*. I have hung in three capitals now and not one of the national art galleries have come forward to buy. Hal Missingham [Director, AGNSW] was up on press day. Said he'd be back but did not make an offer. I know Ashton was disappointed. He said: "You should see some of the stuff they've been buying lately." I *have* seen it, some nice but quite a lot of my pictures knock it all into a cocked hat.

When all the smoke had cleared away there was Dave Wildy still sitting in a corner waiting for me to come and have a drink with him – which I did. He got me a couple of bottles to bring over to Kirribilli where I was having dinner with the Brahams …

Well, this morning I went to see art dealers here called Morley & Tonda, two Austrians, rooms in St James building. Ted Cranston [photographer] said they knew all about me, were coming to the show. Well, they didn't know about me and I didn't or was in no mood to tell them this morning but invited them to see the show. Morley going on holidays but will call in when in town on Thursday. Tonda said he would come. Not bad little fellows, gather they are dealing with a few chaps work here and in prints of van Gogh etc, hope to get a gallery soon, did seem to have some art sense.

On Monday I make a broadcast from the gallery at 9.00am for 2GB. I don't know what about. Gather they'll be there and ask a few questions. Will then try and get to see Fairfax, though he may be hard to get into, will have to, however. Tuesday, I regard the Father Thomas appointment to see the pictures of great importance, it is bad luck that the Cardinal is away on holidays. Your suggestion about his coming was what I intended however seeing Father Thomas was next best thing. Will see if they can fit you in here [unnamed hotel] if you decide to come to Sydney at end of week.

I shall use every day to the utmost now the pictures are hanging and will welcome any suggestions from you. Morley & Tonda may, I think, take a couple on sale or return but even this is doubtful. I shall be glad to break it up now, it has served its purpose as far as I'm concerned. It was a beginning. I am now a lot wiser and certainly no sadder although unless I sell one or two of the bigger ones it is far from being a financial success, perhaps I never will be.

George Finey was up once earlier when I was not there, did not leave a message. The art reviewing here is not the regular business it is in Melbourne, as far as I know. *The Tele* has not been up, nor *The Mirror*. That is the point, as Bernard Smith emphasised to me. The *Herald* is the only regular and consistent art review in the city and therefore of such importance.

Called on A&R this morning. Cousens said he'd have 'a report' ready about TRAL [*They Reached a Land* – original title for Mary Durack's *Kings in Grass Castles*] on about Wednesday. Didn't like the sound of it much. Oh dear, as one poor little artist said to me yesterday, after telling me about a picture of a boat he had been trying to sell to the Orient Co. for 3 years: "We artists have a hard road to hoe."

Hope you continue to be not unreasonably uncomfortable at 127 Millswyn Street. Do they know of anything there. Frank, don't leave letters around. I almost feel like asking you to send this on to Mary as I feel I can't go over all this ground again at once, perhaps you would, she would return it to you if you wanted it. I got a letter from her yesterday, some press comment that Coverley was going to have a headache. Kim in Broome, oh dear, I wish he could get in. [Standing as an Independent for Kimberley in the March 1947 State election. He was narrowly defeated.]

No more now dear, will post this and call on Abbey, I think. We might have some coffee, too late for dinner now. Well, what do you think of everything?

ever your loving,
Elizabeth

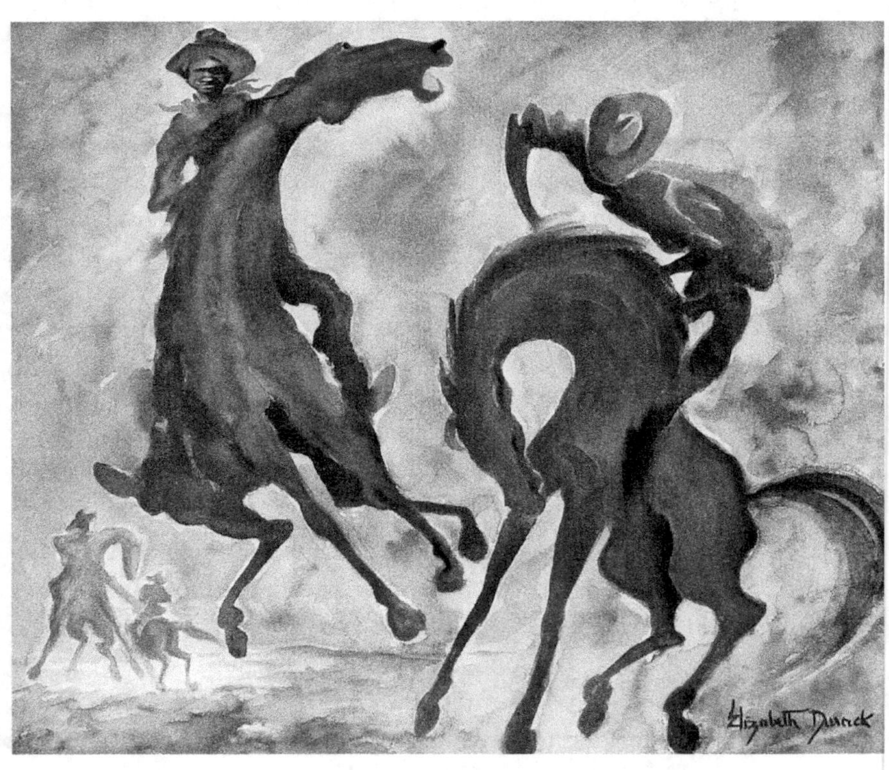

Breaking Colts 1947
watercolour 55 x 65 cm, private collection

Letter: Elizabeth Durack on Ivanhoe (after four years' absence) to Kim Durack in Perth, 11 May 1947

Dearest Brother

Yes, it is both a terrible and terrifying country. I think I learned a lot about it today. It is a country that demands of all who enter it – surrender – but for one who refuses surrender and masters it there is no limit to the glory of the fruits of victory. The morning started as a hundred million Ivanhoe mornings – still, blue, rose madder. The first haha haha of cockatoos. Ice-smooth water on the billabong, purple shadow, then later the wind. I wandered around drinking in the strangeness of familiarity. More wind, some dust. The dust and the voices and the temptation, insistent, to do nothing; to spend the day unpacking, fiddling.

But now all thought has stopped because Norman has turned on the wireless, the football. [Norman and Thelma Bridge were managers of Ivanhoe Station through most of the 1940s.] This is going to be one of the hardest things of all to contend with. It is hard to analyse why my loathing for this machine is so intense. But what I was going to say was that I drove right in against the wind, against an imagined heightening of fever and felt all the sensations of actual battle as I plunged into a composition: *Breaking Colts*. I seem to have laid two enemies at once, first my fear of the country and its potent drug of inertia and secondly my fear of not being able to deal with stock …

I cannot help feeling how at this stage our careers are, if not linked, at least parallel. And oh Kim, what a country for the castle, nothing less, the sheer wonder and beauty is shattering to the senses, and the insult that all construction is to this beauty comes with renewed realisation.[12] Also the actual *mildness* of the climate. The way buildings, furniture etc although always originally of the cheapest, worst quality – *last*. There is not a stick or stay that was not here ten years ago (and goodness knows how many decades before that) and yet the deterioration is actually very slight despite little care taken and many hands handling it.

But the feeling of drift, the drift and aimlessness of everything. I gather from Norman that 'The Farm' [the government-run Kimberley Research Station, established 1946] is doing nothing but growing sugar grass. As he says, no one knows what they're doing and he's sure they don't know themselves, vague talk of 'new construction'. The Bridges, like everyone else here who does not get the hell out or who is not just biding time to do so are a typical example of the surrender, because the surrender is so complete and so abject the country suffers them, tolerates them and they fall into the general enormous pattern of Drift …

Well, Dot, the eternally inarticulate, has found her tongue. She wants Mother to take little Joan: "No more want'm go longa mission."

"What's a matter mission, Dot?"

"Mission marry'm black, missus. I want'm go longa sous, missus – marry'm white. Black no give'm dress, no give'm shoe, nothin'."

She is very proud of the child who is a pretty little thing really very like herself. I told her I would tell Mary. What we can do I don't know. It would be best to build the castle and adopt her here where she could be lifted out of camp conditions and yet not be impossibly separated from her people. That is the longest sentence I have ever heard Dot make in all the years I've known her. There is something very strong and persuasive about it, and of course she is so right …

I hope there will be a letter for me from you all. This time last week we were listening to the concert. I wish I did not always have to be subject to these violent contrasts. It would be better if we had the castle and everything smooth and orderly and waiting only for the arrival of one of those small aeroplanes that I see advertised in *Time* that even a fool can fly.

I am in the room diagonally opposite the Bridges – the most private actually although no one will understand how I must be alone and how I cannot be watched or interrupted. There is a misconception (understandable, I suppose) that drawing or painting is play.

It is bad, there is no turps or linseed oil so all canvas preparation and oil painting has to wait till some pain in the neck arrangement can be made to get some from Wyndham. In the end I couldn't get the frame aboard the plane, damn shame, but Norman got Ernie [Chapman, head stockman, Ivanhoe] to make a wooden board which will be very useful.

One thing, it is almost with love that the blacks have welcomed me here. Old Tommy, Mundi, all the girls, old Jinny on the edge of life and death. Plenty of pics, mostly little girls.

Norman and Mrs B have just gone to bed so the wireless now off and only the sound of the blowfly drone remains …

Well, the plane dropped me down. Did not stop the engines. Pulled out my stuff and stood it in a pile on the 'drome. I felt pretty forlorn. Norman came riding over. I could see figures on the goat hill. Three black boys came to pick up the stuff and Michael and I walked over to the house. I thought Bob was due straight down and so wrote a few letters right away including a very scrappy little one to Mary but will write again presently and most of this for you both. So give her my love again and explain the hurry I wrote in and how I have worked all day. I wish you were here …

The ascetelyn [sic] lamp, a blond praying mantis climbing very slowly up a spikey oleander leaf, flying ants, faint smell of rotten sardines from an extinguished lamp, the night noises. Michael asleep, the little white moth with the red and black spots – Write or give me some news of things somehow. I guess this is what it means by 'cut off' …

I really don't want to go to bed. I could talk if anyone were here.

Oh Kim, please call at my bank and tell them to forward any mail to me here. I forgot to do this.

Well, goodnight – ever your loving sister
Elizabeth

Letter: Elizabeth Durack on Ivanhoe to Mary Durack in Perth, 21 May 1947

Dearest sister

When once one starts writing a letter it's not difficult to continue even though I have none from you to answer. Actually a lot of things about the work done, and some discoveries made, I have written to Frank and much of what I say on such subjects goes for both of you but it is not possible, quite, to make copies of such letters as one only really writes to one person at a time – unless one is writing as [cousin] Edith (and that is advisable too).

One main thing I discover is the mobility of the sky. The whole thing is not that flat unbroken surface of glazed blue that Streeton and von Guerard have us believe. A clear sunlit sky is completely mobile and precisely where it comes in contact with any object it throws off diamonds of light if the object is dark, or whorls of brighter blue, if the object is light. In this way the whole of the sky surface can be used to add rhythm to the whole composition. Oh lots of the time I am learning [indecipherable word] while I just look, so that every waking moment is all a part of some unpainted picture. I did not give you my ideas concerning the necessity of exploring the anatomy of isolation in order to arrive at something approaching a new vision. I have gone into this more fully writing to Frank, the whole point being that not only do we observe objects, people, everything, with a pair of sensitised eyes but when once we raise pencil or brush to delineate them then a thousand dead men's eyes and hands and thoughts crowd in upon us to direct our movement. In order to escape, at any rate, in part, such a shackling it is necessary to explore completely, within the limits of one's principal and mental ability – *isolation*, *aloneness*.

Also, I am using the *earth itself* in great *handfuls* on my pictures. I am only tickling the surface of this game. When we were kids Dad brought down a bottle once with layers of different coloured earth in it, red, grey, brown, mauve. These colours must be collected, not by the ounce but by the pound, and sifted and mixed to form the basis of serious compositions. Also it is no longer enough to continue drawing and painting the natives in their clothes. I must use them naked against these colours, using the colour of their skin I will use the colour of the earth that raised them. In this way some unity may be arrived at, some harmony of idea and colour and form.

This is another reason why it is necessary for me to set up in some independent establishment. While I am here I am part of the white man's machine for the natives' betterment (if you will); for their exploitation (if you like). I don't want to be part of anything. I want to be completely independent but capable of observing. I don't want to preach. I don't want to uplift. I don't want to do anything except pursue what I feel I must and what now I can feel I can. But to repeat, it really can't be done quickly, feverishly. I can't rush up here for a few weeks, collect a pile of superficial paintings and mass of notes and then rush somewhere else, busy and bussling [sic] and bursting with vivacity. It must be calm, considered. One must move and feel with the colour of the earth itself. I must be idle for long periods if I want to. Not even doing anything except looking.

I think I might be able to establish a kind of grass house – *casino della gramigna* [for myself and the children] and yet keep somewhat in touch with the station to the extent of the gins doing our washing and getting some water for us which would have to be put in drums. I could pay them in tobacco for this. There are tons of them here and all they do is water those damn dreary creepers that Mrs Bridge has got planted all around the place shutting out the glorious glare. How I hate creepers and how they hate growing here too. I would not mind having a few cactus or anything that grows without effort and meaningless toil. Dot, Maree, Sheba, Roco, Peggy, Gwenny, Naida and goodness knows how many more. I do not want them living near me or feeling responsible for them. It would be good if we could have a kero refrigerator but unless this were donated by someone it is out of the question so we would have to make do with a meat safe hanging on a hook.

I have just about finished a painting of Roger. It's pretty big and really the best I've done to date here, mostly for what it opens up for me in regards to the disposition of form and colour.

Saw Jeff [Chunuma] this morning passing through with Argyle drovers. He is a good-looking kid – I can still see the child there. You remember how Jeff could look uninteresting and bedraggled sometimes if unanimated. Jeff looked quite smart but the verve was not in evidence and yet I suspect it was not far under. He has a very beautifully developed pair of arms.

Letter: Elizabeth Durack on Ivanhoe to Mary Durack in Perth, 22 May 1947

Dearest sister

With what great pleasure I have just finished reading your letter just delivered by Hector, the first news I have had for the full two weeks. Am interested in all you have to say about everything. Certainly do understand the paragraph wherein you describe our sensations towards this land. The acute personalness of it all and [indecipherable word] the detachment (which as you will see from this and former letter I wish to make more corporally complete). Glad to hear you are progressing so well with BSR ['Black Swan River' manuscript]. I don't know what you mean by saying you did a Jack Sorenson [poet/friend] of it on me when I was vitally interested in hearing it from the time of my arrival. You know I suggested it several times and did not want to officiously ask as thought you might not want to read it yet (as I often don't want people looking at something when only sketched in and when I know it is going to be recast) and certainly did enjoy the short time we did eventually squeeze out in which to read it.

Of course very interested in news of Kim. This sounds good. Yes, the boy has my complete confidence. Will be most anxious to hear of further news on this and when will he be up?

Went for a walk to the river, in fact just returned, and for the first time I told someone – Gwenny – that I was going to build a house on the river bank. Instead of the *storm* of protest opposition that I will have to meet with as soon as I voice to Dad, or any of the whites, she cottoned on *immediately* and we spent an hour discussing and examining the different spots (Roger's camp, Drover's camp, Martin's camp) and considering their relative advantages and disadvantages, their positions when river in flood etcetera.

Finally decided on the spot I have had in mind for ages. It's on the right hand side of *Chement* [Ord River Crossing] going towards Argyle just through the horse paddock fence, lovely spot, high and safe from flood, good trees. Gwenny saw no difficulties in the way *at all* and it was funny. I kept saying that I was going to build it all of bush timber only big and high and she kept telling me of all the places where I could get *iron*: "Plenty iron longa 3 Mile, where 'e bin hav'm fire *be*fore." Explaining to me that the home Ernie had built himself here behind the stables was all built of 3 Mile scrap iron. It's an atrocity of an erection but apparently highly regarded by the blacks. Then Gwenny told me how I could get a pump to get the water up the hill. In fact, she had nearly as many grandiose ideas as Kim on the subject. But it was really very nice and warming to talk to her. I feel as a result of this morning's conversation that there are less difficulties in my way than ever. If only Dad will agree and let me have the services of Ernie and Johnny Walker[13] for a couple of weeks. Gwenny saw immediately how we could: "Make'm ebery where all-about mak'm level – good clean place." And I told her that she and the others could help me collect river stones to cover the floor with. Oh yes, she grasped this right away too: "Plenty good flat stone there – longa Crossing." And this set her off on another train of thought how I could have: "A *chement* floor – plenty good sand longa station creek." So you see the blacks are as thoroughly conditioned to the idea of importing materials into this country, already so gloriously and naturally endowed, as the whites. I found a boab nut and am sure that if they could be sized or lacquered inside they would make lovely cups. I am going to write to Alf Morgan [Pearling Master] in Broome and ask him to send some nice big mother of pearl shells. They would make lovely plates. Even if the boab nuts are not good to drink out of they would make cute ash trays and mixing bowls for my paints. (Know this sounds like some pages torn from May Gibbs.)

We had a lovely swim in our pool. It was like heaven. Gwenny found some nice little spiralled shells of which we collected a lot and carried back in my bloomers. Intend to make a necklace of if I can make a little hole in them. She also found some pretty rocks, they are always looking for pretty things, one piece like a bit of fossilized wood and may be too. They would make very nice paperweights because the wind is pretty constant.

This is my idea for the house:

From ground to ceiling to be as high as possible, say 10 feet, if such timber is available for the mainstays. Then grass and boughs for the roof and sides, much of which is open. This then leads out onto a courtyard, as big as possible and this will have to be covered with boughs for shade too. Tables and chairs (out of greenhide) are arranged here and a barbecue for grilling fish and meat as I will only have a primus in the kitchen.

Anyway, enough of this now. I did a drawing of Gwenny without clothes and am now hastening to get on to it. The skin is exactly the same colour as the river rocks though more vibrant.

My love to you all.

8.00pm: Tell Kim I hear from everyone, even when they don't know who I am, nice things expressive of respect and confidence in him. He will ask who. The Roads Board people, the men who were taking the river levels at Mons Mont (Reid, Emil). Norman regrets that he didn't get in [as an Independent MP]. I always say I am glad he didn't and that his work is developing in more fruitful channels (or something vague like this. You needn't say this to Kim if it may annoy him but I generally give it around with a statement of confidence that he will *come again* and stronger. I think this advisable).

The whole experimental business is a meaningless fiasco to Norman and indeed it could be if Kim cannot get control and direct this machine he started operating in the first place. [Kim had initiated the agricultural potential of Kimberley producing crops irrigated from the Ord.] Norman says: "Oh, give them a year or two and there'll be a nice little auction sale over the river." Actually it is the statement of the general reaction to the idea of change or progress. I know Kim has a soft spot for the Bridges and I suppose I have too but Jesus they're hopeless.

Am glad Mick was helpful about the administration talk with Kim, no doubt talked better than if I'd been around, as I certainly work better when he is not but hell, I wish he was or that he could be some way regularly or irregularly.

Well, Mary – *Venus* – rearing up between the great rocks. The colour of the rock itself – a part of it. Big 5 x 3 [feet]. Am on to it now and trust and hope it will be my best work to date. Finally, Mary, and in the end what it is all about apparently is the GLORY – my vision and my day. I feel the glory coming through now. Coming through like sunshine, the sheer joy of beholding, the sheer living, throbbing beauty.

Ever your loving,

Bet

Address of Mr Howe: c/- Collins Publishing Company Sydney. See Sydney telephone book. GPO. Mary do not feel impatient about this publication. A turn of the wheel for Kim or me and the whole thing trebles in interest.

PS How is everyone? I am wondering when Kim is going north. It was wonderful seeing him like that. How was poor old Neville [AO Neville, WA Commissioner for Native Affairs, 1930s-40s] when you left, very disconsolate? Did Mick ring you, or anything? I will never write. I will do the only thing possible and reasonable under the circumstances. I shall force myself to forget him. But just how, I don't know. When I pass the [Wyndham] Post Office I think I could ring Perth now and talk to him but of course I walk on and will continue to walk on.

Frank did not have six pence when we arrived. It is too silly and boring. At the same time he has this regular fortnightly money and it is the only present source of income to the four of us so I must be sensible and what not. But at the same time – hurry – always the urgency.

I hope I hear from you this week. Tell me everything about you and Horry and how the children are and how Broome is if you are there and how are you.

Ever my love,

Bumbles [family name for Elizabeth]

And if you get to Auvergne special love to Dad, Reg, etc.

Letter: Elizabeth Durack on Ivanhoe to Reg Durack on Auvergne, 5 June 1947

Dear Brother

Thank you very much for the goods sent by Bob [Skuthorpe], it is very good of you to have done this for me and I can well understand what it meant finding bottles and boxes in all the rush of arranging unpacking and plant-setting out etc.

A long pause here since commencing this after lunch, now evening and have just cleaned up poor little Michael and got him to sleep after a bilious attack, the result of stupid Mrs Bridge giving him sweets, biscuits etc during the day. I have protested about it before but will now have to be very firm. It is amazing how utterly stupid some people are and how little is understood of correct feeding either of themselves or others. A child, unless it is bored, shouldn't even think of food between meals. Even if it asks for sweets its mind can be quickly diverted by giving it something interesting to do or see.

Dad and Norman have been out since yesterday riding a fence or such. By the way that Reeve chap dropped in here a couple of days ago and says he'll be here again about Monday when there is a chance of his dropping Dad over at your place for a few hours (he has a 'plane you gather). So just be suitably surprised if this occurs. Personally I loathe surprises of such a nature but perhaps everyone does not.

My grass box proceeds. They have a wall done now, batons on the other three sides and the top. It is going to look exactly like a square haystack. I tried very hard to get it rectangular but the idea of the square seemed to get riveted in Dad's mind and it was not a thing to fight about. I am fortunate to get anything no doubt. It will not look so bad when a few windows are cut in it and if an extension in the way of open shade is built on to it. As it is, I defy anyone to see it without laughing.

It could be finished by now but I think Ernie and the blacks have turned it into a hunting expedition as well, as I met them coming back home this evening with two kangaroos and some eaglehawks' eggs. I am terribly impatient for them to finish it and go down twice a day and hover for a while. I am frightened Dad might panic and say they have been on it long enough and then everyone would be nowhere.

The following are a few items that I thought you may be able to lend lease me. I realise that having taken nearly a decade to get a few of the amenities of living about you, you may be disinclined to part with anything and I do not expect you to but if any of these items happen to be there and not in use I would take good care of them till I see a bit where I am which will probably not be until the exhibition in September (if then) though in a couple of months' time I should feel a little less uncertain. I simply hate asking the Bridges here for anything. For one thing they have hardly anything of the regular routine things that you would think every station would have such as tacks and also there is in them the fear of the little man. What is it? It is rather pathetic in a way. One can sense with Norman the fear that he might be asked or expected to cope with something which he knows he couldn't. For instance, he doesn't want electric light or even good light, nor a pedal radio, nor even a truck because surely if he did and could really utilise such things he would have had them here 'ere this. To understand all may not be always to forgive all but it certainly makes it harder for one to dislike anyone completely. The same with Mrs Bridge. The slovenliness and the insolent stomach and navel are really a pitiful defence. All these things, they sadden and depress me. It is better alone. At the same time to make an official divorcement from the homestead without providing, even moderately, in my *casino gramigna* would be stupid. The list:

a primus or blue flame stove;
two cups and two saucers;
two iron greenhide or canvas beds;
a lamp (preferably one that does not blow up I have an awful phobia of explosion. What lamp is best to get from Wyndham if you have not a spare one – a pendant one?);
a hurricane lamp (for walking at night to and from my place – a torch is a pest with batteries);
a chair or two (I can't imagine you'd have such a thing to spare so skip this);
a couple of saucepans, frypan, kettle or any odd kitchen gear, spoon, fork, knife;
a meat safe (I will get one that hangs from Finlays as I have a memory of Auvergne and a big safe-building project when I was there);
any odd small table;
any spare kerosene boxes or wood boxes – I guess these are precious and scarce anywhere;
any sheets etc – I am sure no one has such a thing to spare since rationing;
any jars or bottles or useful things to put things in;
a few yards of thin wire. I thought this would be a good idea to tie on to bottles and tins and sink them in the swimming pool and fish them out cold as I would have no cooling apparatus. On pearling luggers they do this.

Do you know anyone prepared to loan or sell a gramophone? I want a simple basic selection of records from Mozart to Tchechowisky [sic].

Reg, this is just a list of what I see I would need almost immediately.

If you could put a tick to an item or two, well and good. After that I will see what Wyndham offers. Heavens, in how many places have I set up the impedimenta of living. All the things I want here (or most of them) I got in Broome, Brisbane, Sydney, Melbourne. In Melbourne I have in store, chests of cedar drawers, beds, crockery, silver, linen, glassware. However the delay and expense at the moment of getting them sent would be terrific.

Thank you for the information about the mud-brick construction at Forrest River. On further enquiry I learn that ant-bed and stone would make an ideal construction. But to commence such a task one would want at best a truck or at least a horse and cart. However I may proceed to collect little kilns of stone and dot them about but all the same if once I get this grass box completed and a few things in it I better lie low for a while and plug at the painting. It is amazing how extraordinarily difficult it is to reconcile painting and living. In fact the two are practically irreconcilable – completely. To live, one must compromise; to paint one must apparently be so utterly ruthless that any sane person would see immediately that the game is not worth the candle. Still it burns brightly and sweetly.

My fondest love to Enid, little David and Anne (is the 'e' right?). I hope you are all well and that the baby has by now settled into its new routine and surroundings.

Ever your loving sister,

Elizabeth

PS: A little letter from Mary. Little news. No word from Kim. Mary was typing out a detailed report he had prepared for the Premier as a result of his interviews and says she thought something would come of it in a few weeks. It is very slow. No doubt that boy has a fine nerve. Nothing less could stand the strain under which he has been living for weeks now.

Letter: Elizabeth Durack on Ivanhoe to Reg Durack on Auvergne, 12 June1947

Dear Brother

I was going to enclose a few paintings with this as samples but don't think I will now as I don't know really if you talk much to Eddie [Connellan of Connellan Airways, Alice Springs] these days or even if he stops long enough of a Friday for any indirect conversation to arise. It occurs to me that as he is taking tourists on his plane these days he might like to have a few of my paintings. I am a bit vague about it all but it seemed to me a kind of a tie-up but not the sort of thing that the artist himself can actually suggest although it is quite a simple proposition. I know, or rather I learnt from my contacts in Melbourne and Sydney, that a certain amount of hedging about was really essential to the art game or at least to its commercialisation. I mean it's not the point of a person being anxious to sell anything. It would be more that, under persuasion, someone might consider the idea. A great gag among the eastern states blokes is to kid they don't want to sell any more pictures because the taxation makes it not worthwhile. This always sounded a hotty to me because I would like to find the taxation department, for all its omnipotent mechanism, that could catch up with an artist.

How to deal with this landscape is at last coming to me. Having got my grass house with the one idea in my mind, that of putting as much space between the good Mrs Bridge and myself as was workably possible, I suddenly realised that the whole idea was definitely one of the most inconvenient ones I could have thought up. Poor Mrs B suddenly became so jealous of the blacks that she developed a most extraordinary attitude (a long and tedious and typically nor'west story) the upshot of which was that I had to beast-of-burden all my stuff down to the river and will probably not bother to have or ask the women here to pose for me. Too ridiculous really and in a way I blame myself.

So there we are down on the bank of the river, paints and canvas around us, dust blowing in clouds through the doorway, branches rustling in the south wind. Otherwise very quiet, not a model within miles. All my ideas of the girl who would bring my lunch down and then drape herself for me for an hour or so, blasted. I sat all day frowning at the glare and feeling very sad and sorry for myself and very indignant, very self-righteous. All of a sudden I started to see something – Grass! The great unknown, the great unseen grasslands of Australia!

Grass. Before the grass all other features of the landscape take a subservient position. Grass massed and folded in a dense foreground, grass sweeping not only to the horizon but waving far above the horizon, every landscape cut with the soaring shafts of grass, mountains, trees, rivers, lowered before it. It was an exciting discovery. So far only two little paintings have been done but this is the beginning of a presentation of the countryside – the grasslands. For so long I have worried. I saw the mountains and I saw how little different they were from those so well depicted by the desert artists but the desert character is different again and yet I could not, until yesterday, quite put my hand on the difference. Now I see where the sameness ends and the difference begins. The whole character of dealing with this land is through the treatment and portrayal of its grass.

Oh I am tired of human beings. Every face that screams its awful message at me – how can one ever hope to attain to the formal and the pure if one deals with human faces. Look at me, love me, hate me, fear me, pity me, feed me, bury me, faces say things all the time. I am tired of all that can be said by a human face. I know every inflection of its contours, every fleeting transient thought that darts like fish through the open windows of the eyes, the little fears, the little scorn, the little hope, but grass says nothing. It just folds and unfolds itself, leans and turns in a glory of formal patterning, leaps suddenly skyward in a crescendo of excitement.

Really, Reg, I am sorry about all this but just had to tell someone about it. I guess you are out in the camp and having a worrying time and wishing that there was someone trustworthy to leave in charge of it and that you were at home with your family. I hope Enid, David and little Anne are well and that it will not be necessary to be much away from them all, and from the thousand and one things that make it necessary for you to be at the house.

This goes with Dad. He is very much looking forward to seeing you all. He has been very good to me over all my nuisancing, wonderfully so, and I am very grateful to him. I have had no news or letters from Perth or the East. Kim is still waiting the reception to his extensive report that was presented to the Premier last week. The boy is a genius; an administrative genius and during this trying time we must do all we can to help him in whatever way lies in our power. He would very much appreciate a letter from you reassuring him of your faith in him. The loneliness and isolation of the boy is a big burden for him to carry, his nerves are very strained but I have great faith in his ability to maintain control.

All well here. Apparently it got a bit [indecipherable word] so Norman went out today. Dad will be giving all immediate news. Mrs Bridge just came in. Sends kind regards to you and Enid and hopes the baby is doing well.

Well, a lot of people seem to be moving in and out so I shut up, put down the lid, push in the bolt. I am tired of all this discipline. As a matter of fact I am getting *thirsty*. I would have liked to have told you about my complicated love life but the time was not opportune. Not that I want advice. It has gone beyond that now. It all broke up but I pick up nice chips from time to time and delude myself it is a whole jug.

My love to you all,

Bumbles

PS: Do you think Eddie would be interested in the idea, paragraph one? 20% on sales. Small pictures about 18 x 12 inches selling at from 4 to 6 guineas?

A book on loan would be welcome. Have you got Edmund Wilson's *Hecate County*?

Letter: Elizabeth Durack on Ivanhoe to Mary Durack in Perth, 25 July 1948

My own Darling Sister

By this time you are, no doubt, up to the armpits in another Wonder Book and probably the one you left at Ivanhoe has receded a little into the background. However, if Ivanhoe has dimmed for you believe me you have not dimmed here. The repercussions and rumblings go on like the sound of thunder in the early part of the Wet – and like these sounds too they portend an eventual, if not an immediate, storm and deluge …

Yes, she [Mrs Bridge] knows she has made a mistake though nothing in my attitude or manner could give her any cause for alarm. I am impassive, completely impassive. Completely, I am even light and pleasant, nothing has happened.

As your truck pulled away I walked across the plain and did not feel the ground beneath my feet until I hit the Black Rock. In solitude and quietness I communed with my soul and prayed and wept and drank the secret waters … The day passed swiftly and when I emerged from the evening shade I was strengthened and refreshed and calm and strong again. Ah! The secret heart of the bush that I fly to now as another flies to the arms of a beloved for succour and sustenance. Do I say I hate it? I love it with the core of me and because I see that love incarnated in the blacks I love them too as my children and myself, this is the tie-up.

There was a strange atmosphere as I approached the house. The blacks met me declaring they had been worried about me:

"No got a dinner. Nothing. *All-about* [pidgin for 'all of us'] bin think you fall down, broken you leg …" Break it down, break it down, I kept saying to myself as I extricated myself from them. But they were not being as tactless as I thought. Mrs Bridge was not there.

A truck was pulled up: Bill Flinders (he thought your little article on his Dad v good and sends his k. regards) and Charles Pretlove on board. No, on the verandah, pretty drunk telling me they were waiting for me. Norman almost in the horrors. We had tea. I thanked them but declined the invitation either to drink or be driven over the 'The Farm' where a Salvation Army (?!) Padre was giving a sermon and where Mrs Bridge had betaken herself. In the end it turned out to be a very pleasant evening. Pretty light, but strong. I decided to show a few pictures. Norman by now stoomed [sic]. Drink was forgotten and conversation, although pretty moronic, free and easy. I enjoyed it, defending the cause of Art against the philistine, for – for all their lack of knowledge etc, they both had that clear and open mind of the not greatly lettered.

The next morning was the first time I have done anything ever, here. I got breakfast, though poor Norman, to do him justice, was trying to rally.

However, Mrs B returned before dinner, surprisingly sober and normal and things have been so ever since. A page has been turned over. It will not be referred to again … yet no return to sobriety, no return to routine or normality, can alter the now changed position. It is both tragic yet inevitable.

I think Ivanhoe needed your visit, Mary. I think it was long overdue. Or timed exactly.

Mary, there are forces working and at work in the country at present that are bigger than ourselves. The air is suddenly electric in a way it has never been in the past.

I have been considering the whole position, no, not the whole position, the particular position of ourselves in relation to the blacks – and this business of *respect*. Mary, I believe (for all our general acceptance of their chameleon attitude towards all people) that they do really deeply and fundamentally respect us. And I do not take credit for this upon ourselves but basically because of Dad and his position in the early days when whatever deeds were performed by him to obtain mastery and safety for the white. There is something, an echo of something deeper and older in the attitude of the blacks towards us than our generation. And this is basically how I account for it: there is the Boss (no matter how Dad has evaded responsibility in the past or present) he is still *the original Old Man*.[14] When they call Norman or Eric '*Ol' Man*' they know they are sure to get a bite, that it will please etc, but in their hearts there is only one *Ol' Man* and that is Dad and we, as his daughters (you particularly – I am more oblique both to black and white) are "my Missus prop'ly" and no amount of soft handouts, no amount of cruel control can ever alter this. "My Missus prop'ly, before now – long time …"

I hope you come back. For *face* reasons – I hope and consider it advisable that you come back – for a day, two days, for morning tea.

your ever loving sister,

Bet

PS: I missed Bob as out today. Believe you had punctures. You will no doubt be telling me of your trip – though I am sure you will agree that punctures, heat, breakdowns and what have you on the part of a truck are nothing as compared to similar eventualities in human relationships.

My love to Reg. I hope some basis of cooperative conversation is continuing there. I am getting the strongest vibrations from Kim. There is nothing to do but swing in with every moral weapon we have behind him. He has virtually become so much the future of the north and the new pattern soon to be spread over it that it will be difficult for historians and biographers to separate the two. If there is any further suggestion of sale of the stations or if such a wicked and foolish and traitorous act would ever be put through I shall simply cut my wrists and melt into the sand.[15]

Letter continues Elizabeth to Mary, 27 July 1948

Your letter yesterday, per Hector. You apparently had a real old-fashioned grape of a trip but sounded in good spirit, amused at all your comment and snatches of conversation.

Am sitting beside the Black Rock pool and have just had a heavenly swim. This is a lovely place, open and clear and inducive to direct and level contemplation. I am sorry we did not have a chance to revisit these places together but they are too far for children to walk and yet it is best to walk to them; one misses too much any other way. Also there are various ways of walking, sometimes with the eyes and sometimes with the ears.

All quiet at the house. The quiet of a hangover which no doubt will continue for a couple of days longer till 'after the boat' brings its quota of people and refreshment. This is as bad a hangover as I have seen Norman with and he looks sick and miserable, officially he has 'a cold'. All recedes, but the name of 'Mary' by tacit consent joins the lists of the unmentionables. I have, of course, said as normally as possible, that I had a note from you and you had a strenuous journey but the atmosphere is not yet sufficiently purged for even this to pass without reverberations of electricity and now embarrassment on Mrs B's part. However, as the poor soul chose to make a major issue of a four day visit from one sister to another to discuss mutual interests she must be prepared to take the consequences.

I quite believe the whole incident was contrived and evolved purely by the blacks – the black devils – driving their wedges between white and white, feeding on the jealousy, fear and suspicion among them. Disunity, friction, anger is the very breath of life to the blacks. As much as anything I am angry at Mrs B for falling into such a trap. She had only to be quiet and pleasant during the ridiculously short period of your stay and they would have been thwarted. Instead of that the foolish woman with a liver enlarged from days of drinking and her ego swollen from what must have been a huge nip that she had before descending into the kitchen blundered and fell into the net. For sheer stupidity there is no excuse … Oh it is all too ridiculous. However I have foregrounded the whole thing in this letter from the point of view of general interest and the germs that lie in it of a novel about the north that could carry the reflection of the whole in one small glass …

My main object now is to infuse a little ease and reassurance into the everyday life, little as I see of it, being as I am so much away, living my own life secret and of a happiness that is now increasing. I do not talk about where I go, what I see, what I do during these days I spend among the hills. I too have my little jealousies. They [many of the whites in the north] have lived here for years and years and have seen nothing, created nothing but the desert around each little settlement and the desert in their own hearts wherein they can lull themselves with alcohol to sleep. Let them sleep. I do not wish to open their eyes.

But there are other eyes that are coming into the north and that will soon be coming in ever-increasing numbers, eyes that are already open, hearts that are not a desert. You met one in Moira Ronan; there is also Shirley Horstman, alive, seeing something, seeing the north in relation to other places.

PS I would like you to see *High and Inaccessible*. Definitely not one I can show – wish you were here – as the work incorporates thought, idea and philosophy more and more my isolation increases – only temporarily however and this suits me too because I must have quiet and isolation now in which to think.

Yet I am not all removed. I even envisage ways wherein the work (on another level and scale) could be utilised as an *active factor* towards incorporating into the natives' heart that loss of personal respect that

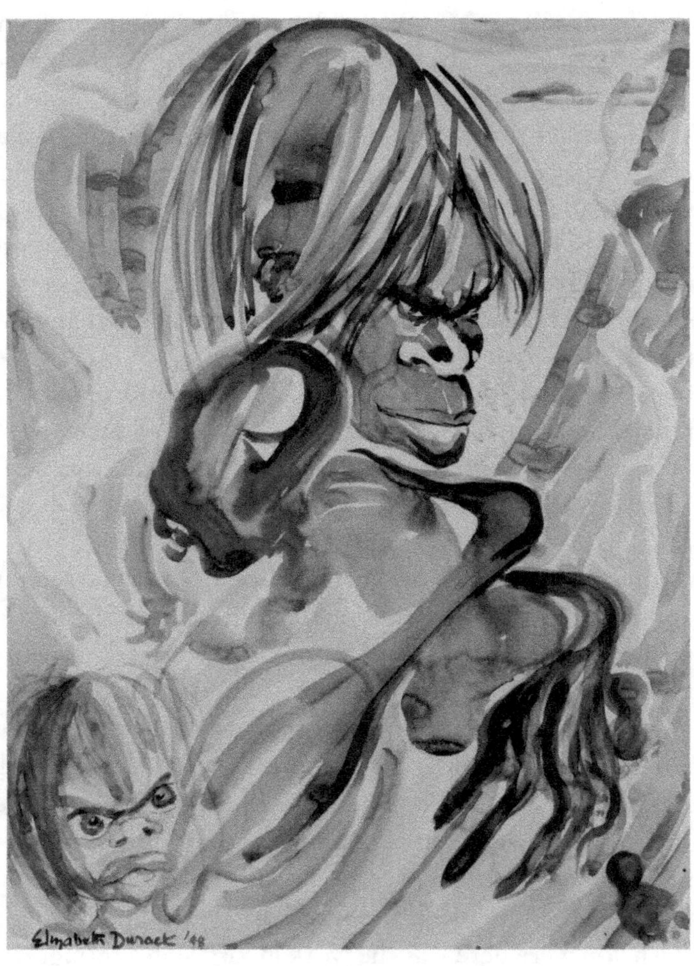

High and Inaccessible 1948
watercolour 73 x 52 cm, estate of Elizabeth Durack

the influx of this [white] colour has, to a large extent, induced. They love the baby with the toys; are now almost too eager for me to paint their young. They make an extra effort with their clothes, hurriedly change them, do their hair, wipe their faces when they see me coming – but sensitive always, are not a nuisance with their eagerness. I did one of Dot's little Colin in this way. Also I can imagine some institution somewhere (unlike any we yet know of) wherein black children painted like this would decorate the nursery and where a vast industry of ceramics would be organised and generated by themselves for themselves. Self-respect, confidence, wholesome and clean children, and this carefully nourished 'problem', so dear to the heart of the white, would die of malnutrition. But these are not the lines I pursue with a torch through the dark places.

Do hope, dear, you are finding it possible to get on to the re-organisation of TRAL. Know it is going to be better than ever before once you get down to it. But at the same time if you cannot find the right corner do not strive and worry – let everything glide over. It may be that the corner still is at 12 Bellevue Avenue [Mary's home in Nedlands] but what you could gain from a period of mental and spiritual relaxation would be invaluable. Continued industry is often as much a fault as a virtue.

ever your loving
Bumbles

Essay: extracts from *Signature – Reflections on art and life – and a part reply to critics.*

The Black Rock, Ivanhoe, August 1948

… The hardest single thing that I have had to contend with when showing pictures is not that people in the Australian cities know nothing about the aborigines, but that they all do know something. They come to my exhibitions with minds pre-conditioned – by something they have heard: some brief personal experience, some book they have read – prepared to see reason for some vague sensation of guilt. Sometimes, as when some ancient family secret is stirred, active antipathy …

Perhaps because of this mental pre-conditioning I speak of, and the vexed social issues now gathering momentum around 'the natives', they are not the most fortunate choice of subject matter. However, I can neither help nor be concerned with this. It would be, in fact, nearer the truth to say not so much that I have chosen them but that they have chosen me, for among the many reasons why I turn continually to them – or they to me, perhaps – is that I am able in one bound as it were to get at the things I want, simple basic things, qualities inherent in the hearts of all peoples; but which often, with civilised people, are so camouflaged – so overlaid with impenetrable mazes of undergrowth – that any attempt to pierce such formidable defences would be thwarted …

Although it is redundant to speak today of the close relationship of all living races, the oneness of the human family and the comparatively recent yesterday when the wandering tribes in a wave or waves reached Australia, that which is not perhaps felt or realised with the same intensity as I experience, is how, when once here, the land itself took part in their shaping and development …

It is this fusing and shaping on the part of the land itself – of living human flesh and bone – that make the aborigines for me an object of such constant joy, excitement and wonder. They are the very land incarnate, the very colour of the earth in its hundred shades and inflections, from golden sand to vermilion to deepest blue and purple. I never use any other colour to paint their skin but that which is on my brush from painting the ground beneath their feet. The harmony is exact and identical. The crevices of the rocks or sodden plains, the fire-spared summits or the charred limbs of the trees, the elbow in its loose peculiar articulation, the yellow flowered kapok and the highlight upon flesh, the down of grass at noon over the flesh-soft, hard-baked bone of the desert, and in the evening the muted purples of the hills wrapping alike themselves and their people in slumberous coitus.

This affinity between the land and the people, and between myself to the land through the people, one which I have arrived at through long and dispassionate association, seemed to me at first to be something I had alighted upon independently. In fact it is only what has been occurring all through – although Nature's results have been more tangible and lovely than my puny pictures – and the large, increasing population of half-white half-aboriginal people represents one of the healthiest and most heartening aspects in this part of Australia.

The affinity between black and white lies in their relation to the land. The black is of the country before time; the white bridges the gap between a strange, stark, alien land and home, and it is the peace and acceptance of home that pervades the heart. For the black a home inherited by instinct and long association; for the white a home acquired by effort. In this, black and white can be in harmony. Nature makes no mistakes. If social codes and laws lag behind, prejudice and phobias overshadowing, they will catch up in time …

1950s

If this sounds cynical then the words belie me[16]

After almost twenty years working in the north, exhibiting in capital cities, criss-crossing the continent with no corner of it to call her own, Elizabeth received a sum of £3,000 from her father, Michael Patrick Durack, shortly before his death in September 1950. The amount was sufficient to buy a block in the Perth suburb of Dalkeith and to build a modest home upon it.

We moved in – mother, Michael and myself – to 47 Browne Avenue in time for Christmas 1950. Looking back on the 1950s, those years were, in effect, our own Amber Decade *– safe, secure and relatively untroubled.*

Our Miller cousins, Mary and Horry's children – six of them – lived a short distance away. We all rode bicycles to school, attended classes and spent most of our free time together. Our mothers were forever at work – on drawing board or typewriter. The strong bond between them and our Uncle Kim we took for granted at the time. We would hear regularly from our father in Sydney and wrote back. Our Uncle Horry would appear occasionally from Broome. Other aunts, uncles and cousins were very much part of our lives as well, while the pre-eminent presence all through the 1950s and for many years after that was 'Gran Central' – Bess Ida Muriel Durack – *our maternal grandmother.*

PDC

Poem: Storm Day, *at 47 Browne Avenue, March 1953*

It thundered early and
wild wind-torn cloud
forded the morning
entry, through the just
opened doors of night.

Lightning spattered the grey
cloud blankets
with glittering tripods
as though Neptune
threw them in a fit
of the jitters – and the cat
crept under a chair.

Thunder broke right in our eardrums
then went rumbling off like a bull
waiting the next chance to charge.
The lights fused and when the phone rang:
"Lord, what a day," said Mary,
just audible above the hail.

And all day long like unwilling
spectators to an ill-timed quarrel
we could not for a moment forget
the wild discord of the heavens
nor find escape from it
(pity the postman).

Too sudden, after the long
languor of summer the season broke
and
sitting on the lawn drinking tea
cleaving to shade and brushing
flies became 'last year'.

Yet, even as we sat talking
and dozing through the gold hours

(storing its fierce energies and shrill dissent)
the heavens, blue and enormous,
boded not peace,
but this storm day.

Letter: Elizabeth Durack from '47' to Ida Mann[17] living nearby, 3 November 1954

Dear Ida

The Cockney and the Crocodile [MS] makes such bright delightful reading I feel regret to come to page 50 of this section of it and although you are dealing really with grave things close to your heart and mind the lightness of your pen lends a poignancy to this which makes it so convincing. It is all so fresh and the touches of sharpness very refreshing after the habits of continual 'back-slapping' that have settled like a pall over Australian factual writing. How quickly and with what ease you can create the atmosphere of each place – Darwin, the monks, Forrest River. I love some of your similes – Wyndham 'with its toes in the muddy water' and the new born baby 'slowly turning black at the tips like a negative in the developing bath'. And I enjoy the backgrounding that you give to our local scene with the comparisons etc that your wide travelling enables you to give. I should say any publisher here or in England would welcome the chance of publishing this and I hope you have plans afoot on these lines.

Apropos of our brief conversation this evening – Yes, I do agree with you and do consider that anything on the lines of something rather more 'enlightened' (dreadful word) than the sub-standard Missions should be endorsed. Yet, as you'd know as well as I, there are practical reasons for the State's present policy of Mission support. Also it won't last long, say about ten years, and the pendulum will swing precisely in the direction you foresee as, at present, desirable. Native encampments, settlements and reserves will sprout anthropologists and psychiatrists, vocation guiders like mushrooms and by and large the position generally will probably be little better than when the Bible thumpers held sway while Commonwealth funds will be tremendously depleted by paying big salaries to the newcomers for what, under the Missions, they are getting done free.

The Australian Aboriginal in his present phase of evolution is not adjusted:

to wearing clothes – or – going naked
to medical care – or – physical neglect
to 'higher education' – or – illiteracy
to a 'useful trade' – or – throwing a spear
to the 20th century – or – the Stone Age
to Jesus Christ – or – Biame
to urban life – or – sequestered Reserve
and so on ad infinitum.

But what he is *adjusted* to (and that most happily and even serenely – and I think it is a little necessary to grasp this point) is *his mal–adjustment.* Are we to take this too from him? Can, in fact, we reasonably hope to do so? Within this particular and qualified adjustment he stands as gloriously remote as before the first European ships tipped his sanctuary.

And can we be so sure of the fixity of our perilously poised civilization to force him into the Faith in the unbroken thrust of (shall we say) Western Civilization? And by Faith, I mean it in the broadest sense, the thing that gets us up in the morning – yes, if you like, the alarm clock.

But if this sounds cynical then the words belie me, for the very eyes which you are healing have pierced so deeply into my soul (if I have one) that I now look outward through them.

Nor do I condone a policy of defeatism or non-activity, far from it. It is part of our Faith that we should ACT – and act we all do and shall and must, (even as passivity is essentially the core of a philosophy of adjustment to mal-adjustment). The issues at stake are as big as Life itself and as small. Because they are so big we must strive for perspective; because they are so small we must be continually active. Bandage the sore foot, divide the tobacco stick *exactly* in two. And if we are to espouse Causes let us do so with all our strength but let us realise that in so doing we feed the need within ourselves, not within the Cause. And let us be happy in the realisation because if we are not no one else will be.

For the Child Crusade of the 11th century is each one of us in microcosm, for some got lost and died on the way, some were sold into slavery and some became wealthy traders while all, by Papal Encyclical, received the Martyr's Crown – a warming consolation to the bereft Mothers.

I am sorry to have run on at such irrelevant length (the effect of a rare early night) and words, not being my medium, convey only partially and imperfectly my meaning. Sometimes in paint I seem to get through to a true expression and I hope eventually it may be clearer. What? Simply, I think, enjoyment. Enjoyment of the whole bang lot of it, and most of all enjoyment of the bewildering, perplexing, funny, sad, human animal on his zig-zag march from camp to camp and sometimes sitting in the shade.

With all best wishes and thanks for letting me see the MS so far – also thank you for the very enjoyable lunch on Monday.

Elizabeth

Poem: Song of the Travellers Returned, *1954*

They all go away
and they all come back
then, scarcely before
they begin to unpack
(whether they be Australian born
or ones who fled Europe all forlorn)
the chorus starts up
from all their throats
like a creek full of frogs
or a yard full of goats:

"London is hateful
we didn't like Rome
oh, we're terribly grateful
to be back home.
The food was funny,
the people stank,

we couldn't get money
out of the bank.
It was dirty and dark
and bitt-er-ly cold
dingy and stark
and de-crepidly old.
Paris was not
gay and delightful
and as for Berlin
it's simply a spot
to avoid being in.
Spain is just frightful
the cabmen there robbed us
and going through Naples
the porters all mobbed us.
Theatres? oh yes, and music and shows
plenty of that the Lord only knows
but everywhere crowds – you couldn't draw breath
and on a diet of culture we'd soon starve to death.
The people looked hungry and frightened and thin.
Laughing in London is almost a sin.
The pavements were filthy beneath all those feet
and worst of the lot we couldn't get meat.
The pavements were damp
we couldn't buy meat –
all the beds gave us cramp
and we couldn't get MEAT …"

Then when we told them
we're going home to stay
(now this'll rock you)
what did they say –
standing there in that London stew
with their chill-blained hands and noses blue?
You'll hardly believe it, but "Oh," said they,
"We teddibly, teddibly sorry for you!"

Letter: Elizabeth Durack in Sydney responds to her critics: 'Hate Hocus–Pocus on LOVE MAGIC'.

An open letter, never sent, to Paul Haefliger (Sydney Morning Herald) and James Gleeson (Sydney Sun) November 1954.

When an artist exhibits his work he invites criticism in general and criticism in particular from the representatives of the various newspapers in whatever city the work may be on display. The latter are within their rights to make any statement they choose, favourable or otherwise, within the boundary of what is known as 'fair comment'.

The story of artists' reaction to hostile criticism is a long and not unamusing one. Whistler resorted to affectations of rudeness towards his critics which became a delight to Londoners. Matisse, stung to retaliate at various times, advised: "If you would reply cut your tongue out – an artist should speak only with his brush." Then he promptly flew into print with his *Notes of a Painter* in an endeavour to justify and elucidate his work. Others more sensitive became unhinged – ran pencils through their hearts or dropped into chilly dawn waters. Picasso, the wisest old man of all, did not exhibit before a solid reinforcement of eclectic literature and a good deal of private investment had conditioned the world into a receptive state. The 'Art Colony' or clique is itself a defence against the outside world and the barbs of the critic who is usually, in such cases, made an integrate part within the group.

At a recent exhibition of some work of mine at Anthony Hordens' Art Gallery in Sydney (ah! you were right in sensing this was coming), I am quite prepared to accept in good grace that I cannot paint, that I cannot draw, that this despoiling of surfaces that has apparently been going on far too long is all something less than Art. The critic is expressing his opinion as he is entitled to do and, as in the interests of possible public exploitation, he has a duty to do. However I have one small dart in an otherwise empty quiver so I can let it fly into the No Man's Land between the trenches – for what it is worth.

I wish to, and am within my rights to correct a misstatement: The decorative mural *Love Magic* – a sequence of ten pictures – is NOT "a copy of Aboriginal bark paintings".

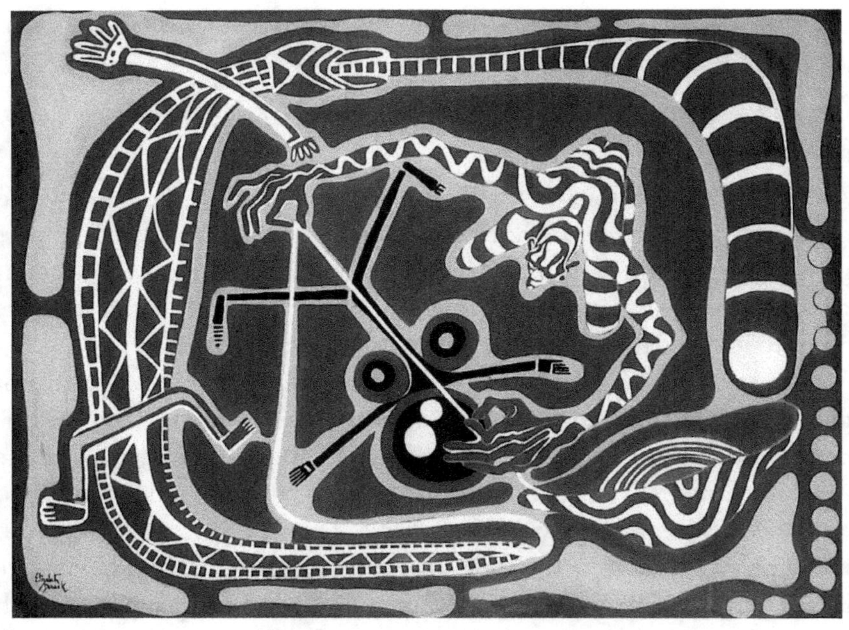

Drawing Death 1954 from the series *Love Magic*
oil on board 94 x 125 cm, private collection

The critics of two leading Sydney newspapers assert that it is and a third implies it. I ask them to produce the bark paintings from which this work is copied. May I suggest that in asserting that this particular work of mine is a copy they reveal the fact that not only are they unaware of what I have done but that they are completely ignorant of the bark paintings of the Aboriginals themselves. As one of the best collections of these paintings can be found in Berlin, it is regrettable that 'Our Art Critic' of *The Sydney Morning Herald* did not avail himself of an opportunity of seeing them before he left home to give Australia the benefits of his erudition.

Apart from some photographs my own knowledge of the subject had to be acquired the hard way. I have seen only local collections and the work of the few remaining artists in the far northern regions of our continent. As for the comment about my self-conscious attitude of "White Meets Black", I can only say that three generations of my family in these remote parts probably makes any of us less self-conscious about

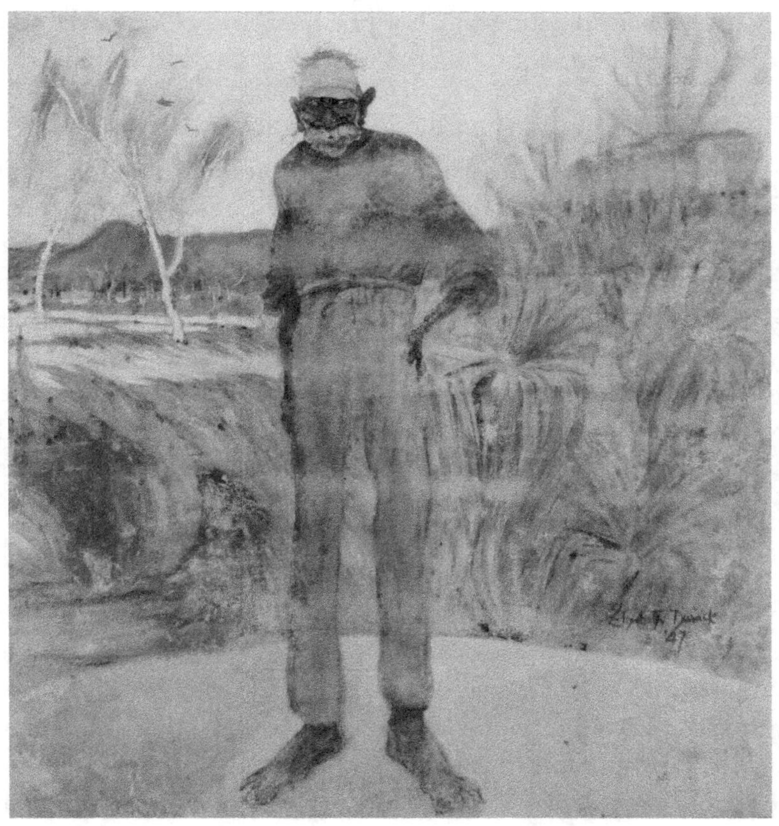

Jubul 1947
oil on canvas approx 90 x 70 cm, private collection

the Aborigine than we would care to admit socially.

All this in itself however would not give sufficient confidence in developing my ideas had it not been for my acquaintance with an old Aboriginal artist called Jubul who I knew in the Kimberley district of Western Australia. He used to come to my studio on the banks of the Ord River and watch me painting. Usually his reaction, particularly to portraits, was one of great merriment. One day, chiefly to get rid of him, I gave him some paper and pencils and told him to go away and draw something for me. He quickly lost patience with these materials and on another visit came equipped with his own. I learned then that he was an old hand at the game as he came originally from Arnhem Land but because bark painting was not practised in the Kimberleys he had not bothered about it for years or to work without the stimulation of 'the colony'.

It was an exciting experience to see him go to work on a piece of prepared bark with his paper-bark brushes and his tins of ochres mixed with urine and blood. He explained carefully to me that what he was doing was simply "play-about" art and had no connection with the paintings in the sacred caves which we had, on occasions, visited together. That of course was the *real* thing; this was more a pleasant way of filling in the hot hours between camps. The subject matter would be some incident of the day, the hunt or the dance. He drew an aeroplane with the same aplomb as a crow. A verbal explanation always accompanied his pictures, much laughter and hand waving. Dots and lines were used to fill in the parts that were "too hard" to draw.

Before he commenced work he seemed to have a very clear picture in his mind of what he was going to put down. I never saw him rub out a line. The whole was a kind of building up ordered by some kind of innate sense of form and design that was never geometrical or precise though always perfectly balanced and satisfying. I would ask him out of curiosity why he had placed a certain form just so and not another way. It was then that the governing factor operating over the whole work became clear. The painting in completion had always to have "Look-Nice" as no matter how interesting it was it was just no good.

"Look-Nice" has been explained in more elaborate terms and at much greater length since the beginning of art comment but never with the same economy and directness as Jubul managed to convey to me. A sort of mutual admiration society went on between us for a long time. We never tried or thought of 'influencing' each other. I continued working with Windsor and Newton, Jubul and his dogs shuffled around outside under a tree. At the end of the day I would exchange his work for some tobacco and he would have his usual good laugh over mine. After a while I had quite a pile of paintings and a lot less tobacco. It is a great sorrow to me that these paintings were later lost when the old Ivanhoe homestead burned down in September 1950.

It is only very recently that I have had any urge to incorporate some of the lessons and methods of this art into my own work. In doing the illustrations for K Langloh Parker's *Australian Legendary Tales* it came to me that really the only possible way of illustrating these stories was by an adaptation of the bark-drawing method. From this I began to work on a larger scale and on themes and sequences.

No art is ever really 'new'. Ideas are more infectious than measles. I make no secret of the fact that this particular section of my work derives from Aboriginal Art but – in no possible definition of the word, is it a copy. That I have found bark paintings a spring of inspiration I admit but so too did the modern French School derive a similar stimulus from African carvings while artists such as van Gogh, Toulouse Lautrec and Gaugin received a fiat from the introduction into Europe of Japanese prints.

The critics in their comments upon my *Love Magic* pictures accuse me of not doing precisely that which I am doing – creating a synthesis of two art forms. Perhaps it is poor and bad, perhaps it is wrong, perhaps it should be stopped here and now before it gets a grip of any part of my imagination or before any more misguided investors want to see it on their walls – but let it be clear: the work is not a copy of bark paintings. Of course, if the critics would be any happier I could make for them some truly faithful copies (they might like to contribute some of the mixing materials for the ochres) but in this case they would really be better advised to choose some other artist more adept at plagiarism. (Did I hear Mr James Gleeson cough?)

All they will ever get from me is something 'curiously hybrid' – an amalgam that tells 'as much about our own world as it does about the Aborigines …' The critics themselves, it appears, have failed to register to either world.

All Love is Magic and the motorcar as powerful a charm as an enchanted shell.

Yours sincerely
Elizabeth Durack

Poem: To the Southern Cross, 5 *November 1955*

Set there an arrow
set in a bow
ready to let fly
at the word go.

Set like a jelly
up side down
set like a smile on
the face of a clown.

Set like four jewels
set in a crown
set like a plaster cast
set in a frown.

Set like a keen high
precision tool
sharpened and pointed
set with a rule.

Aloft in black sky
brand new and bright
kite to forever fly
set in its flight.

Set like the felled tree
set to transfix
St Peter reversed
on his crucifix.

So is the Southern Cross
set in the heaven
tonight as I saw it
at half past eleven.

Elizabeth was an inconsistent diary keeper. When motivated to keep a daily record she usually wrote in blank notebooks which meant that length of entries would range from several pages to simply a line or two. Michael and I were teenagers and still at school in 1957 with our mother supporting the household on an income derived solely from sales of her art – paintings from exhibitions and hand-finished prints. Compared with many subsequent Day Book and Journal entries, 1957 is minimalist. Even so the brief record highlights some preoccupations of the times.

PDC

Diary: 15 April 1957

Will try to keep diary – event and activity only – things sent etc. Dinner at Dr Minc's[18]– ten present – all artists – all hungry.

Diary: 16 April 1957

Out to Houghton's vineyards. Drawing – interesting also romantic – rather too much architecture for me – figures minor to tanks of wine, presses etc – but a wonderful atmosphere. A kind of 'devil's kitchen' – it is more than wines they are making. Sent two felt nib sketches to manager, Jack Mann.

Diary:17 April 1957

Hersey [gardener] came. Into town to bank. Paid in cheque from Alberts [Bookshop] (£22) cheque from Cooper Bros & Goyder – no, someone else returning £5 on house insurance (?) Very little money in bank – would be none if bills all paid up. Bought Henrietta Drake-Brockman's book *The Wicked and the Fair* from Tothill (Library) also a comb from Bairds.

Diary: 18 April 1957

Kids on Easter holidays. Michael fishing with Andrew. Perpetua into town to pictures with Julie. Invitation from Lord Mayor to meet Albert Namatjira – doubt if I'll go. Invitation from Geoff ? Kwinana to meet Albert Namatjira – (Friday 26th 3.00pm) doubt if I'll go.

Diary1: 9 April 1957 – Good Friday

Hersey cut big wattle trees back (£3). Mother left for Adelaide, TAA 11.30pm. Out to airport with Mary, Robin and Julie.

Diary: 21 April 1957 – Easter Sunday

Mass with the kids at Old Men's Home [Subsequently Sunset Hospital, Dalkeith, now awaiting redevelopment]. Quiet day, very wet. Went with Michael to see waves at Cottesloe.

Diary: 22 April 1957

At home – prints – and reading *David Copperfield* to Perpetua. Fires are started.

Diary: 23 April 1957

Into town – kids on holiday – visited Convent. Alberts sold eleven of the sketches delivered to them three weeks ago.

Diary: 24 April 1957

Didn't go to meet Albert Namatjira. (Mary went.) Perpetua on Geography expedition to Armadale with Aquinas College. Wrote to Kim in Sydney.

Diary: 25 April 1957

Anzac Day. Mass with Michael. Tidied caravan and centre room. Posted prints to Verity Bookshop, Canberra. Collected the three remaining pictures from Royal Auto Club. Perpetua's friend, Kerry Riley, here for dinner. Played chess with Michael.

Diary: 26 April 1957

Into town with prints. Down to Kwinana with Mary and Patsy to arrangement there for Albert Namatjira. Only went under pressure and persuasion but I wish I had not, although Albert is impressive.

Diary: 27 April 1957

Watched Head of the River [inter-school rowing] from King's Park, with Michael. Kim arrived from Sydney, staying here.

Diary: 14 May 1957

Into town with children. Shoes for Perpetua, jumper for Michael. Working on print order for Todd & Co this afternoon.

Diary: 16 May 1957

Perpetua posted Todd's order to Melbourne for me – TAA. Stramit and Nu-roof men came to see leak in studio.

Diary: 18 May 1957

P off to Rottnest for weekend. M out. Quiet day. Did two prints and one road picture. Mother and Edith called and stayed for dinner. Got new screen for studio. Seems good.

Diary: 20 May 1957

Into town with Michael to deliver prints to Aherns and post clothes to Perpetua in Rottnest. Rumours this afternoon that Freney's *may* have struck oil. [*Two generations of Duracks built castles in the air on Freney shares – until they ceased to trade in the early 1970s.* PDC]

Diary: 21 May 1957

Lunch with Mr and Mrs Mann (Angela Dolet) at Houghton's vineyards with Michael, Grey Smiths, Pat Jordanoff, two or three others, otherwise no work, and no news of Freney's. Shares up to 4/8 but on 9.00pm news no comment at all. Tomorrow?

Diary: 25 May 1957

House – Met P at Fremantle returning from Rottnest. Dinner with Colebatchs.

Diary: 27 May 1957

Into town with Michael (shoes). Got some small prints (MacDougalls). Worked on them afternoon and evening.

Diary: 31 May 1957

Working on landscapes as Caris Bros asked if I had any. Did 18 from the road notes. Mary came for dinner. Read closing chapters of *Kings in Grass Castles* worked to late on possible cover for same (3.00am now).

Diary: 1 June 1957

Wet day. With Michael to see *War and Peace*. Perpetua has Toni Tully staying the night.

Diary: 2 June 1957

Worked on drawings in morning. Went to *The Reluctant Debutante* in afternoon with Perpetua (English cast in an English play – very poor).

Diary: 6 June 1957

Maps for Mary's book.

Diary: 7 June 1957

Cover for Mary's book. Cold in head. Letter from Kim. Also traffic summons.

Diary: 8 June 1957

Didn't go to Henrietta Drake-Brockman's party yesterday – bad cold. Wrote letters.

Diary: 9 June 1957

Did nothing – bad cold.

Diary: 10 June 1957

Can't work because of bad cold. Cold and wet day.

Diary: 17 June 1957

Completed maps etc Mary's MS.

Diary: 18 June 1957

Sent Mary's MS [*Kings in Grass Castles*] to Florence James, Constables, 10 Orange Street, London. Airmail (£2.12.0) this morning.

Diary: 29 June 1957

— — – – – P X X X [*Translated: P behaving abominably.*]

Diary: 6 July 1957

My birthday. Took P, M and Julie to *Tobias and the Angel* at the Playhouse. Wrote to Kim re David [brother].

Diary: 7 July 1957

Quiet day. Mass at 10.00am Cathedral. Visited Mary in afternoon. Patsy N there. Mary packing for departure tomorrow. With children doing Xwords in evening.

Diary: 26 July 1957

Dentist – wisdom tooth out. Brought three prints to Myrtle Rose White, Wentworth Hotel. Puncture tyre. David evening.

Diary: 4 August 1957

Mass 9.30. Called on Reg and Enid. Mother here for midday meal. Quiet afternoon doing two small prints. Evening, P to Aquinas to hear debate. I reading old journals prior to destroying them. Allan Cook called 10.00pm with the borrowed pictures from the Upper Swan show. Claude Hotchin has bought *The Great Northern Highway* (a big water colour road picture). £21.00 (minus commission). P home 12.00pm – bed.

Diary: 16 August 1957

Tooth out 11.00am.

Diary: 24 August 1957 [*The date has been heavily underlined.* PDC]

Bruce McPherson here for day with Michael. Plans to leave for Ninghan Station tomorrow. Evening meal with Mother.

Diary: 27 August 1957

Dressmaking with P. News of Cecil Durack's death midday. John Dent called 8.00pm with Perpetua's photos.

Diary: 28 August 1957

Requiem Mass for cousin Cecil at the Holy Rosary 9.00am with Perpetua and Mother. Wet day.

Diary: 5 October 1957

Perpetua's *Alliance Française* exam.

Poem: Anniversary *Thursday 10.30pm, 20 November 1958*[19]

Oh I am less sad now
for sorrow
of all of yesterday
than the unburied power
in you
over tomorrow.
This unremitting barrenness
of your persistence
to pursue.
Had you but lived
you could have died
for me
as better men than you
and some more true
that I have buried
of my own accord –
I could have seen
you wed
to some coarse wench
some nag or bore
and patched
a wounded pride with:
"Well matched!"
Or as the years passed
and a string of
nondescript offspring

swung into existence
I could have faced you then
with cool indifference –
or on a chance meeting
(in a pub, on the tarmac,
buying a lettuce)
seen the hand of time
had thickened your face
thinned your mind
and smiling then
consoled myself,
the way we do, with:
"Lucky escape …!"

There are a thousand
ways
you could have died
more utterly
(as better men than you
and some more true)
than as you did –
but with your death
(sudden, preposterous
22 years ago)
in one swift stroke
of cunning
you contrived
in me
your immortality –
and I am shocked
from sadness
into anger
at the long
remorseless
continuity
of your living –
Better men than you

(and some more true)
I've buried in the sands
with these two hands.
Oh I am less sad now
for sorrow
than for this power
you hold
upon tomorrow.

Poem: The death of Albert Namatjira, *9 August 1959*

Marie Rose picked a small blue flower
"I'm allowed, I think, because
I haven't picked the root …"
(we were within the 50 mile
wild flower protection limit).

Robin kicked over a white stone
with her toe: "Quartz," she said,
"but not likely to be gold-bearing."

I was picking dry nuts and brown leaves
that fire had passed through.
Spikey leaves that the fire had
trans-coloured
but not damaged – little
black nuts with cracked laughing mouths
that they had spat the seeds from –
Kim said: "They'll make an
awful mess of the boot."

Then we picked our way down the hill
to where Mother was arranging
a small posy
of white, flat-faced, tiny flowers –
the ones that smell honey-sweet.

Big grey cloud raced overhead
and a grey rain mist
smudged its way
slowly over the valley below
like an accident to a watercolour.

"You saw about Albert," said Mother.
"Albert … you know, I can never
pronounce his name –
you saw where he died yesterday …"

But I saw nothing, nothing
except a white tree
twisting and weeping
amid alien grey …
and Mother putting down her posy
gently in a safe place
before she lifted the lid of the picnic basket.

1960s

I AM, I THINK, A METAPHYSICAL ARTIST[20]

Elizabeth held eleven solo exhibitions during this decade, six in Melbourne, Sydney and Canberra, five in Perth. She also completed commissions for CRA in the Pilbara and on Bougainville Island. A significant event was in 1961 when Bryan Robertson chose examples of her work for his landmark Recent Australian Painting *at the Whitechapel Gallery, London. Elizabeth was one of only three females in the field of 53.*

By 1963 Mother was back in the north living and working in Broome, Beagle Bay, Wyndham, Kununurra and Kildurk Station. Perpetua and Michael graduated from university and soon left home – Perpetua to teach in Africa, Michael to work as an engineer with WAPET in Western Australia. Frank Clancy died in August 1965. By then Elizabeth too was ready to leave home for a while.

Between 1966-69 she travelled for months at a time through Africa, Europe, the UK, the US, the Pacific and PNG. During her travels she wrote for Australian newspapers and magazines and also commenced the first of her 'seeing through' books: Seeing—through Papua New Guinea, An Artist's Impressions of the Territory *(1968).*

PDC

Letter: Elizabeth Durack in Melbourne – an open letter, never sent, to critics – Alan Warren (The Sun), Alan McCulloch (The Herald), Arnold Shore (The Age), 24 June 1961

Dear Sirs

Because it is ten years since I last exhibited in Melbourne,[21] and because I am, I imagine, unknown to most of you, I thought I might be forgiven on this occasion for addressing the following comment to you.

Some of you may have already seen some of my work in various forms (illustration, prints, murals etc) and already placed me into certain pigeonholes that although justified, perhaps, have been something of a bugbear to me over the years.

I am not an illustrator although some of the work that has given me something of a reputation in this field might seem to contradict this. It did so happen that I illustrated certain books at a time when work of this nature coincided with my artistic development (e.g. *The Way of the Whirlwind* was as far as I could go with expression at the time I did it – now over 20 years ago). I have neither the discipline nor the training to tackle the illustration of a book on any subject such as the true illustrator has at his command.

Neither am I 'a crusader for the aboriginals' – another favourite pigeonhole. I am, to a fault, disinterested in social issues and have always veered away from any move to drag me into taking an active role on such vexed issues as 'citizenship for the aborigines', 'uplift of our depressed minority' etc. Whilst I admire people who can give generously of time and thought to these matters, they are not for me and I have an instinctive sense that the artist bearing a Social Torch, is headed for a bog. (This may not have always been so, but today our boundaries and our dilemmas have stretched.) It simply happened that for years the Aboriginals were (and still are to a large extent) my everyday companions. I got to know them pretty well, got to draw them pretty well – seeing them always as members of the human family as a whole, not as a particular people, of a particular race. Also I have been moved by their beauty – particularly in coincidence with landscape.

(Recently I turned down an offer to exhibit in Moscow because I saw, just in time – the offer was superficially attractive – that the interest in my work was not from an aesthetic point of view but because there was a good deal in it that could be twisted towards 'anti-capitalist' propaganda. To be a tool for political ends is abhorrent to me.)

Yes, I can if I wish, do good decorative mural work and will continue to if I get the chance – realising, however, that 'art as decoration' is only one facet (and a restrictive one at that) of the whole of art. The same goes for 'the document' which I have done with spirit and enjoyment at times and will do so again no doubt. [Refer *Shearing – its Practice and Poetry*; *Look at the State we're in; Meekatharra; Geraldton and the Living Past*; *The Inland Road* et al.]

My development as an artist has been slow – this is partly due to the circumstances of my life and environment, partly because it is almost impossible for me to be influenced by another artist in the way that can so often lead to rapid artistic growth and discovery of individuality. All my influences have been interior spiritually – exterior visually, and I have deplored at times my inability to assimilate or to regard the expression of other artists with more than a sincere, but impersonal admiration. Moreover, during the long and slow process I have been helped to a considerable degree by perspicacious critics – all in negative reaction. It has been enough for a critic to refer to me as 'an illustrator', 'a crusader', 'a documentor', 'a decorator' to build up my responses contra-wise.

Over the last few years, however, a change – a development, rather – has occurred. My reading and study has led me into the fields of mathematics, physics and philosophy and whilst it seemed to me at times that I was getting wider and wider and further and further from my chosen medium of expression, a confluence has occurred where the thought material closest to my heart has united with the heart material closest to my eye and mind.

The present exhibition [of 37 paintings] represents some examples of this development. The delicate antennae of the intuitive and aesthetic stimulus, which only extends in those places of Australia where I can achieve a sense of timelessness and placeless-ness, has at last found upon the familiar material a support to curve and lace itself. In short, I have started painting – painting in a state of semi-somnolism where manual manipulation is automatic and almost unconscious. While much of the work remains conscious and awake I feel more and more drawn towards the sleeping areas where symbolism and the contrived accident will finally bring me to peace and towards a heightened realism.

Still, I enjoy drawing – and nor would I try to convince myself or others that I am airborne, until such time as I actually am. But the boundaries which have held me enthralled for so long are collapsing on all sides. Dividing lines no longer exist. Horizons have dissolved (have in fact become obsolete with the elevated perspective). The recurrent surface image and human symbol moves on – where? That is the question.

To this question I can only give my particular answer within the limitations of my time and my country: sufficient that there is *procession.* Do not ask where we are going – we only know we are going on. For the present this is enough … and represents a faith enlarged considerably from a previous belief that continuance necessitated annihilation.

Later this procession – this going on of substance and non-substance – will make more sense than it does either to me or to others at the moment. I am, I think, a metaphysical artist and when my material output justifies this label I shall have played my role.

I am dependent upon comprehension at the moment from the critics, for the Press represents almost the only bridge between artist and public. I look for the type of perspicacity that can elucidate my work and build confidence – my own as well as public confidence – in order that I may be able to continue to do what I must.

Yours sincerely
Elizabeth Durack

Letter: Elizabeth Durack from The Bishop's House, Broome to Perpetua at '47', 3 January 1963

My darling Perpetua

I haven't started yet, haven't unpacked my paints but will be doing so today. Everything else is unpacked and in pretty good order and all my things are clean and tidy. Had a hectic day yesterday shunting all the hideous dirty old furniture out of sight (more or less) into the sleep-out and now all three rooms are practically empty and look much better. There is not a great deal more I can do to them that does not entail spending money – painting walls etc which I am just not going to do at present and will soon get my mind off the housewifely tack and on to essentials. I made out an inventory of everything and have written to Marie McDaniel and sent a month's rent. Of course I am rather nervous and strung up and a bit anxious but basically, Perpetua, I am just thrilled about this place. I feel I don't want anyone to know just how much I love it and how much I wish (wreck and derelict as it is) that I owned it. Even its very decrepidness [sic] appeals to me in some strange way. I just hate the State Housing jobs – little neat boxes where life is reduced to the level of gadgets and mod cons and stripped of everything else. I love these wide verandahs and the breathtaking glimpses of Roebuck Bay through the corroded and slipping wrought iron. I love the big empty rooms, the high ceilings and the French doors and the mad bits of broken coloured glass around the front door – yellow – bright yellow and in the morning the sun streams through it and lights everything up and sends all the ghosts of the night hours spinning. But don't tell anyone any of this (and I will tell Julie not to either) [Julie Miller, ED's niece had accompanied her on the drive from Perth to Broome] because if I am talking about it at all I just pull a long face and say: "It's sad. It's terribly sad – the poor old place is just a wreck." And of course it is too but if I can see any daylight ahead over the next few months or weeks I'll make an offer for the place and try to get hold of it. At least that's how I feel at the moment. But I'll want it dead cheap and to get it that way I must continually depress and deflate it. I can't see that it is of any use to *anyone* but me. It would be awful as a family house with small kids, it is useless for a bachelor, worse for a spinster or any young person but ideal for me – and to furnish these empty rooms with paintings is a challenge. I am writing this in the empty empty room in which I'll work. I've got the big wood table in here now, an old bookcase for paint pots and it should not be long before the gun goes off. Julie has just come in. She flies back shortly. She wants to spend the night with you tonight and will give you all the news.

I saw the Males on New Year's night. They send special love to you.

Sam recalls you with particular affection and tells about your asking if you can smoke a cigarette and how he said: "Yes. And what will you drink with it, Perpetua – gin, whiskey, beer?" He told this story about three times. They are being brave and bright over their loss but in fact they are both on the brink of tears most of the time and it is terribly tragic.[22] I know you would be welcome there any time and of course, compared – this is a blacks' camp as regards comfort etc …

Perpetua, I don't know if I'll be able to get anything down in time for the Perth Prize. It won't matter much if I don't and I don't want to send anything I'm not sure of feeling ill-used if it doesn't win (which it wouldn't anyway) but I'll want to know all about it and, if you see and speak to Laurie Thomas [art critic and judge], you can just say I'm living and working in Broome. It would be fun to see him again and give him my fond regards. Will be glad of any news of 'the art world' when you get going at the Skinner [Galleries] again …

It is a grey day here today. It throws up the whites of everything. There is talk of the Queen's visit and Broome has gone vinca happy what with the latter and the new water (good). The Q will only be here one hour or so. They will see the school kids etc – then just a quick drive along two streets and off.

Fondest love darling, loving thoughts, love always
mummm

Letter: Elizabeth Durack in Broome to Perpetua at '47', 5 January 1963

My darling Perpetua

I was delighted to get two letters from you this morning from PO (2 and 4 Jan). No, mail is not delivered here, but you can address letters 'Bishop's House' as it is well for the PO to know my address in case of wires etc. As regards yours of 2 Jan, how clever of you to sell those pictures. I haven't got the faintest recollection of what *Settlement – Post Atomic* is (unless it is a picture painted by my subconscious of Bishop's House and wafted down to 47 Browne Ave tele-pathetically). However, that doesn't matter. Yes, please pop everything into ANZ kitty 68 St George's Terrace and send receipt slip to me and I'll pop it among 'the papers'. (I note time-payment arrangements. That's OK. Did you learn this tip from Rose [Skinner – gallery owner]? Did you also obtain his name and address and enter it in the Visitor's Book so as to be able to jog his memory in 6 months' time?)

Glad you heard from David [Ledger] and interested in the Mornington [Station] business. Suppose he is pretty busy over collection of plant etc just now. Yes – old Pip [Dunkley] same old butterfly drip apparently. But P don't, if he breezes up one day, flatter him with the cold shoulder. Just greet him with the same sort of cordiality as you would the milkman if he'd let up on the deliveries. Think this will get you further quicker and more dignified, also remember me kindly to him.

It's good to know Julie arrived home safely and that you have had some good talks with her. She is a wonderful old pal to us all and always loyal and loving. Hope she has been able to deal with the squatters in her place. She owes no loyalty to them and they are just imposing on her.

Glad to hear you are coping with the house and getting at some cupboards. If the Craven As turn up in big quantities you might send them on as I find I am giving a good few away here, e.g. to the 'ill Mob [Kennedy's Hill, camping ground] for digging me out of a sand bog (which I should have had more sense than to get into) and to the prisoners.

There is a chap at the gaol here called Wherra Jack.[23] He carves boab nuts and emu eggs. Wonderful work, true folk art and he can knock the famous Eskimo-walrus-tusk artists into a cocked hat. He is in for life for a tribal murder, *Kadaitcha* stuff, and I called and had a talk with him this morning. His face is a mask of resignation and his eyes like sleeping coals. He has put on too much weight on the prison fare and was heavy and leaden in his talk and so docile that when I asked him to stay still for a few moments while I drew him he just petrified and moved not so much as an eyelash and I think had asked him to stay like that for three hours it would have been the same. Consequently I was able pretty easily to depict this rather monolithic shape. I showed it to him and a quick change came over him, his face lit up and he smiled and looked suddenly quite young and boyish. He immediately asked the Warden if he could get his drawings to show me. As it turns out these are rather

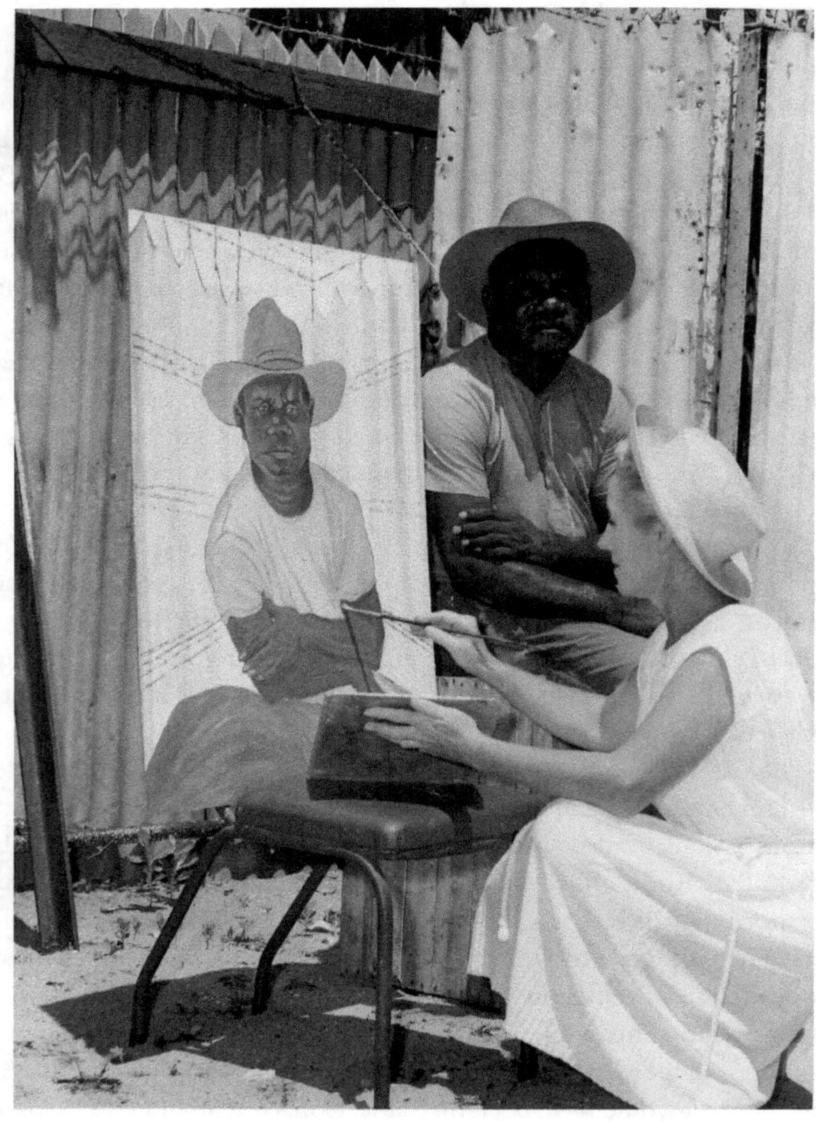

Elizabeth Durack painting Wherra Jack,
Broome Gaol 1963, ©photo courtesy WA Newspapers

feeble watercolours on drawing book cartridge, but feeble in a very particular and heart-breaking way. "My country like that," landscapes of the King George – Munga area done in his cell from memory. Rocks, a waterfall, palm trees and one with a pink sky and waterlilies, "Sun go down." They did not have the craftsmanship of the boab nut carvings and none of the fun of the latter as these carved ones are all genera stuff, blackfellows spearing kangaroos, hunting dugong, dogs chasing and tumbling kangaroos etc. Anyway, a portrait of Wherra Jack is the first painting I've done and have just knocked off working on it to rattle this to you. I don't know yet whether it is any good or not but it is a start and I loved doing it and worked very fast and sure, and the old turtle just went on croaking in a slow deep monotonous voice. It is getting rather dark now and I shall have to have a shower directly as I am having a meal with Celia de Pedro at 7.45 – just me, as Roy is v sick and feeble and she wants to get him to bed first.

A big storm here last night and what a scatter. If there were any ghosts in the place they must have blown away leaving only me who must have looked very like one running up and down the long verandahs in a shorty nightie blowing over my head shutting shutters and doors. A lot of mess and debris this morning but I am v relieved to discover that, although every gutter and verandah roof leaks, in this room where I am working and in the room where I am sleeping, not a drop. The old beaten sheet iron has weathered the test of time pretty marvellously as it must be 70 years old.

Glad to hear you liked *Duveen* [by S.N. Behrman], what a man, eh, and how cleverly this book is written holding the excitement and interest right through. Also glad you went to the races with Diane, that you are not minding the solitude of the house on your own too much and that you are going to the play with the Yank. Tell me all about it. I really don't want to lose touch completely with the goings on down there, although I really doubt I'll make anything for that Perth Prize this year. The sheer EFFORT of getting the tiniest job done here in Broome makes me think I'd never get Gould [local carpenter] to rig a frame for me over the next 5 or 6 days. I gave my iron to an electrician last Monday and it and the electrician have disappeared off the face of the earth. When I tell people this they just laugh and say: "You haven't waited a year yet, we waited a year for our iron to come back." This man also goes on blind drunks, I wish someone had warned me as I am wearing my shirts rough dry.

But on Tuesday I am having the GANG down from the gaol for a clean up. This has also taken much tortuous negotiating but at least the gaoler is in one piece and only a party drunk and rather a jolly old boy although he went rather blue when I handed him a typed list of what I wanted done in the day [see below]. I know I opened my mouth pretty wide but I thought it best that way as even if they only do a quarter it will help.

Must leave this now, dear. I haven't heard from Michael since arriving. Glad you had a letter from him [on Cockatoo Island, Yampi Sound]. I'll write again tomorrow. I see Uncle Horry of an evening. When he is not out on Dampier Downs [Station] he drops in for a wee low-pressure talk and I make responses also at low-pressure. He has lent me a hammer and a screwdriver which I think v nice of him. I put the lid of my car up if I see him coming in the hope he'll look inside it for me (the oil) but he hasn't taken the hint yet. I dread to think what sort of complication there will be getting a simple mechanical job done. However, am only creeping around in 2 – 3 mile laps here at present. Not that there is much wrong with the car but it should be looked at after the big run [373 miles (600 kms) on unsealed road] from Port Hedland.

I am feeling very well and although I miss you very much and darling Gran and Michael and all the kids I am really very happy Perpetua and enjoying everything here and particularly this strange energy that I have. Love to everyone –

Always your loving
Mummm x x x x x x

January 1963
TO: Mr Ferridge – Prisoner liaison, Broome Gaol
RE: Clean-up 'Bishop's House'

Implements required:
Rakes, spades, picks, clippers, secateurs, hoes, sickles, wire

rope – (for dislodgment of leaning tanks. May not be possible with man-power and may require a truck).
Front section, east:
general rake over
define garden path from gate by removing weeds and grass
turn soil in beds along verandah base and trim edges
turn soil around oleander hedge
Southside section: same as above
Back and west section:
gather all rubbish – rusty tins, old drums, old copper etc etc and place in heap for collection by Council
dismantle leaning tanks from broken stand and place with adjacent rubbish pile ditto old rubble under stands
empty grease trap (bury refuse) and scour out with caustic soda and disinfectant (to be provided)
remove cement plant pots from verandah (west side) and place as directed
cut back long grass around old lavatory and remove all rubble from this section and place with pile – rake and tidy around present rubbish drums
dig 4 foot square pit for future rubbish hole in place to be indicated

1963 marked HRH Queen Elizabeth II and Prince Phillip's second visit to Australia. In addition to capital cities, the Royal Visit included stopovers in Darwin, Kununurra, Cockatoo Island/Yampi Sound and, on 21 March, Broome.

PDC

Letter: Elizabeth Durack in Broome to Perpetua at '47', 22 March 1963

Dearest Perpetua

Broome feels this morning like a piece of tightly extended elastic that has suddenly been let go – I myself have not showered yet although 8.45am but thought I'd rattle this before other things blot out the excitements of yesterday.

These atmospheres and feelings-in-the-air are not just figures of speech. They are strange. I wonder what they consist of chemically. Yesterday began for me very early. The little man who is supposed to be painting the roof here was on it before light. Apparently Terry [McDaniel] had told him that if he didn't get it done by 'The Day' he wouldn't pay him. It still is far from finished but he did do a lot of rapid splashing around from 3.30am to 8 o'clock. The intricacies of 'the contract' will no doubt be thrashed out over endless Bar conversations. I'll be surprised now if another brush of Talorite is lifted to this roof – ever.

It was a lovely morning. A breeze from the west came in early and the sky was full of puffs of mauve cloud. Some days this month have been real panters and tongue-lollers but not yesterday. The air was quite light. There was a sort of hush in it. This was probably because the bull-dozers, graders etc were silent for the first time since I've been here. A few cars were wizzing [sic] around containing busy last-minuters not yet 'dressed'. Celia de Pedro dropped in about 6.30 on her way to the Roads Board Hall to arrange some flowers and to tell me she had read the story about Wherra Jack. She seemed rather excited about it. I was bored. I had asked them [*The West Australian*] not to print anything until and unless anything was actually finalised but this was pretty useless as they obviously intended to and knew about it [the imminent Royal Pardon] before seeing me for the photo.

I drove Celia to the Roads Board Hall and saw people running up their flags. One opposite, Mr Knox the butcher, (one of Derm's 'men') [Derm Farrell, Shire President], The Conti Hotel [The Mercure now stands on the site of the old Continental Hotel], Bishop Frewer's house, the Cross of St George, Blue Ensigns, Union Jacks, Aussie flags. About half past eight the blacks started straggling along on their way to the

[Primary State] school where they had been told to assemble. A big group passed here – men, women, kids and babies – in sparkling new bright clothes. The run-through of sketches will about give you the picture. I don't know what to do with these and would be glad of any suggestions. I had thought of *The Sketch*, London, but I simply don't know whether they'd want them and whether to bring them further along (the work in them) or leave them as they are, or all in b and w or to colour them?

Broome people sometimes say that the coloured people hang back from occasions such as this – but not yesterday. They were around in hundreds and they actually emphasised the enormous disparity of numbers between coloured and white people in this town. To get even a little block of whites it had been arranged that a nest of chairs for them be placed in front of the dais at the school. They must have taken their places there early because by the time I got to the school it was just a mass of coloured people – blacks, half-castes, Malays, Chinese, Japanese – milling around on foot behind the white 'nest' and the rows of school children and completely obliterating them.

I'll try and get a copy of Derm's Speech of Welcome. It was a corker for an all time low-level in this type of tripe. He prattled on about 'beef roads', rice growing on the Fitzroy (??!), iron ore in the Pilbara, and God knows what else. Anything, in fact, but about Broome, the honour the Queen was paying the town or any of the obvious things that should have gone into such a speech. The Queen's was just about as bad. While Derm was speaking she had her head down reading her reply. Then she got up and read it out from a piece of paper. I suppose these people have to be careful but wouldn't you think that after all these years of practice she could rattle off a few words of innocuous pleasantries without reading from a sheet. (Eve Farrell told me Derm's speech was written before Christmas, sent to Buckingham Palace and the Queen's reply made up there from it.) The Queen too spoke of beefroads, using the term as though it was a new kind of surface the engineers had thought up. They've tried gravel, stones, cobbles, jarrah blocks, bitumen and now – beef. Then she made allusion to the brave men doing all the brave things in developing the country and the brave women who go with them making homes in the wilderness for their men. You never heard such nonsense. It might have been a speech made by Queen Victoria or a George 100 years ago just when they broke over the Blue Mountains for all the relationship it had with life in northern Australia today. Still, it had the saving grace of being brief.

They descended the platform and made their way along the path to the gate (they planted a tree – I didn't see this). The 'nest' of whites was somewhere behind but invisible. The pathway was lined with the multi-hued from coal black to tanned yellow, some of the Chinese had very good cameras and were trying to get a shot. The Queen was wearing a nice little dress, there were many like it among the coloured girls jostling me as I watched, and a white cloth halo beret hat. She carried a posy of bravadia and frangipani (only a last minute decision made by someone strong enough to say *Broome flowers* rather than a bouquet that was going to be ordered and flown up from Perth).

This is the part where they do their little Act, turning to people in the crowd and having a passing word. The Queen was a bit lucky here, she spotted a chap in uniform, which of course she can recognise as quick as we can pick a Utrillo from a Matisse and she had a few words with him. The Duke wasn't so lucky. I saw him give a kind of desperate glance over the massed faces. He had to alight on someone so he said to one: "You from Broome?" Perhaps he thought he was a visitor just flown in from the Orient for the occasion. The chap replied: "I born here." The Duke had another go. He got the same reply. He gave up. It was only another three yards to the gate and the black car that slid in to release them momentarily. The Royal Progress set off to make the loop through the town. They were mighty quick because by the time I got into my car, picking up Mr Ferridge, who was wanting to run up the Standard at the Roads Board Hall in a hurry, and drove the few hundred yards to the Hall, parked the car (there was no crush of cars) the Royal Party was already in the Hall. Sam and Phyll were the only Official Introduction. And I think that's just about all it was. Usually, I suppose, the Queen copes with a few hundred of these at a go. I looked through the window from the verandah, only Official Party, one Press, one Photographer and Mrs McDaniel. I think that's all were allowed in the Hall at this time. The Queen looked pretty bored. I really think it is People not Things that they want when they are Out. They come Out to meet People – they're prepared for it and it's what they want. They want to do their little Act that they are so good at doing. I saw Phyll and Sam standing together in the near empty Hall looking a bit abashed. I think Phyll may have thought that you get introduced and then it all becomes jolly and matey and you can chat together in a merry party. Not so. The Queen looked at a few shells and a moment later I saw poor old Mrs Mac also on an island looking a bit crest-fallen.

Derm had insisted I show a few portraits. He said he wanted Paddy [Djagween] particularly as a talking point prior to a possible introduction of the old boy. As this is what I wanted too for Paddy I eventually agreed. So, stuck on a couple of kindergarten easels, two on the floor, with drooping ferns on the dais behind them, jammed in a corner between the last shell and carved boab nut were five ED's – unframed and looking as I knew they would – damn awful. As I told Derm, there was simply no room for paintings. However, then I gave up and ceased to care. I saw Eve having a little say about these – and the Queen did look faintly interested.

Then she moved on to THE DIVER – all my own work. At the last minute Phyll got sick and asked me to take over THE TABLEAU she had been planning for weeks to strike the NOTE that Broome was PEARLING. There wasn't much I could do. With a terrible struggle – it caused ill-feeling with Jock de Castilla, and practically called for a Special Meeting of the Council – I got THE DIVER moved off the dais where Jock had set it up, looking madder than mad, a colossal dummy in a new diving suit, and had it put in a corner on the floor. It's terribly heavy and had to be suspended from the rafters with wire. On the dais it had stood in lop-sided isolation between two big flags under the prints of the Q and the J[uke]. In the corner, at least, I was able to muck around with the shell grit, shells, palms for sea-weed etc and it made a little nitch, at least, but of course, still looked utterly Mad.

It didn't seem long before the Q escaped from this. Oh, I forgot to say that working till midnight on Wednesday I managed to get the kids' paintings up on the still wet screens that Gould eventually rigged for them.[24] There are some beauties and really, despite the bric-a-brac with which the rest of the Hall was crammed, these screens set apart from the rest (and if you shut your eyes to the rest) didn't look bad. But the break in taste(?) idea(?) was too much as an ensemble. The paintings are, of course, with their bright colours and freedom – *Modern.* The rest of the junk was Early Victorian. The two tastes(?) ideas(?) clashed badly. I saw the Q and J pause to look at them and make some remarks but I wasn't looking through the windows all the time. I was also chatting to various people on the verandahs – including Frank Wise [former WA Premier] who looked sheepish when I greeted him (or perhaps on his guard – as he might well be – as might well be all politicians as far as I'm concerned), but I did see the Duke with Derm for a moment look at the paintings (mine – just a quick look. It was, as I said to you long ago, they (the Q and the J) must be very used and bored with having that bit of 'Art' flung unartlessly in their path and, like anyone else, would be impressed with an exhibition at the Leicester or Redfern in London but not with the Village fare at the Fair. However, I don't care. As you know I did my best, my level best, not to be in on this personally. When to have continued to refuse would have been being unpleasant, I gave up.

But the students' exhibition has pleased the Nuns a lot, I know. The whole idea of it did not please Broome (this gives me satisfaction) and really to add genuine interest to the kids' work a few of them should have been in the Hall sitting there beside their paintings. Little Henry Dia is terrifically gifted. He is a bright, shy little chap not much bigger than Johnny [Mary's youngest son] and I found it fascinating to watch him work. His sense of colour and composition is innate and instinctive. Also the moment he faces a problem he drops his brush, Sister says he always does this. It's not that he's lazy over it, he will work at a painting for hours after school and ask to come back at night sometimes – but he never plods on if he's uncertain. He leaves it. The next day, or two days later, he'll come back to it and finish it quite quickly. Sister says she's often seen him do this. He goes away and thinks about it or talks to his brother – older and also v gifted – about it. Really the Dia boys are the only ones when it comes to outstanding talent, but several are very good …

Well, the Q eventually made the verandah where she did the Act. I kept well out of the way during all this. I watched from the ground the tense jossling [sic].

Standing by the big cattle-train was old Paddy. He was fairly quivering with excitement. He had on a new white shirt, trousers and a big blue tie. He was standing as straight as his old bent back and legs could let him. The Queen looked at the cattle-train. She passed by him. I nearly died – and then – oh, thank goodness – she turned back a shade and had a word with him. The cameramen closed in. I was never so relieved about anything in my life. I think Paddy would have died of a broken heart if she hadn't spoken to him. It would have been really tragic. All the little snakes and vipers which I can feel rising around the town in the inevitable tangle of post-Royal Visit post-mortems are trivial – just jealousies, spites. (I saw some of them on Mr Tresize's face yesterday afternoon. He has to deal with them as Road Board Secretary.) But to have not spoken to Paddy would have been a tragedy. It meant *everything* to him. Almost more than anyone in the town he has been keyed up about this nonsense.

Then the Derby kids – bogged at Langi Crossing – just made the Hall. The Q delayed a few minutes getting into the car (now drawn up) to talk with them and then – the door of the air-conditioned car shut. (This car was flown into here by RAAF freighter last week. Its transport alone has cost thousands.) A cheer, a wave and wizz. It was over. They did 40 [mph] to the jetty. (All this had been timed dozens of times over the last few days) and I guess it was only minutes later that the Queen was on board *Britannia* again and no doubt doing the same as everyone else, saying: "Phew" – and taking off her shoes.

I went to see Phyll and Sam as they had asked me. The Rowells and others were there … Collingworth, Perpetua, who met you at the Dunham [Station, East Kimberley] and asked to be remembered to you. His father, Phil Collingworth, used to manage Pardoo [Station] and helped dig Kim and me out of the sand the time we went up with the caravan [in 1950]. Also the de Pledges – Mrs and son Joe. They are nice. Also I got to know and like young Kim [Male] better over the DIVER set-up. He was good and helpful (also really tipped me off about the

FEELING I would arouse if I moved it: "You'll have to have Dad here when you tell Uncle Jock you want it moved.")

So there you are. That's Royal Visits to small towns. I guess they are much the same the world over.

An Anne Matherson, Perpetua, may contact you or may have contacted you ere this. She is *Woman's Weekly* representative in London. I liked her. But how would you answer this one:

"Doesn't it depress you to see so much poverty and misery?" looking at the Broome scene.

I didn't know where to BEGIN to answer this one. Of course there's poverty, an organic poverty in the town and the North generally. I'm very concerned and depressed about it. Misery? There's not MUCH misery (as it's usually understood) – but mainly the thing that rocked me was that she asked this question on the DAY when, as Broome thought, Solomon in all his glory was not so arrayed.

Love dear and love to all – particularly darling Gran who will, I know, be interested in bits in this letter. I'll try and think what's best to do with my sketches. I wish I had someone to talk to about them with. I came back from the Males and worked till 12 on them last night. I will get a proper painting out of it but at this stage it's just field sketches. A bright Dufy-ish painting or two I could easily do *from* them – but not immediately.

Love dear
Mum x x x

From Broome Elizabeth drove northeast to Kununurra, a distance of some 1000 kms again on unsealed roads. The town of Kununurra, excised from former Ivanhoe Station – and long before that from Mirrawong-Gadjerrong country – had been officially gazetted two years earlier. ED's impressions of the new town were not favourable. She was particularly sceptical of the extent of State and Commonwealth support made available to the first farmers. It was decades before Kununurra produced viable commercial crops. The Diversion Dam at Bandicoot Bar had been completed shortly before she arrived and, despite informed predictions of serious difficulties ahead, negotiations were already underway to construct 'Top Dam' some 70 kms southeast of the town.

PDC

Letter: Elizabeth Durack in Kununurra to Kim Durack in Canberra, 19 June 1963

Dearest Kim

I have just returned from a run up to the Dam site so I will tell you about it before answering your letter received yesterday. I went with Brigadier and Mrs Hussey (he is one of the four engineers attached to PWD; has been here over the years and is a very nice person – ex Army, retired. A sort of smaller edition of Geoffrey Drake-Brockman and took on this job in preference to complete retirement. I mention the retirement because it removes him somewhat from the more avid grouping of the younger engineers who have been brainwashed over this whole set-up. He may see a few more years out in Perth office and then the garden and bridge in the new house they will be building in Perth shortly. Mrs H also v nice – ex Army matron. They have been v kind and hospitable to me here and I regard them as new friends); also the Deputy Leader of the Opposition, Whitlam, and Calwell's Press Secretary, a Mr [Graham] Freudenberg, a sort of European edition of John what's-his-name [Wheeldon], Marianna Korwill's friend.[25]

Now this is not near as exciting as it sounds. I started the day off brightly by saying we were ready for questions, would do our best to answer them and if we didn't know the answer would admit it. But no questions were forthcoming. Nature – the trees, the spinifex pigeon on the road – was as far as conversation reached on the way up. I mentioned the bit about your expedition to the spot [in 1940] with Russell Dumas[26] but although the Husseys knew who this was, the name meant not a thing to the visitors. A road has been made about two miles turning west about two miles south of Thompson's Spring – pretty good road too – the whole journey there taking about an hour and a half. At the dam site resides Jackie Savill known in these parts as a full-blood Aboriginal but picked by me in a flash as having a splash of Timor pony, three parts thoroughbred at least and such as are by mountain surveyors prized. He lives there alone in quite a goodish house (that is to say about 100 times better than Bob Skuthorpe's house at the 20 mile) but, in terms of the Kununurra-ites, a shack. Whitlam made one rather amusing comment as we drew up: "Funny place to put it." This in reference to what in fact did look exactly like a little outback lav on top of a water tower, level-gauger.

From Jackie's house we ran down half a mile or so to the SPOT [selected as a suitable dam site by Kim Durack in 1937]. Here I squatted on the ground and started a sketch. A respectful awe fell over the party and they withdrew leaving me to my artistic contemplation – which was what I intended as I did not in any way wish to interfere or intrude with any possible hot talk that Hussey may have wanted to get across. Two big paint strokes have been made across the rock face on the west side, representing height of the dam. Below this is a hole/tunnel – an excavated test on rock solidity. With the party fairly well away I crossed the river – only ankle deep but rather muddy – and climbed up to this hole. It goes in about 100 feet. Not a difficult climb but a lot of loose rock rather slippery. Inside the tunnel it was very warm. It was full of bats and festooned with wasps nests to which I gave a wide berth. Yard by yard the structure of the rock deteriorates – from the entrance smooth and hard towards crumbling slate and shale and finally into almost pure clay. The latter so soft that it would hardly take a charcoal lettering of 'ED' that some vulgar impulse urged me to imprint. I was anxious to ask Hussey possible significance of this rock deterioration. But I refrained myself. From an engineering point of view, I guess it could be overcome, but it will take a hell of a lot of filling, if not require a complete concrete capping and filling of this entire rock structure.

I have no idea how advanced plans and tests are on this whole project but I suspect (only suspect – 'don't quote me') not very far.

I tell you Kim, the whole GREATER ORD RIVER SCHEME is based on a kid's dream of a quarter of a century ago. Thought here has not budged one inch since 1937. But what has happened is that Politics and Public Spending has caught up with it, too late, far too late. And without any comprehension of the shift in the structure of

Kimberley's basic product, its increased value and the position of this product (beef) in the Australian economic structure and its potential within the diplomatic-economic structure (Australia-America).

What worries me quite a bit is my growing fear that, in your drive for up-lift for Kimberley, via captured water and agriculture, you have, quite unwittingly, led the Nation up a gum tree.

Yes, this worries me a lot because I feel now that my thought is tending towards disloyalty to you. It's all very well for you to say, in your last letter, that you never intended that successful agriculture could or would solve Kimberley's problems. What did you intend it to do when you unlocked the door? Would you ever have lifted the lid off Pandora's box had you foreseen that a low-grade Ivanhoe beast would net £40 to the Christiani Nielsen canteen?[27] Would Dad, had he foreseen the same thing, ever have dreamed of selling out for a song at the very moment, almost, that 60 years of frustrated hopes were about to be realised?

Yet would any of this have occurred had you not acted as you did?

Who negated who?

What is Progress?

WHITHER Agriculture in Kimberley? (Answer me this CK Simmons.)

Right.

There are no answers.

History moves forward not backwards. Later the Academy (Geoff Bolton) [WA historian and friend] can retrace the steps and discover the HOW and the WHY.

What is the HOW and the WHY of Court's blind, lemur-ish drive to obtain sanction for the spending of £5,000,000 on water conservation directly related to fixed intensive Agriculture on the Ivanhoe river frontages?[28]

At one time (perhaps it was yesterday or the day before) I might have been prepared to say: because an influx of Commonwealth money at a defined point was a money spinner for Geraldton, Welshpool, and St George's Terrace. Now I can't say this with any genuine inner assurance.

Back at Jackie's house for morning tea Whitlam had his head buried in a copy of *Man* [magazine]. The cake is passed round. Mrs Hussey and I are cooing and arring over some agates that Jackie says we can have. To examine them better, I ask if I can borrow the glasses that Mr Freudenberg is wearing. "You will never see through them." The colour mounts in his pale face. "They are very strong. I have them changed every six months. I am going blind, though they may have arrested it." His face pales to the colour of the piece of quartz I hold in my hand.

On the way back, Mrs H and I talk 'women's talk', the picnic she last had at Thompson's Spring. Everyone else is silent. Whitlam dozes in the front seat. Hussey is driving too fast, taking the gravel bends churned by the cattle trains, too fast. He wants to get them back in time for the Hostel lunch. At the tick of 12 we pull up at the Club Hostel. "Well," I say. "That's 100 miles of it. Square that and add six naughts and that's Kimberley's cut of it on the Australian map." But they are tired and bored.

In answer to your letter received yesterday: description of brief meeting with Mary and your feeling of deflation at her departure. Glad to know a letter from me, and a letter to me filled a little gap in the void. But don't worry, Kim. History moves forward not backward. PERHAPS you have played your role in this section of it. Yet this I cannot really believe. And I am not romantic and am the least starry-eyed inhabitant of the model modern town of Kununurra. God, what a bog hole, the more I see of it the more I hate it, for its meanness and its squalor and its mean, squalid tiny boxes of mod-con houses set in a sand tray. Mid centre of the town, the ORD RIVER IRRIGATION SCHEME PWD office building looks at the Club Hostel. The Club Hostel looks at the ORIS PWD office. From this it corkscrews outwards until you come to the outer suburbs in which I am writing this. Everyday the corkscrew goes down another inch or so into the sand.

For relief, of an evening, I go to the crisp stony rise beyond the Dunham Bridge (what a beauty) and look back at the curve of the Diversion Dam, the Gantry crane, the trees, the hills and Kununurra, an ellipse of dust in the evening light, from the point, in fact, on which a town *should* have been built. What a disaster. And one which could have been avoided had the most incompetent (even) bushman in Kimberley been consulted about location.

Kim, the longer I am here the harder it becomes to 'write an article' on the place. Perhaps I shall be able to do so when in remove. In Perth, I pictured a sort of rather controlled hot-under-the-collar expose. But to my disconcertion: *c'est expose ça-meme*. (In case my French is inaccurate what I mean to say is: the place exposes itself.)

I had no idea it would be so evident. Tragically evident. I had an idea that one might be able to put one's finger on a few Soft Spots. I had no idea that one would be able to *put the finger right through them*.

THE DAM

£3 to 5,000,000 worth of concrete and steel to capture 80,000 acre feet of water.

Me to Mr Vynof (engineer for CNC): "You are, of course, Mr Vynof, purely Construction Engineers in this undertaking?"

Mr Vynof to me: "In this undertaking, yes, purely constructional. We worked from the plans and the designs submitted to us by the PWD of WA."

Me to Mr Vynof: "Sometimes you are both Consultant and Constructional engineers?"

Mr V to me: "That is right."

Me to Mr V: "As Consultant engineers, say for a private organisation, would you have considered the expenditure of £3 to 5 million a rather excessive cost in consideration of the amount of water actually held by the structure?"

Mr V to me: "Expensive – yes – very expensive. In normal circumstances, yes, excessive. But on matters of DEEEvelopment of a backward area …" A shrug. The big shoulder moves forward to pick up a cup of coffee. He takes a sip. He looks at me. I look at him.

Me to Mr V: "I trust your Firm has found, however, the undertaking well worthwhile?"

Mr V to me: "Unfortunately, no. Only, we weeel – as you say – break even. The Unions, Meesus Clancy, you follow the activities of the Unions eeen this country? Two Representatives sent out especially. We were at their mercy. Either we hold out and default in our contract to deeeliver the water to the Farmers by March or we give in. We must weigh. We geeeve in. From Russia, Meeesus Clancy – you understand. You follow the Unions in your country?"

THE FARMERS

Well, Kim, I could give you this one in conversation piece too. In a nutshell it looks as if they will be ploughing in the 200 acres of each of the five farms (1,000 acres all told) of safflower and I think (I am not sure of this) the government is going to re-coup this loss to the tune of £2,000 per farm. It is infested with *Prodenia* [a species of caterpillar] in plague proportions.

Now I am on really touchy ground and do not take for fact what I say here. I am merely trying to give you the facts as accurately as I can under the circumstances where it is practically *impossible* to obtain any facts.

The farmers have planted no cotton.

Cotton has been planted on Northern Developments land – whether leased or a grant of land, who knows?[29]

But this cotton has been planted by a Mr Toms attached to the Ag Department (WA, yes) especially seconded for the job, sent abroad to America for a couple of months to bone up on it. Toms planted 80 acres of cotton on Northern Developments land in November. A section of this was destroyed by aerial spraying it with an insecticide deadly to the plant (at what cost of effectiveness I do not know) and this cotton is at present being harvested. I watched the picker in operation yesterday and did drawings of it. It is badly infected with *Prodenia* but even so I understand it is giving a good yield per acre. It is a good type of cotton, apparently – long fibred. This cotton is being placed in a shed opposite the field.

To whom this cotton belongs I do not know.

Nor, I think, does anyone else.

It is practically open talk here that Northern Developments as the Pilot Farm is a dead loss. It has failed utterly in its promise (contract?) to steer the private farmers through the shoals and reefs of initial production into clear water. Mr Cole, head of Ag Dept WA, has been pretty outspoken in his criticism of Northern Dev and has got into hot water as a consequence. (He comes from New Guinea. Has a fine collection of PNG art and met his wife, a missionary, when there. They won't be here much longer.) He is not a bad young man. It was just unfortunate that I should have blown my top at him the other night when they kindly asked me round to dinner. I had no intention of blowing my top. But this whole thing caught me unawares. He made insulting, inaccurate, uninformed remarks about the Pastoralists. As I say, before I knew I was saying what I said – He said: "And they don't even know what cattle they've got – over-stocking, exploiting the land."

"It's a pity," I said, "about their not knowing what cattle they've got. I hope you realise that sales are assessed on head of cattle. There are the branding checks and the marketing checks – and let consideration be given before a quarter of the best pastoral proposition in Kimberley is put under water to give way for a worms picnic." Right-O, I said it – but I doubt it went very deep anywhere except with me. Mrs Cole, a missionary, a kindergarten teacher, then said very nicely and lovely: "I think Mrs Clancy should represent the Pastoralists." And the evening fizzled out. Cole left with an entomologist to examine the night habits of the *Prodenia*. A child cried in its bed and only I made an exit shaken to the core.

POPULATION

Kim, re your letter: 'measure the Indigenous population'.

Right.

Well, forget the blacks, the half-castes, the public servants, the Ag Dept officials (State and Commonwealth), the engineers, the contractors, (Keath's Melbourne doing more channelling), the Hostel staff, the AIM [Australian Inland Mission] nurses, the this that and the other thing that comprises population here at present, there is only ONE indigenous population here now of any significance and that is the FARMERS, some of whom have staked their all in this insane undertaking.

I'll give you the framework:

No 1 Farm

A syndicate, Bank subsidised.

Don Beech; Clive Massey (WA Manager of KRS [Kimberley Research Station]); Noel Tolson; Arthur Grey – all four ex (or still with) KRS

No 2 Farm
Jim Arbuckle; Don Arbuckle (son)
No 3 Farm
B Arbuckle; Roger Arbuckle (son)
No 4 Farm
W Dougal; and son
No 5 Farm
David Revell; Ronan Revell (brothers)

Altogether 12 (odd) Farmers. They have grouped themselves into the Ord River District Association of which Jim Arbuckle is the Chairman. I think he represents them on the Council. Meetings being held through Kimberley towns at intervals this year (Charles Court and new Administrator etc). The resurrected ghost of your original Council.

At present Jim Arbuckle is in Perth having been called there (I learn from his wife, a very fine nice person) for TOP LEVEL talks. One day I saw her and she reminded me of Lawson's *Past Carin'* (*I married two and buried two, and now I am past carin'*). Then the next day she was all smiles: "… and he (Court) told Jim that they have the BEST BRAINS looking into our problems – So that's nice to know, isn't it? And Jim's going to Perth …"

Right at this minute Jim is being bought or sold by the Politics behind the set-up.

It is, of course, worrying the Politicians. The five Farmers that were to meet Menzies next month with smiles and glowing reports of promise will, by that time, have just about buried their first crop. This is the WORST that can happen at the present time. And every effort is now being made to somehow silence or placate the Farmers.

If the Powers that Be succeed in doing this then the Farmers of the Ord become *another thing* from farmers anywhere else.

I am a bit inclined to think Court will succeed in this. Just imagine it, a market gardener from Balcatta being wined and dined by the Highest in the Land. I hardly think he will be strong enough to stand out. He just might. But, oh, I doubt it.

I have felt myself that THIS is a core to work on and had even thought of 'addressing' them myself. In fact I called on Mrs Arbuckle (senior) with this in view but by the time I called she had had the news that Jim had been 'called to Perth' and was already packing his case.

Kim, this is not a proper answer to your letter but it has taken most of the afternoon to write and I must now shower and go to KRS [Kimberley Research Station] where an evening party has been arranged for Whitlam to which I have been invited. I am rather too tired to go but this may be a good thing as it will tend to keep my ugly mouth shut, which I am determined to try to do. Will keep you advised. About What??? History? Or its making? Somewhere through all this there is a Tiller – I mean a ship's Tiller – but where???

love,
Elizabeth

Poem: Prayer to the Road God, *26 April 1964*
(3.00am – on waiting for Michael to come home, but I'll be asleep when he does.)

Oh dreadful Mason
Oh terrible Builder
You who use flesh and blood
for mortar
and human bone for binding straw.
Oh awful one of the long arm
and the long blinding eye
who tumbles your building blocks
of metal and broken glass
into spiralling castles
of siren-hideous, screaming-silent,
night-lightning,
panic.

Oh fearful Mason
who sits cross-legged
at cross walks,
supine
at level crossings

who, serpent-scaled, and
slippery when wet
entwines the
winding road
and hides curved in the
curves.

You with the blinding
yellow eye
who, perched on
crest
cunningly replaces
left for right
and scatters the
cats eyes
in a dizzy confusion
of rubble foundation
for an up-building
of a new castle
of
siren-hideous,
white-black,
screaming-silent
night-lighted
terror.

Oh terrible Mason
build not of the flesh
of my flesh
bind not with the bone
of my bone
that the teeth of my teeth
may not bite forever
in petrified anguish
upon your lime-encrusted hand

Spare him, spare him …

Letter: Elizabeth Durack from Kim's flat in Canberra to Michael in Perth, 1 December 1966

My Darling Michael

I heard from Hooker's [Real Estate Agents] confirming what you had told me about '47's' vacancy on December 20, ['47' had been rented for nine months while Elizabeth was travelling abroad] so here just a few dull but practical:

Provided it can be fitted into your own work programme I think it would be best to aim to up-end from '203' [Michael's flat] about this date thus avoiding a joint muck and muddle of arrival and also eliminating the necessity of a shut-down (milk, frig, paper and/or light and water). In other words what I would like, selfishly, is to arrive into a going concern with an absolute minimum of dirty socks, half-empty suitcases, unmade beds, broken LPs, muddy boots, oily overalls, unopened love-letters, unusable shave-masters, souvenir corks, bottle tops, hard hats, soft butter, wire, stale bread, steak (smelly, but still usable if curried), slide rules, dud biros, battered bark paintings, unfiled filings, unidentified rocks, unread classics, un-scrapped scrapbooks, brand new shirts, useful pots to put things in, rare coins, common denominators and all the usual impedimenta of your daily day to day living – neatly stuffed away in a state of semi-invisibility awaiting further sorting and attention, consideration and disposal. If you get the picture. However, if this is not possible, or convenient, forget it; it is by no means worrying or urgent.

Glad to hear on the news this morning of WAPET's expansion and continued effort for next year into subterranean mysteries. No doubt this is due to the advantages of that firm having you on the staff. Should anyone at the top there happen to overlook this I would not hesitate to point it out.

So the elections are over and at the moment the only political news is the Labor Party's convulsions of further self-destruction [the Calwell–Whitlam in-fighting]. Something tragic about this, I like Whitlam and never understand his extreme unpopularity which will deprive him, I think, of what would logically be the inheritance of the Labor Party if, indeed, such a party still exists which at the moment is doubtful. The forecast of 'a major Cabinet reshuffle' hasn't yet clarified Paul Hasluck's continuance in External Affairs. But I think he'll stay where he is and should know next week when the eagles will gather for a brief pre-Christmas shindy in Parliament House.

Michael, you must get and read the Sept '66 issue of *Scientific American* – all on the computer. It is enough to make even the most hardened Molesworth stop in his tracks [the Geoffrey Willans/Ronald Searle Molesworth books had been some of Michael's favourite schoolboy reading] and so out-dates all our previous methods of communication as to make this letter seem like some remote and obsolete contraption only comparable to the heiliogriphics [sic] incised on an ancient Egyptian tomb and extends the old brain into the airiest levels of the improbable, possible and the yet unchartered Future – exciting.

Dear, have not much actual news at the moment. Will be in touch again soon. Give my love to Gran and all family. Hope all well. Hope all extra well with you.

Ever your loving
xxx mum xxx

1970s

It takes a little time in New York[30]

While '47' remained Elizabeth's studio and home base for 50 years (less so for Michael after his marriage to Margaret Parker in 1972), we all used to make extended and extensive excursions away. I was away the longest – all up, almost 30 years.

Yet whether in Lusaka, Athens, London, Tokyo, New York, Sydney or Broome – mother and I remained in regular contact through an often irregular airmail service. Occasionally, en route or after visiting me, mother would find reasons to stop at places that were off the beaten track for the times. In 1970 she was in Iran and Nigeria; a few years later in Indonesia and in 1979 in the US, exhibiting in New York.

Once back at '47', Elizabeth would feel the limitations of Perth. She would speak of selling, of moving to Mauritius, Zanzibar, Canberra, Sydney – anywhere but Perth. At such times I'd plead with her not to sell. From a distance, often from a great distance, '47' remained a blissful haven. So mother never sold '47' – although she may well have found a better haven for herself had she ignored my pleas.

PDC

Travelogue: Coming into Enugu
[September 1970, six months after the ceasefire of the Nigerian Civil War][31]

The bus on which I was travelling was crowded with men, women and babies, some fowls, a pile of high-smelling skins and a goat that kept investigating the back of my neck with its wet nose. I had paid a double fare for the privilege of sitting up in front with the driver and my unfeigned enjoyment of the expedition proved infectious. The driver himself was solemn and careful but the rest of us were in a merry mood. A helpful young man explained things as we passed.

"It is a dance," he said, "a dance for young men, for this time of year," as, near a small village, we passed a group wearing ostrich feather headdresses and swinging fibre skirts. A little further on a figure transformed to some man-monster came lumbering down a jungle path. At the sight of the apparition with its great horned head and bulging eyes the passengers all began to laugh and cheer.

"This is harvest time for yams," explained the young man. "There will be a feast here today with many like this," and he wrote the name of the festival in my notebook when he saw me struggling with the double 'O's.

As we approached the outer perimeter of Enugu the architecture of the houses changed dramatically. The rectangular red mud-brick houses now disappeared and we passed large two-storey homes, their upper balconies flanked with slender columns and shuttered windows. Sometimes a gracious set of steps led up to a porch also set about with slim Doric-type pillars. *What's this? What's this? Where has Africa gone*? I turned to the man but my amazement was too complicated to explain and obviously he saw nothing odd about the places we were passing. All of these houses were deserted and badly war-scarred. On one, a big sign lettered *Chief Shan* had been hacked savagely in two, and long grass was taking over in what once had been a garden.

Later, on the west side of the Niger along the approach roads to Lagos, I would see again similar houses. There they are called 'Yoruba houses' but these along the Enugu road were the first I saw of this distinctly Chinese-derived architecture which had been lifted straight out of the landscape anywhere in rural China. Between the dwellings and stretching for long distances were schools and churches while signposts marked the way to monasteries, training colleges, hospitals and maternity clinics. Many Christian sects were represented and the Catholic predominated.

We came to a large sign, *St Mary's Diocese of Enugu,* and we were in the near suburbs of the capital of Eastern Central State. Here a wilderness of ripple-iron shanties, the size of dog kennels, now spread out and about as far as the eye could see. These dreadful improvisations have mushroomed all over eastern Nigeria as more and more crowd into the urban areas to live parasitically off the huge army camps splayed out under canvas and in Nissan huts along the roadways. One of the mysteries of developing countries is how mothers manage, out of such dreadful slums, to present their children clean and in clean clothes for the school day. As we passed children were emerging – little girls in bright dresses, boys in pants and white shirts.

At the northern limits of the city, soldiers in jungle-green and russet-blotted uniforms waved our bus ceremoniously to a stop. I popped my notebook out of sight and tried to chameleon into the landscape but I was horribly conspicuous and, almost instantly, a young soldier put his head through the window and said: "Please, I want to see your Pass." I presented my passport, but this he said, was not sufficient. As a foreigner it was necessary to have 'Permit to progress beyond this point'. Otherwise I must return to place of embarkation.

"But," I said, "in Lagos I was assured that the road was open and Passes no longer required." While this was going on a heavy hush fell over the entire bus. The driver began to tremble and the pockmarks on his face seemed to deepen. I saw the eyes of the young man who had been so helpful and informative roll away like billiard balls and fall silently into the string-bag of his out-stretched newspaper. The woman with the baby to whom I had given bread and who had passed me, smiling, a half orange in return now hung her head and commenced to feed her infant. The bus driver's talkative bilingual off-sider who had been haggling over fares all along the way was struck dumb. From being, so recently, a rather charming novelty, I had become *persona non grata.*

Eventually, after insisting that I see their superior officer, the young soldier got into the bus beside me and we drove off in an atmosphere pregnant with apprehension. A mile or two further on we stopped at the Military Headquarters of the East Central State. The soldier alighted, bumping and scratching his rifle against the bus to the further dismay of the terrified driver. I delayed my own descent to fossick in my handbag for compact and comb; every action was watched. I sensed a certain response to these small vanities. I asked the driver to wait assuring him that I would not be long at all, that there was just some little mistake. He looked ahead with an expression stony and unresponsive but his off-sider said it would be alright. With such a loose thread is Africa tied to Time that not one passenger demurred or objected to a wait, that, for all they knew, might have lasted hours.

In an enclosed area set about with white-painted stones, several young soldiers were hanging around. They leapt to attention at this welcome diversion, clutched their rifles and made a wobbly salute. One of them rushed into a shed and came out with a visitor's book. Africa is the most Visitor's Book conscious in the world.

Destination – Home (*DV*) [*Deo volente* – God willing], Purpose of visit – Pleasure. And all the while, to my amused self-contempt, my hand was shaking so much I could hardly form the letters.

These courtesies discharged, we proceeded towards a large wooden building, accompanied now by two more armed escorts. (At the best of times and even on bush picnics I'm nervous of guns and the way they were now being slung all around me in such cavalier fashion challenged composure.) We came now to a very smart guard wearing a red and gold cap and white pullover sleeves, such as are donned to direct traffic at a garden party. He led us to a flight of stairs.

Inside, domino-like, a group of officers sprang to attention at the arrival of our contingent. I was shown into an anteroom and there left waiting for what seemed a very long time. I feared the bus would move on with my case on board and my Fulani hat, and my boab nut and the lizard-skin purses from Zalganga, and the post-cards from the Jos Museum, and my half bottle of duty-free, and I began to feel sorry for myself.

At last someone appeared and in sepulchral tones said: "Come!" Together we entered another office and, at sight of the man at the desk, my escort went through a strange assortment of actions. His right hand came up to his brow; he lifted his foot until the knee touched his chin and, after swaying in this position for a second or two, he brought his heavily booted foot down with a resounding thump onto the loose boards of the floor. From the ceiling a small piece of dry-rotten wood fell into my hair. The officer before me rose, stretched out his hand and said: "Welcome!" I could think of no response that properly fitted so I said nothing. Very slowly I removed the wood chip from my hair. I examined it for a moment, looked around for a receptacle in which to drop it and finding none placed the offending chip on the edge of the desk. My hand, free at last, I then extended to the now completely bewildered young man before me.

"Yours is a culturalmissin," he said, making one word of it and stressing the second syllable. I did not know what he meant and he began to fear I could not understand English. At the best of times it is agony for an African not to communicate and I saw an expression of desperation pass over his face.

"A culturalmissin," he repeated. I still didn't respond. "A culturalmissin!" he shouted now, "our antiquities, our art, our museums, our scenic beauties …"

"Your friendly happy people …" I enjoined.

"Exactly!" His face broke into a broad smile. He was so relieved at having at last got through to me that he would have agreed with anything and wanted somehow to make amends.

"We regret this inconvenience. Yes, the road is open but only for the past week and from time to time we close it in the interests of peace and order. But your passport is all in order, and I see you carry this letter from my government. And now," he turned to the young soldier, "accompany Mrs Elizabeth to her vehicles and ensure that she has safe conduct to her place of residence." And with a lordly wave of the hand he bowed me out. Back in the bus I sensed something of anti-climax, disappointment even, among the passengers. Perhaps I had deprived them of a good firelight story: "… and we never saw her again, which goes to prove that you should never really trust the *Onitcha*."

About Nigerian Art

The term *Nigerian Art* covers a very wide area and if, along with art, we are to include crafts – objects of practical use as well as those for embellishment of person and domicile – the field of reference is extensive. Like the country itself, like its people, like the climate, like the vegetation and, interlocked with all, the artistic expression of that area that has come to be known as *Nigerian* is rich, varied and reaches back to the roots of human life itself. Needless to say it does not confine itself to any political boundary. It is multi-cephalous and tips over, prodigally, extravagantly, in all directions. However, for our purpose here, we shall try to remain as close as possible within Nigeria itself.

The most ancient examples of Nigerian art are to be found on rocky outcrops in the high plateau area of northeastern Nigeria. Here we see evidence of that characterising reflective urge as Man depicts himself and his animal contemporaries in a series of drawings and engravings that date back 50 to 100,000 years and which link with other rock engravings and paintings throughout the continent and elsewhere in the world. A uniformly high level of skill distinguishes the art of these early hunters. For millions and millions of years there is nothing. Perhaps the bird's song; nothing more. Then, suddenly, *Adam* is here. He has arrived. With fanfare and flourish Adam signs rock faces in all hemispheres. Letting out the secret he marks them unmistakably with his powers of observation, his masterly drawing, with realism, movement, colour and composition.

A common and significant feature of early rock art is the positioning of Man himself in the overall scheme of things. Without exception he is always self-depicted as small but cunning. He outwits all the creatures around him, he has *named* them, and is linked in mystic ways with the supernatural which he can persuade and induce to remain on his side.

There is not a progressive upward gradation in human evolution from hunting to farming as is sometimes postulated. It could be argued that small-scale agriculture was in fact, a backward step. However, the truth is that the two overlap. Sometimes they complement each other but more often they remain in competition indefinitely. The Cain and Abel legend is ubiquitous. Sometimes hunting preceded farming; sometimes farming communities return to hunting after an era of more sedentary existence. The switch from foraging the surface of the earth to digging into it results always in moral and artistic decline. Something other and essentially female takes over from the wider well-ventilated male domain of the hunt. Discarding the brave, accurate, deadly pointed weapons for clumsy-headed tools, the act of tilling becomes entangled with fertility rites, superstitions and a demi-human spirit-world in which Man lives out a haunted, fear-ridden existence. And Man himself, now only half man, becomes big, swollen, monstrous, a mindless sinister shape. He stands out in ghastly contrast to Man as depicted by the early hunters – tiny, frail, stick-like, winning the contest with the animals that he so tellingly brings down, spot-on, through accurately positioned hearts.

The gloomy, fire-lit, enclosed and shadow world – the slow, restricted, in-turning world of the vegeculturist and the subsistence farmer, the wait between sowing (conception) and harvest (birth) is essentially a female canton. Woman here has the upper hand. Obese matriarchies with the power to dispense, spider-like, with the male, hold sway. Magic spells, witchcraft, sorcery, fetishism, hoodoo, voodoo, motivate the art of the subsistence farmer …

Letter: Elizabeth Durack from '47' to Perpetua, job-hunting in Sydney, 7 August 1975

P dear

I thought you might like to read the enclosed ['The Long Story of One Manuscript', *The Australian Author*, July 1975] over a c of coffee – perhaps between appointments.

I really wonder where all this accumulated frustration on the part of writers is leading. It further highlights what I mentioned in writing to Michael and Margaret (as *we* know) that the publishing world is in crisis. The big-multi-group-*push* books are *so profitable* and the old-style (writer sends MS to a publisher, the latter approves, accepts, or rejects) *so unprofitable* that the publishers do not know if they are going or coming. But the trouble is they won't own up to it or be honest to the writer about their position. They seem to prefer to *torture* the writer quite mercilessly and in a way that would be totally rejected by any other business (or human) relationship …

Further confusing the whole picture is the dreadful government subsidy to publishers – and for that matter, to authors. I am getting v anti 'The Grant'. This will not stop me from going on playing the 'putting-in-for' game but I don't like it and God knows where it is leading. The old pragmatic profit and loss system, for all its evils, is surely better than all these *crutches*. Also a buoyant economic situation can be adequate to satisfy an artist (that is, sales at exhibitions which result from a confident public, bright and responsive). As things are, even the doctors (the bulwark of the artists' sales factor) are going to be turned into nervous public servants with their hands continually out for refunds from the public purse …

loving thoughts – mummmm

Letter: Elizabeth Durack at '47' to Perpetua in Sydney, 19 September 1975

Darling girl

Oh, did you hear the good 'Books and Ideas' program on ABC last evening on [Xavier Herbert's] *Poor Fellow My Country*? The whole thing fell into place for me suddenly.

Poor Fellow My Country is the book Gough wishes he could have written but that God graced him into law and politics. Explains why $20,000 of Aus taxpayers' money went into the subsidisation of its publicity. It is a clutch-bag of defunct left-of-left *old* ideas all connected by a rambling yarn – half-fact, half-symbol. There will be Part 2 of this review next Thursday. The review is *all* favourable. The book is rubbish but a literary and historic curiosity – collector's value.

Like you, telling me the bit about '246' [apartment in central Sydney] last, I've left the best till last too. *The work has come good. The flightless birds achieve lift-off* has suddenly jelled. I knew it was too good to let slip but it wouldn't come right. The place is a litter of sketches – of emus. (I know all the places around Perth where they are. The best is not the zoo but an animal sanctuary not far from Jandakot in which locality also is the most fabulous depository of ruined cars I have ever seen – hidden – and not easy to come by (info) or find (locality). Miles of them, in seried ranks. Stacked five high and gradually being pancaked for export to the mills of Nippon – the ultimate in man-made desolation. Well, that is the background but it was hard to get it together and all the ones I did, too dark. Actually it was 'Michael Toowoomba' [a nephew, Bill's second son] who put me on the lead of a paper I am now using and which makes all the difference (he suggested it for another purpose but I haven't used it for that yet). It's 30" x 40" and gives that extra play as c.f. the 23" x 36" size I've used for so long.

I have only done four as yet and in fact am having a bit of a spell writing this to you as it is a big area (not big compared with big, but big compared with small) to cover and plays up with my shoulder muscles – but this is nothing. I think these are good – and I haven't felt this about anything till *now* – yesterday. Actually 10 of these + 20 small 'sources' could suffice for Canberra, I think. If I can keep it up, and if it doesn't evade me again. We'll see.

As I mentioned to you in previous note, I see Canberra as that 'try-out-in-the-provinces' and the November exhibition is not really as demanding or as important as Sydney but it would be a bit of a foot in.

As the catalogues etc etc roll in from you I begin to feel the 'enormity of the lost tempo' in my being in Perth so long. One is really only a mug to stay in Perth if one has any artistic ambition. I note the biographic notes of all those young men from far and wide who 'came to Sydney, 1968' etc etc. It is surely the nearest thing to a New York Australia will ever have. What do you think?

(You'll have noted with interest that Pattie Hearst's Freedom Stand has come to an end. I suppose she fell out of love and it got boring and uncomfortable.)

Other bits, but I'll press on. The week is over, nearly over – so little done. The weekend somehow causes a pause even when one has no plans for it. An enforced break – the paper buckles badly. That is one worry – however 'bridge by bridge'. Let's adopt that for the time being.

love, mummmmm

Bonney Prince Charlie in Goroka yesterday. I hope M & M & L [Liam, first grandson] saw him.

Letter: Elizabeth Durack at local Laundromat to Perpetua in Sydney, 9.00am, 29 September 1975

Perpetua dear

I'll tell you what I am thinking so you can think about it too and direct your art exploration accordingly.

I think that in a week or two's time I'll get Doug [nephew, Reg's third son] or Sivyers to photograph this new work and send photos to you and I would like you to take them to Watters and Macquarie, or any comparable gallery, and see if you could get a booking for early '76 (April or so).

Like you, I go on having misgivings about Prouds [Sydney gallery] and then put them aside. Neither Prouds nor Solander is what I/we want. Joy Warren went to some pains to explain to me (as if I didn't know) that the average Canberra gallery goer/buyer was the average Canberra new home-owner who, as you said, really doesn't know anything about Art but wants an original at a moderate price. But hell, I've been absorbing this message for 30 years. It is the message I am trying desperately to escape from. Of course a big percentage of my work fits/can fit/can be made to fit almost exactly to this category attracting the same category of patrons every time – including the 'Sonias' and the 'Dr and Mrs' etc. But I want to be known as the artist of Wrack and Ruin and it is in this area of wild paintings that I feel I can get somewhere – personally – in expression. They are tremendous fun. They are even funny. James Joyce is funny. An iconoclast, a wrecker – of language. I absorbed the message of Joyce over 30 years ago and it has been gestating for a long time – un-be-knowns to anyone who has ever bought an Elizabeth D to hang on a suburban wall in Hawthorn or Camberwell or Nedlands because of 'the expression in the eyes'. (The wrecker, of course, finally wrecks him/herself – but this is part of the fun.)

Anyway, Perpetua, I would like you to start making a bridge with the Macquarie (which I think we both feel differently about since the Fairweather exhibition). It is Australia's oldest, almost classic gallery. I thought it was dying but then it may have more kick in it that given credit for. Also that other, Watters gallery and/or any that you might visit with a higher *noospheric* grading than Prouds (but not Barry Stern or

Rudy Komon. These belong to some other category/thing. I don't know what really, but it isn't *me*). But I won't reject Prouds completely. I know how to have, almost exactly, a 'successful exhibition at Prouds' and it remains tempting to do so (although also, in my present mood, *very hard* too). Also, of course, nice Mr James is quite cluey and he himself would know well all the gradings/ratings/levels of art (and particularly the latter) of the Sydney public.

Why Sydney? one might well ask but then I believe your researches there have shown that it has a real Art core and furthermore, links and bridges to 'the outside world'. All those young men seem to have gone to New York, Florence, Rome, London etc almost as a matter of course and will no doubt continue to do so all their lives.

The position of WA – its total isolation in the Art world (in the world, beside the quarry) becomes clearer and clearer …

The maddening part for me in all this is that what I am now trying for – a place, a tiny, tiny slot in the general Art picture of Australia – should lie *behind* me and the full realisation that if I don't act now I shall never get even this, is to a large degree both annoying and time-wasting (that in 20 or 30 years time there will be some WAIT [WA Institute of Technology, now Curtin University] 'Fine Art' student who will dredge up 'Art in WA 1940–1970' in which the work of ED will be included as an item on page … blow this). I mean, it seems to have dawned on me, conclusively now, WA's place in the scheme of things. I have known it a long time but have been circumventing action in very diverse ways. 'Going overseas' on my own steam only to return to WA to sense the isolation and the *bog* in an ever-increasing intensity. Since this last trip to laughing Africa my restlessness knows no bounds. If I can't get into Sydney I think I'll migrate to that continent.

Well, there really wasn't very much to say that wasn't repetition but it has filled in the time and the washing now through. A wild blustery day here for the [Royal Agricultural] Show.

Did you hear Meg Thatcher talking from Washington: "If this (the US) is failure (of the Western world, of Capitalism) what, in heaven's name, is *success*?" The *bon*est *mot* I heard for a long time.

love, mummmmmm

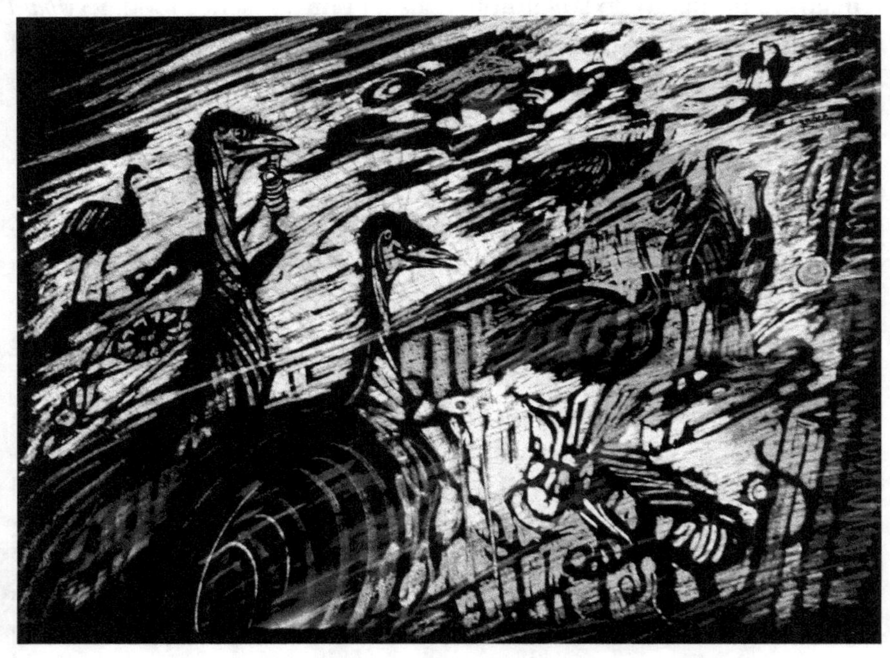

Flightless birds achieve lift off (No 1 of a sequence of 10) 1975
mixed media on paper 92 x 122 cm, private collection

Letter: Elizabeth Durack at '47' to Perpetua in Sydney, 30 September 1975

Dear

Just to acknowledge your welcome note of 27th re 'busy weekend'. Delighted to know you enjoyed the opera and had done 'homework' on beforehand and that Japan book arrived and that Park Regis is 'moving' (I hope).

Doug came this morning and took 20 b & w photos of the *Flightless birds achieve lift-off* … set and 12 of same for colour prints. I should have these in hand by about October 12th – a long time but Doug pretty busy and it's good he was able to come as soon as he could. I'll send on to you and you can, if you like, *play* around with them. I say 'play' because that is all one really could expect to do. The more I think about it the more I come to the conclusion that there has been a lot of innocence on our part re Sydney and the big galleries. (The old style was that a gallery became interested in the work of an artist and proceeded to put on an exhibition. I think this lies in the past – as 19th century style publishers which it takes a bit of adjusting to realise they no longer exist. However you can talk to galleries and make bridges and learn and pass on info to me.) My thought is assisted by your comment and info generally – but just as 'the critics' are, probably, 'corrupt'/corruptible, so too the galleries. I don't really mean 'corrupt' but you know, perhaps, what I do mean.

That Laurence Hope exhibition was particularly illuminating. In this case, with so little actually for sale, the Holdsworth [Sydney gallery] must have received a worthwhile *exhibiting fee*; and, no doubt, also for the Bali man (what's his name? [Donald Friend] we saw tail end of show) and really, this is only reasonable. And when I said that the Laurence Hope exhibition would have cost 3 to 5 thousand dollars to put up it might have been a good bit more – e.g. I had never heard of him (he has been away a lot) and now I *have*.

$10,000 would be a reasonable fee/price for ventilation such as the work got (and deserves). Perhaps he got one of the $10,000 Australia Council grants for: 'Artists Who Think They Have Not Received Sufficient Recognition' (I think they have eliminated this category. It was one I did *not* 'put-in-for' thinking it was a trick or a leg-pull) and he simply proceeded to organise a good exhibition from there – the same with publishers. I would never have got *Face Value* published on face value but for the government subsidy to Ure Smith (they undertook to buy 2000 copies) and actually Ure Smith chased *me* (can you believe) when I was dragging my feet …

In a nutshell, satisfactory exhibiting for me in Sydney depends on money, finance – government or private 'angle' backing. I haven't got it so that's all there is to it. *But* it does not rule out Prouds and all it represents (*sale*, small popular paintings at low prices) and I shall be guided about Prouds by the Solander exhibition in November which I shall try to proceed with. *Three* negatives have come in now from the Aus Council put-in-fors and to make matters worse I see an ad for October *Quadrant* that has neither 'put me in nor made me brave' [a quote from the Molesworth books] however, WA Arts Council still a *possibility*. [*It wasn't. Detailed Application rejected.* PDC] I think a *Wailing party* should be organised for all those who didn't get grants – and special prizes for those who can show greatest number of unsuccessful applications. As you know I don't care/feel much about this but it is surely terribly bad for any creative person – the hope, the anticipation – followed so devastatingly by the negation. Better not to have raised hope at all; better to find *another way* of helping the artist/writer: reward, payment, sale of work done – real assistance with bridging the publisher gap.

Lovely spring day here. I am scribbling this before getting, again, into the shed. The sweet peas are coming out and a joy – thanks to you and Michael. All well here. Mary in Darwin.

cheers,

love, mummmmmm

Letter: Elizabeth Durack from New York NY to Perpetua in Sydney, 11 November 1979

Perpetua, darling girl …

Long ere this reaches you I shall have phoned, so some of the news will be a reiteration – the main being that the exhibition ended on Friday – and turned into a wild international romp. There in the [World Trade Center] Lobby, adjacent to my *Explorers and Discoverers*, the Volzhanka

Folk Dance Ensemble put on a wild display of prancing and dancing while above, on the Concourse, a huge Chinese trade exhibition was being assembled – under heavy guard – as there had been warning that the Chinese might throw something at the Russians.

I tried to get a photo from the top of the escalators on the Concourse but the black guards wouldn't let anyone stand still, even for a moment. "Keep moving, keep moving there."

"I just want to take a photo of my exhibition with the dancers in the foreground."

"Your exhibition, sweetheart? Where's your ID?"

"Well, will you take the photo for me and I'll move down the escalators and back again and collect my camera?" The big bully conceded to this so it remains to be seen if there is any result. By 2.30 the fun was all over. By 3.00 my packer had arrived and by 5.00pm *ED '79* was in wraps.

There is a really hectic week ahead but by a blessed dispensation this Sunday is free. I even have the Metropolitan exhibition *Art from the Aegean* behind me – thank goodness, as it was one not to be missed … As I left the crowds were disgorging all with Met bags full of souvenirs and postcards. The bus was packed and rain was coming through the roof. I got off at 53rd and went into MOMA to enquire and check on the staff and office hours. MOMA as you know open on Sat afternoons and all 57th Street galleries too. Yes, Elizabeth Streibert [Senior Curator] is still there and a Mr Waldo Rasmussen, head of International Programs. I am getting quite good attention from Info desk attendants because by this time I have learned to carry around in my hand my (long out of date from Canberra days) Press Card/Pass. Press is good news in New York. Artists are bad news. They are a drug on the market and for that matter mainly sustained by drugs. You should *see* some of the rubbish that *only* the drugged and doped could come up with – in words and line.

I am not having much difficulty in getting comment on my exhibition although Piers' [Akerman] request for this came late and many wonderful opportunities have been lost. Many galleries have been helpful. Some not, of course. I have already told you that 'Modern/Contemporary' paintings are the most prolific in New York and at the greatest discount.

Quote Max Hutchinson [Australian–US art dealer]: "Why, there are 30,000 artists, all working within a radius of a mile of this gallery … some of them good artists. You are trying to do the impossible. You'll never get an exhibition up. Sure, plenty have 'plans' – but they never get an exhibition up." This was at our first meeting (a year ago). Anyway, I did get the exhibition up and I know that this both surprised and, yes, impressed Max H. He came to see the exhibition the day after he returned from Houston.

In my innocence I kept thinking that the critics would turn up or that a review would occur in one of the papers, magazines and journals to which I had sent invitations etc. This is not the way art criticism works in New York today. For a start there is hardly any of it – art criticism – and what there is, is on the decline. The big names in art criticism have become so big (and certainly too big for their boots to carry them to any exhibition – let alone that of a foreigner, a loner, at a downtown part of New York – although the World Trade Center is a prestigious place) that they are living in the rarified atmosphere of internationalism. For example, the Pompidou Museum in Paris might – all expenses paid, Concorde's champagne flight etc etc – get one of them to review a certain show that would then obtain international press exposure through an international press release network. Bob Hughes has, to a lesser degree, slotted himself into this lane but I think he has a pretty precarious hold. He really only got on to the ladder in 1970 with his break with *Time*. Before that I think there was a long limbo.

Yet – when a Big Name – like Hilton Kramer [leading NY art critic] – is approached from another angle, access can be obtained. I have this appointment to call at his office on Tues Nov 13th at 11.

As I write this I am looking south to the Twin Towers of the World Trade Center – shrouded in rain. In some ways I am immensely relieved the exhibition is over. In other ways I wish I had another week or two to run there. On Tuesday I go back to make my last contact with Alf Pettanati & Co. Thank goodness no mishaps and no ill will. All the crazy insurance that they insisted upon has been simply another set of papers in my over-loaded swag.

Letter: Elizabeth Durack from New York to Perpetua in Sydney, 14 November 1979

Perpetua, darling girl

Such is the power of the press that Hilton Kramer's first words to me this morning were ones of apology for keeping me waiting. I was at the offices of *The New York Times*, 229 W 43rd St pretty well on the dot of 11.00am – a little early and just as well as the security on this great edifice is *conspicuous*. Guards at the door, a telephone arrangement before one can take the elevator etc. However, once through this the third floor area opened up into a huge, fairly easy-going area with a good-natured desk attendant who gave me the day's paper to read while I sat on a comfortable sofa and taking it all in: the oil painting portrait of some former editor, the list of recent awards to Ms X for her outstanding photo of Pope John Paul that captured the spirit of the Pontiff's visit to New York, and the comings and goings of the staff – many of them women and many of them black.

"I am so sorry to keep you waiting. You would not believe that it took me as long to drive down Manhattan as it did to get on to the bridge from Connecticut …" His office was small and Ned Murray of the Bodley Gallery was dead right when he said he had a picture of HK's desk. It was simply a mountain of papers – but I can't believe that he has three secretaries as not even one could have been at work on the total confusion of stacked material not only on the desk but all around the narrow perimeter of the small office. He only had one small chair but he dragged another in from an adjoining office and the 'interview' commenced. Thank goodness I did have the basic background facts – of his life and career – but he filled in that he was born and raised in the US, in Massachusetts, and that both his parents were German Russians. And no, I was wrong that there were other Kramers in the arts – not that he knew of (*Who's Who* said differently). Both his brothers were doctors. He was the youngest in the family … we got through all this and then I moved in with a few questions.

He's written a book – or rather, his book was a compilation of his essays and crits on art called *The Age of the Avant-Garde*: *1956–1972* so my first question was what would he regard as 'avant-garde' today. And this opened the whole conversation up and the talk ran on well and easily but unfortunately just at this moment in time I seem to have forgotten most of it. He is not a funny or entertaining person to talk with – as e.g. Max Hutchinson, and yet he would be a sounder character and much more sincere and reliable. He knew Robert Coates and Edmund Wilson although I prefaced my question on these personalities by saying: "You'd be too young to remember R Coates?" Then, perhaps because of this, he seemed to take it that I knew a lot of the personalities in the New York art world and he started running on and throwing in names like Susan Caldwell and Phyllis ? and Andrew Ritchie and it was hard for me to keep up with much of this. It was interesting when he spoke of NY when he first came to work at the *NYT* in the 1950s. He said that one could see all the galleries in a day and that the explosion of galleries is comparatively recent. We had both registered to the deal recently put through between Citibank and Sotheby's Parke-Bernet. This has further boosted the art for investment and the value of the Old Masters and antiques etc etc. People buying paintings over the phone, stacking them in a bank vault without even looking at them.

Only at the end of the talk when he asked how long I'd be in New York did I say I was here on two jobs: talks like this for my paper with 'outstanding voices and personalities in the NY art world' and because of an exhibition of my paintings at the World Trade Center, just concluded, that was coincided with Western Australia's 150th Year. I pulled out the catalogue from my bag in one swift gesture. He looked through it quickly and said: "Interesting – now if you come back to New York let me know well ahead and I'd like to see it." Then I spoke or asked another few questions and then his telephone started ringing. I got a flash photo of him which he seemed quite pleased to sit for – looking serious – not smiling. He is really a serious man. I would not say he had a highly developed sense of play – as, for instance, myself – but he would be very trustworthy. There was a nice part in the conversation earlier when we were talking of the Whitney and I said I thought some of their current exhibits were rubbish and he said: "Well, if you've read my comment on them – you know I said the same …" He said I should not miss the Baron Thyssen-Bornemisza at the National in Washington DC etc etc. We talked also about the Aegean exhibition at the Met. He said he saw no big single names emerging – just a proliferation of ideas, styles and artists.

Letter: Elizabeth Durack from New York on Thanksgiving Day 1979 to Perpetua in Sydney

Last Sunday I met up with Lucille [Durack, American cousin] at the midday Mass at St Patrick's. No mean feat as it is a very big cathedral and was very crowded – both with genuine worshippers and with the ever-moving crowds of tourists that they try to control with ropes (I don't mean flogging them in the Temple but with cordoned-off aisles) during the Consecration. I took her to the Mus of Mod Art – which isn't bad on Sunday – although, as everywhere, the cut-down on staff makes serving slow. Lucille has lived in New York all her life yet it was the first time she had been to this museum. After lunch I suggested we take a turn together through *The Art of the 20s* exhibition but I could see quickly she didn't want to do this – so I walked very very slowly with her back to 51st Street. We said goodbye at the corner. She is a dear gallant little soul – looks well – but is, I think, paler and more shaky than last year.

Then I caught the Madison Avenue bus up to 90th Street and the Guggenheim and my first encounter with the overwhelming avalanche of Joseph Beuys' art. You said on the phone that you were familiar with it from your reading there – but the actual physical confrontation with it is almost beyond description. This exhibition is a huge retrospective and includes both drawings and sculpture. How they ever got it across the Atlantic God only knows. The exhibition takes up the entire museum (with the exception of the smaller galleries off on the 4th circuit) and I have never seen an exhibition look so splendid at the Gug as this one. It must surely be the show for which Frank L Wright designed the building and just as the Gug is, in a sense, an architectural revolution and an assault and an affront to conventional planned construction so too is the art of Joseph Beuys a total revolution as well as total assault and affront. This is by far the most outstanding exhibition I have seen all this time in NY. Beside it everything sinks into insignificance — and I shall try and collect my thoughts later (on return) and use this as a central theme from which periphery can … peripherate … As for STUNT – J Beuys is *Total Stunt* – but never deviates (even in such extravagances as 'Dialogue with a Coyote' – when he spent a week in a room with a live coyote) from also being *Total Art.* Even his scratchy small drawings pack a terrible and frightening punch. The work of course is all terror, all frightening and all punch. It left me drunk – punch drunk – and, by gum, it has to be pretty strong stuff to do this to me – as I have an acutely selective, critical, cynical and even destructive art stomach. Also I bore easily – but the bells were ringing and the guards were cross and impatient before they got me out of the place.

When I stepped out, at last, into the luminous twilight of Park Avenue in an absolute daze – I looked down and saw what I thought was one of Beuys' drawings of the female pelvic region. It was a leaf pressed to the pavement. All the week his work has been echoing and re-echoing in my head and before my eyes. I went back again yesterday for another look and to buy the catalogue – also to see darling Ward Jackson again [Guggenheim archivist and Director of Viewing Programs] – (not by appointment as my day had been too full for this. I just took a chance and asked if I could see him at the admin counter when buying the catalogue). He came up from his under-nether region right away and I got one of the attendants to take a photo of us together. I hope it comes out. I said I was giving him the highest marks as the kindest, most patient man in the NY art world. This seemed to please him. Ward Jackson is almost child-like in his gentleness and yet controlling such an important area of NY's high *noospheric* life. He asked me how the exhibition went and I told him it was a grand experience. He said: "That's good, that's good. I was afraid you might be disappointed or discouraged – don't be – it takes a little time in New York. Come back again – and write to me."

1980s

It is our world, not theirs, not a world[32]

Our grandmother, Gran Central, died in her 97th year at the start of this decade. The event had wide repercussions for the family as a whole. For years Gran had kept in touch with all of us – her own children and her 20 grandchildren – wherever we were in the world. She kept up a diary of family comings and goings (that included cousin Robin Miller's flights across the Pacific in a single-engine – or was it a twin-engine? – plane and various lesser achievements).

Each month the diary was copied and distributed which meant we all had a fair idea of what each of us was up to. With Gran's death there was no one to take her place. The family soon fragmented and nowadays few of us have any idea of what the others are doing.

Rex Hobcroft and I somehow managed to purchase Gran's old home in Nedlands. Soon after, Rex retired as Director of the Sydney Conservatorium of Music and we returned to Perth. 66 Kingsway was not far from '47'. This proved mutually satisfactory for Elizabeth, myself and Rex – we could continue to make forays abroad, or within Australia, while one or the other kept an eye on our homes.

PDC

Diary: 30 December 1980

The year is running out in a strange subdued atmosphere – grey, mysterious. The cyclone *Felix* which threatened yesterday has turned into a rain depression.

I am worried about the story that three years ago I tentatively called 'Episode'. I'll find a title because it is a good story – but I have a timing problem: if Maurice won the Crossing Cup on *Demon Lover* in 1930 and his sister Catherine came north in 1934, and JJ makes his entry that same year, there is still too long a span of time from 1934 to 1939 when I had intended to have him killed in the War. Also Australia's participation would not have been that great in 1939, though the North African campaign (Rommel etc) is a good place (Tobruk – Rats of etc). But it is too long 1934 –1939 and *far* too long to Feb 1942 and the Fall of Singapore (when the War started to take on real significance for Australia).

I could have JJ killed in the Spanish Civil War, but I very much doubt if he was politically motivated enough to have had any desire to assist the government side in one of the detachments from Australia that joined other countries in support of the government. JJ would more likely have joined voluntary aid to France, I imagine, and I doubt any Australians did this, although some from England, certainly.

The story has to move quickly, and end with a bang for JJ, and the total disruption of the lives of Maurice and Cat. Perhaps I can make it the Spanish Civil War? JJ could be going through Fremantle and write to Catherine and give her an approx. date. It would not have been a troop ship. It may have been just a group of men who had done a crash course in guerrilla tactics outside Sydney. It is all very worrying. More so because I don't slog at a story. It does, or it doesn't fall out – ripe, as it were.

The story has been gestating for three years now (though God knows how much longer). When I read the three-year-old beginning of it I was going to chuck it out. Then it grabbed me and has had me in its grip for about four or five days now.

[*'Episode' was soon completed as 'The Survivor': a radio play for two voices.* PDC]

Letter: Elizabeth Durack in Sydney to Perpetua in Perth, 10 January 1981

Perpetua, dear

When I said that it was a good Opening I referred mainly to the setting and the fact that a big crowd constitutes, usually, 'a good opening'. Apart from this I feel even more separated from the philosophy of The Treaty than ever, and everything said or reasoned in support of it sounded more and more unreasonable to me. Really how a historian, as Manning Clark is supposed to be, could give support to such a skewy concept, historically skewy, is beyond comprehension.

In conversation at dinner, again in a heavenly setting, *au plein air* outside 'The Warehouse' with a big liner floating off and the Bridge picked out in green light, none of the eight young people who made up the party (plus senior self) were anything but scathing to sceptical, albeit well enough aware of historical abuses to the old Abs *et al.* However Dibbs Mather Brown stuck out for Coombs being "no fool" and that there must be "more behind the Treaty than meets the eye. And *none* that can come to any *good* to anyone, black, white or Australia generally." Surely the old boy Coombs isn't a latter day Trotskyist? using the Treaty as a tool towards 'permanent revolution'? Anyway, although old now he looks fit, more so than his wife who was with him, and the reverse applies to Manning Clark and Dymphna. The latter now has a fine determination to sit in on the exhibition for the next three weeks, presumably proselytising.

Jill Wran had on a buff–coloured linen dress. Sleeveless, stockingless, very brown arms and legs. She is as slim as a piece of paper and looked very composed, so too did Neville Wran. He looked well, didn't speak and they didn't stay very long. I didn't speak to them, was too shy to bowl up and when someone said they'd introduce me they'd gone. Thea Waddell was her characteristic slow-speaking self. She seemed to be counting money at the desk. I don't know what role she plays in this but had a very vague look, asked after you and sends love.

A very great number of people knew me, to my complete surprise. I didn't know them. One called Kane Savage from Port Moresby said: "I just love your books," and I said, "I think you mean my sister Mary's books." "Oh no," he said, "your books, *Seeing—through* ... I've read them over and over again particularly the one on Papua New Guinea." Big surprise to me as I never think anyone ever reads these modest inconsequential little books. Robin Amadio(?) from the *Women's Weekly* was there and they took photos of me and Dibbs by *The Rim* … which, if they ever show up, which is unlikely, will be awful as they were taken from *underneath*.

After Manning Clark had given his opening speech, Margaret Valadian spoke. She is a very fine young woman with both the features and the fine, precise articulation of an Indian, but she has affiliated with the Aboriginal movement. I went out of my way, out of interest, to meet her mother, Olive Valadian, who Margaret referred to. Olive V does not appear to be Aboriginal – looked more Pacific Islander.

Then me, being smart, addressed myself to a man, v dark-skinned with fizzy hair and a big hooked nose: "Are you visiting from Papua New Guinea?" "No. I'm a Torres Strait Islander." However, the dancers themselves were unquestionably Aussie Aboriginal, and nice.

By the way, the two streams of the Australian population not on the buses and conspicuous by their absence from the coaches on the long Australian road hauls, are babies and blacks. Both privileged types, they only fly everywhere nowadays, and the dancers had just flown in from Arnhem Land a day or two before. They've forgotten the art of body paint (slopped on white and v ugly) but not the steps, and some brilliant miming of a hunting incident. The body painting art has been passed on to white children and several had painted faces. I know it's supposed to be fun but it gives me the creeps like *Lord of the Flies* gives me the creeps.

I tried to take some photos of all this fun and games but won't have them back till Monday and then none may have come out. Diana Fisher is very pretty and Judy Cassab looked v nice too in a Double Bay model. There were quite a number of the legal frat. there, Labor legal bods I gather, and one buttonholed me on Land Rights – with which he seemed to be v much involved. [Al] Grassby was kissing anyone with a black face, man or woman. Our Dawkins was slicing into a huge wedge of cheese. We referred to our last meeting at Ferry Korwill's exhibition. He seemed sort of slap-happy with parliamentary privilege and the gold pass, it was all I could do to restrain from saying: "You could be quite good looking if you watched your weight." There was some way-out dressing. A beautiful couple in Indian white cloth, the man in a hat with hair tied behind. Barefoot but clean which does not usually go with this ensemble. And there was of course the majority in the most ordinary drab Hay/Pitt St ensembles. The party lasted a good 2 ½ hours. I can't tell you anything about the paintings (hardly a thing: Judy Cassab's very ordinary watercolour of a lumpy woman and child; a repetitive Dickerson and Crooke) as I really only saw my own which in fact dominated the show and was commented on a lot, the actual content/significance/meaning of the painting not, of course, being understood. Had it been, I can't see how the Aboriginal Treaty Committee would ever have hung it.

I have tended your fern and the bamboo and the former responds already. I cut off dead and droopy fronds. There are five quite good separate plants but the one in the middle is dead consequently only the fronds along the rim of the container are developed. I have stood it on one of your stools and it's much happier with the fronds dangling their full-length rather than bungled up on the corner of the bookshelf. Another fern is alive but not too happy. They were both sitting in their own drainage which is terrible for anything. The bamboo is okay. I cut off all the dead leaves but it wants to get out and away. Its roots had penetrated the container and can't find anything to get into, but (as *I* know) a plant can survive in this condition almost indefinitely.

Yesterday I did the classic Sydney 'culture loop': the Museum and its Arid Zone gallery, new, and very good; St Mary's Cathedral (to burn a candle for our intentions); and the Art Gallery. Pompeii is on there and an exhibition of clothing, very meretricious and ugly but as a plus a very interesting exhibition of old photos of New South Wales by a photographer, Charles Kerry, deserves more than the cursory glance I gave them en route to the restaurant. It's too late today now to tackle Paddington perhaps tomorrow. I'm pretty tired after the late night. Although I asked Dibbs to drop me back after dinner, *de*–clining the invitation 'to go on to the fabulous transvestite show in the Cross' with the rest of the party.

There are a great number of Asians here, Japanese yes and Chinese women with children and babies and many Pacific Islanders. Dozens of them in Hyde Park all beautifully dressed at the current festivities there, part of Sydney Festival now current although really the latter seems to be something non-stop in this city.

I'll structure my Melbourne appointments before leaving here as once I do I'm at the mercy of the Vic in Little Collins or the Lyceum Club in Collins. More anon. Fondest love to darling Mary. Many affectionate enquiries of her last night, the audience for the exhibition more writery than paintery.

ever your loving
mummm

Letter: Elizabeth Durack, from Derby to Perpetua in Nedlands, 5 April 1981

Perpetua darling girl

As if we did not know it already, as if we needed to be told. The road north is long, hazardous, monotonous, lonely and hot, and, into the bargain, through a howling wilderness.

How 'tourism' is ever game to broach this lot, I don't know. I guess the north does have 'winter sunshine' and I guess it can count on a biggish public on a once-in-a-lifetime, always-wanted-to-see-the-north – hop-kick.

Sure, in the Spring there are also *patches* of wildflowers, and there are a few tiny snippets of relief: a few white gums in the bed of the Fortescue and the three-armed Gascoyne [rivers], a few swift glimpses of 'wild life'. Though alas, most of the wildlife seen lies in decomposing splotches upon the surface of the road. Kangaroos-a-plenty. Every fortnight the Shire trucks do a run and scrape them off into the scrub, eagles, goannas and the exotics: sheep and cattle. The real cattle areas lie still ahead of me and I am *warned.* Also two thirds have remarked upon my not carrying a 'roo-bar.

The end of summer time through the agricultural areas which were a sea of pale ochre, until the Murchison, a sea of mulga and red dirt. Your optimistic comment about the car radio did not prove accurate. There is nothing from about Bulls Brook on. (We will have to wait four or five years until the satellite gets into orbit, which is not to say there would not be available some v good car radios that might function ex-urbia.) So the best I could do was 'thinky-backy'. And there is plenty of that for the Murchison since I did that first run with the mailman from Wubin to Payne's Find when that long road was a two-wheel track through the sand. Past Mt Gibson Station and Ninghan with its long memories of the MacPhersons, the MacDougalls, you, Michael and Forbie (of all odd ones). Thinky-backy the drive north with Julie in the early '60s. Thinky-backy the goldfields – Kalgoorlie (Ian Salmon) and the trips, also with you and Michael and later with Michael alone, through and around and in and out. Menzies, Laverton, Sandstone, Wiluna (what about our run to Wiluna not so long ago and the 'suite' at the Wiluna Hotel?), Lake Darlot, the Mulga Queen – Not forgetting Cun-da-lee … et al … et al … et al …

The Inland Road did not prove me to be as smart as I thought (sometimes think) I am, and although it does give that quick lift out of the southwest environment and looks, on the map, to cut off Dirk Hartog's belly (as it does, of course) there is the *catch* of the stretch between Newman and the coast (Port Hedland) which I underestimated.

The seal holds all the way to Newman, a fine road though it varies in width and there was nought going to induce me to overtake long transports with veering off onto the side gravel (no fear!) so this slows one down waiting for a safe overtake place.

I did not do as well as cousins Jim and Peg Durack that first day. They made Newman in the day and although I left Perth at 4.00am and travelled with only one very brief stop (by the way your sandwiches were delicious and lasted two days. They were nice and soft finally … the tomato, home-grown? was really good) for 13 hours, I called it a day at the Kumarina Roadhouse 150 kms south of Newman. (A rough place but they were quite friendly and kindly, into *quickly*, the total mess and muck of the north, cracked and broken concrete, broken taps, frogs in the w.c., mess, mess, mess: tins, piping, broken vehicles, flies and the hideous roar of the power engine.) I was on the road again by 7.00am. Not a brilliant start and the sun was high as compared with the previous day when I saw it rise in a wonder of pink and gold, like Bishop Salvado's dream, coming into New Norcia.

A beautiful long view of the eternal mountains. Blue and majestic on the horizon against a bland sky c.9.00am. Just one difference: a thin scarf of dust over Mt Newman, the hand of man. Did not go into Newman this time (only thinky-backy, Margaret Halid and my two trips to Jigalong).

A few kms on – bang! Off the seal and on to some of the most horrible stuff imaginable: corrugations wide, deep and studded with sharp stones, the road to Nullagine and Marble Bar. Suddenly everything was in an uproar. The car was hot. I was hot, the exertion of holding it on the road. Dust was pouring in. No thinky-backy, only thinky-forward which was: "I don't think I can cope with this."

I ran on, if one could call it running, crossing from the left side to the right in search of any ease for the tyres, hardly able to hold the wheel at all. Then I recalled, a bit back, seeing a notice: 'Private Road: Trespassers will be Prosecuted' and I remembered a similar Notice around the Tom Price area a few years ago and daring the 'Prosecution' on that occasion. It was an awful decision to make and one I hate doing but I *turned back*. Once on the forbidden road the going was much better, and right beside me this bloody big railway line with cheery drivers waving from their windows, what comfort! It was the Mt Newman Mining Company access road, a road maintained in fair condition for the purpose of servicing the line. It was bad enough, as all dirt roads are, but it was not a *nightmare*, and parts of it, firm sand, were good running though one could not do much better than 80kms per hour. However, the distance was greater than I had expected. In my mind's eye I was picturing (optimistically, I know) Broome by nightfall. There was water on the road and I stuck, down to the springs, in heavy coarse sand. By a fluke I got a tow out of this. There was nothing on the road but this kind young man and a couple of others nearer Port Hedland who told me I could run into Yandy (a mine camp) and get petrol. I was v low on petrol because of all the low gear running.

When I got on to the seal, at last! at last!! (*the sea! the sea!!*) I heard the dreaded roar that told me I'd done in the muffler.

In the interim, Port Hedland, the Ruhr of WA, has taken on the aspect of a city. Contributing mainly to this, the beautiful road system, as fresh and serpentine as anything in Perth, and the swish, swish, swish of cars commuting from old Hedland to South Hedland, for all the world like the convergence from Civic to Red Hill at 5.00pm, everything being, of course, relative.

The Shell garage on the outskirts of town was a hive of activity and yes, they could supply me with a new muffler ($77 on Bankcard, $15 cash for labour). I hosed down the car during the wait and by the time the job was through there was not much sense (indeed it would have been *non*-sense) to go on. The incandescent lights all around the harbour were coming on, a hot sea wind was blowing, there were some fine frangipani trees in full bloom, and the old place looked, really, quite beautiful.

I stayed at the Highway Motel and at the sight of the shower and the bed, if they only knew it, I thought $35 (on Bankcard) cheap at the price. I had been travelling for 12 hours, covering in that time only 583 kms, as compared with 1,022 on the first day.

The ultimate in thinky-backy was, for me, the new Port Hedland–Broome road. The one it took 21 days for Kim and me to *dig* our way through in November 1950. Now it stretches ahead in all its majestic perfection, of blue, red, purple and snowy white. Impeccable, pristine, beautiful, a triumph of modern engineering.

(As far as I'm concerned you can bag up all the old Victoriana/ Edwardiana that still hangs around in Australia and I don't care, much, but if such a feat of road-making as that 615 kms between Port Hedland and Broome ever falls into ruin and decay then I shall protest, from the grave, if need be.)

This is not to say that it is not, still, something of a challenge. It is a long road, and hot and it now induces in one such an attack of Road Fever that one has to keep a grip on oneself, let alone the car. It is not a road to dawdle on and, once on it, one is tied to it. There are (would you believe) 'P[arking]' places but there is no running off it on to the edges which in places are metres from above the surrounding country. How one c r a w l e d from one spinifex heap to the next through the twisting, twining track – through the red hot sand pouring into the wheel tracks. Down, hopelessly down, outside Pardoo Station. The decision, an awful one: Kim to walk back 10 to 15 miles to the station to ask for help, with the waterbag.

"I may not be back till morning."

"Don't worry, I'll be alright."

"Of course you'll be alright, you've got all the water." Kim laughing, because into the bargain, the whole crazy expedition was a sort of fun run.

The bridge, a magnificent new bridge over the mighty de Grey is not yet open. There is a side track and one crosses the river via the Goldsworthy rail bridge, a rickety, scary, narrow job with not only the rail lines but the timbering running vertically and clipping and clicking about. The new bridge standing high and proud on its great steel legs is well seen about 300 metres west of this old job and will be open to traffic next week. (Thinky-backy the snarled-up bits of wire mesh in the river bed held down with a few rocks. Thinky-backy this same run north with Mary and Horry c1953?)

There is no sign yet to indicate that the Sandfire Flats Roadhouse lies ahead, but where? My petrol needle is on zero. Not scary, but a nuisance. I stopped a vehicle. Not a thing I liked doing; nor would do; nor, which today, is easy to do. Pulled up and stood by my car, instead of partly hiding or being in a 'P' place which indicates one is in no need or trouble (the advantages of 'P' places).

"I am sorry to stop you," (everyone has Road Fever, everyone is in a wild hurry) "but how far to the next petrol?" Two easy-going half-castes, thank goodness. "About a mile." Oh, what a relief. "Fill her up."

At the Sandfire Flats Roadhouse there is a big mural of Leichhardt on a camel, setting out, looking at the sand hills and beside a dead camel. The whole thing is not that damn worse than Nolan. I mean, this effort is really no worse than Nolan. I saw the old boy who done it. "I like your mural." His eyes lit up. "Got a couple more in the bar if you'd like to see them." There was also an awful big nude at the Kumarina Road House the previous day. Someone might yet promote this outback bar room art – as for instance, that story we read about Barton/Luna Park.

10.00am Trouble over holding on to this room [at the Boab Inn, Derby]. The irony/comedy of the situation is that in all these countless millions of spare hectares, the moment one gets to a tiny township a few square centimetres of hotel-room-space becomes the most precious/expensive thing in the world.

I would be on the road hours ago but the Royal Flying Doctor Service party arrives here this afternoon. To miss them by what amounts to only a few hours would really be a bit *odd* of me. (I know now I could not make Wyndham by pm today to catch them before they leave for Derby. I thought at one stage, that I might.)

So actually I don't know where I am and this missive comes to a sudden close.

All well … love,

Mum

A bit later: I plan to leave here, Derby, at sparrow fart (M's expression) tomorrow after the function at the RFDS base here this evening at 6.30 when I shall meet Col. Horner and party, Vice Pres RFDS etc. Road Fever permitting I shall try and not hurry too much on the Fitzroy Crossing–Hall's Creek–Wyndham road, and even try to stop for a bit of sketching (always think this, but is it possible? Get there, get there, bugger all else, is what the Fever dictates).

I shall write to Reg. I can't see any real solution to his '81 winter north excursion. Ideally, probably, is to fly. Have a car/ute/wagon in Wyndham. As I said before I left: I've tried it *all* ways … But oh, am I glad to have the car with me in this hot strange little town. I am being dumped out of the Boab and into the Spinifex. Writing on knee.

PS Although not commented on here I am anxious your news: heard from Janet? Direnzo? Sweet peas? And fond love to Rex who will be back from Sydney by now,

and love to all there below parallel 26°.

Essay: Australia's Third World by Ted Zakrovsky* (*Quadrant*, April 1984)
* a *nom de plume*

> *"Well, you see, I worked in India for some years before coming out here so I am used to the Third World."*
> *"But Australia is not a Third World Country."*
> *"I am referring to Aboriginal communities …"*
> (from a conversation between the author and a doctor attached to Pitjand'jara Health, north-west South Australia. August 1983)

Not too many advanced countries in the world today credit themselves with the creation of a Third World. Yet such is Australia's distinction. Our Third World, however, is of a kind that only a very rich country can afford. We finance and subsidise it. Over the past few years this phenomenon has developed to become a specialised national preoccupation – one might almost say a hobby that is growing in popularity as more and more Australians become aware of it and are drawn into the intricacies and refinements of maintaining it.

Furthermore, in a time of high unemployment, our Third World is one of the few growth points for the creation of new jobs as the various Departments of Aboriginal Affairs in all States conform to Parkinson's Law and as the workers in the field put out more flags.

It was when Donald Horne viewed the contrast between Australia and most other countries of the world that he came up with his title: *The Lucky Country*. That was about 1965. In the 1967 Referendum the nation was asked, by the then Liberal government, if it favoured a policy of increased aid to Aboriginals. An answer in the affirmative was returned clear and firm. An ensuing Labor government further endorsed this public response. This was the beginning of the spending spree and the introduction of a whole new set of policies. Assimilation was repudiated and paternalism in any shape or form out-lawed. Aboriginals were to be defined as a separate, self-determining, culturally distinct people within the ideal of a 'Multi-Cultural Australia'.

No one can blame any one else for what has happened since. We're all in this together. Together we can view with surprise and dismay the emergence in our midst of our own fully-fledged Third World complete with an indefinable 'black' minority, privy, suddenly, to international affiliations. Somehow, in the brief span of hardly more than a decade, we have by dint of excruciating mental effort and the expenditure of enormous sums of money, created a situation reflecting faithfully a pattern that, in countries like India and South America, took centuries to set.

In general amazement people are now turning to each other and asking how this came about when, only a short time ago, we had simply an old slack, always-with-us 'Aboriginal problem' which was gradually, albeit too slowly, eroding itself away and which, in any case, represented numerically, less than a quarter of one percent of our total population.

~

Anyone with recall of former days – say from the 1930s and on into the 1960s – will remember when our Aboriginal population was much less and very much more diffused geographically. In outback areas it was an advantage to be part-Aboriginal although no one made a song and dance about it. On pastoral properties 'yella-fellas' were invariably relegated to positions of greater responsibility, though few, if any, ever married white women. (Those with the advantages of education or character melted into the general population almost without comment.)

Half-caste women, on the other hand, either married their own colour or, as was invariably their ambition, had children by white men. They tacitly accepted the fact that such children would be cared for by missions or Native Welfare Departments. If they were in a position to raise them themselves they saw to it that they got some schooling and punished them for playing or co-mingling in any adjacent blacks' camp.

No one called these women 'racist'. They were simply regarded by both black and white as good mothers. Today some of them can watch on television as their sons and daughters take up leading positions as 'Aboriginals' and know with satisfaction that it was because they brought them up white.

Those with no recall and no perspective, young Australians and new migrants, a great many of whom now find themselves working industriously for our Third World, accept the present situation as one of long standing like the doctor from 'Pit' Health. A few may be inclined to view what is happening with alarm but they will not dare to express disquiet for fear that such emotion be labelled 'ethno-centric' and contrary to the over-riding virtues of 'multi-culturalism'.

Moreover, once drawn into the affluent orbit of our Third World, new recruits find themselves stimulated by it, enjoy the experience and the well-paid novelty of it all.

~

The Aboriginal desert settlements are situated on the huge Reserves where three States, Western Australia, South Australia and the Northern Territory join. Access to all settlements is provisional on a Permit of Entry. Originally intended as a protection measure to ensure the seclusion and privacy of the Reserve inhabitants, quite what purpose a Permit serves today is not clear – perhaps so that the depressing situation remains hidden, to be revealed only occasionally and then to suit certain arcane ends and purposes as, for instance, the much publicised World Council of Churches' visit a few years ago.

A large sign-board declaring a 'Liquor Act Warning Prohibited Area' is the first indication one has of having arrived at the threshold of a sanctuary of ancient Dreaming. In all these places the picture that presents itself is depressingly similar and cheerless: a small slum township set in a dust bowl and encircled by a grotesque dereliction of burnt and wrecked motor vehicles, bonnets and boots agape, looking like ancient unclassified monsters marooned by drought. The wind of drought blows through them, in summer scorching hot as the blast of a blow-torch, in winter cold as an Antarctic blizzard.

The millions of dollars lavished on these places is invisible and not a sound or soul is heard or seen to break the low dust-shrouded diorama. High in a cloudless sky a kite-hawk finding an air current moves with out-stretched wings …

~

It does not require a weighty Report nor one of those wordy compilations of the findings of teams of experts to see just how closely *our* Third World conforms to the general pattern elsewhere. Ours, however, contains some special distinguishing elements – notably financial support on a grand scale from the nation's coffers in order to maintain it in all its sanctity and to keep it careening upon its present course.

So we find greatly augmented and concentrated groups of Aboriginals caught in the quagmire of squalor, disease, alcoholism, obesity, illiteracy, malevolence, inertia, tribalism in corrupt form and, consequently, schizophrenia. They are breeding indiscriminately, dying prematurely and have become totally dependent upon the very support that government policies intended they should be proudly independent from.

Saddest of all, child delinquents with self-destructive addictions round out our special Third World's inventory – the sorry lot of it. In this predicament Aboriginals have fallen easy prey to the incursions of the dominant pressure group – anthropological-legalists – working among them with impunity serving science or politics, who knows, other than that they are having a field day.

It takes a little while to appreciate what has happened because it has occurred and is occurring so quickly and so unpredictably. Should any doubts about such a state of affairs exist in anyone's mind a look at Aboriginal settlements almost anywhere in Australia today will soon disperse them.

There are a few exceptions – certain enterprises where rapport between a particular Community and its white Advisor can generate a feeling of stability and hope for the future, or where, at some former mission settlement, an ameliorating hand still persists but they only heighten the contrast elsewhere.

Let us now examine briefly a few of the above aspects of this psycho-physical collapse.

Alcoholism and obesity are areas too obvious for comment and have been long under review by teams of medical men and women, religious, psychologists, dietitians et al.

Illiteracy surfaced more slowly and is a more complex problem. That it should be so widely on the increase is a contradiction in itself considering the enormous expenditure on Aboriginal education in recent years.

The multi-culturalist ideal to 'aboriginalise' education has had the effect of splitting the white teacher attitude and policy down the centre. Some white teachers now argue that *any* conventional education at all is a bad thing. Others strongly oppose such an attitude – we must, at least give them an alternative – the chance to choose. Debate, bitter at times, produces zealots on the one hand and resignations on the other.

Sensing the dichotomy, the kids are simply not turning up to school. In places conscientious teachers have taken to going after their pupils in vehicles on early morning musters through the scattered camps but with scant success. One way or another, for one reason or another, education, in any previous definition of the word is evaporating. The goal is not to read, write or count but simply establishing dole eligibility.

As for the ideal of the old men passing on to the young their old knowledge and wisdom, this simply isn't on. For a start the former are all too busy – either engaged on extensive motorised 'lore pisnis', travelling in one day an area that took their forebears weeks of walking, or else being conveyed interstate or internationally as show pieces and front men.

Unrestrained breeding which has brought forth, during the past two decades, a continual crop of under-sized, under-cared-for children is the direct result of Family Allowances paid to mothers and to 'single-parent' families – the latter proving a particularly attractive bonus for girls of 13 and 14. 'Kid money' is as popular with them as 'Sit-down' money is with the lads – a reward, not support or compensation …

An almost measurable increase in malevolence and violence among Aboriginals themselves – apart from the role alcohol plays – stems from the revival of old tribal feuds and past grievances. On missions and on cattle stations Aboriginal discord had been lulled almost to extinction but now, quite suddenly and unexpectedly, multi-culturalism extols the regurgitation of the past and with it all the long-forgotten differences.

Any malevolence of black towards white is of a secondary nature. When it does occasionally surface in desert communities the reasons for it are extremely hard to find. Without warning, a dedicated and hard-working white Advisor may find himself suddenly and summarily sacked – by a whim of the Council? by some in-fighting among the latter members? Who knows? No white employee has as yet ever contested or won a case for wrongful dismissal from any Aboriginal settlement. Mystified he must simply pack up and go.

Aboriginal society was, traditionally, a male dominated one. In former days, however, some check and balance upon abuse was kept because of the important food-gathering role played by women.

Today sexism reasserts itself without restraint in a wholly dislocated and distorted tribal revival. Many women live in fear and subjection, their presence as aides in schools and hospitals erratic, their voice on Councils a token only. (The success of some part-aboriginal women, freed from the past by circumstances, and their own character and ability, should not here be overlooked. There is an increasing number in this category who have risen to their present status not because of 'multi-culturalism' but in spite of it.)

~

The white inhabitants of the desert settlements who, at present, are all employed by the Aboriginal Councils, consist of an ever-growing team – advisors, teachers, linguists, publishers (of the settlements propaganda periodicals), book-keepers, religious (yes, still there in low-profile), store-keepers, communication operators, maintenance engineers, out-station managers, builders, carpenters, mechanics, road-makers, well-sinkers, pilots (for the Community's private air-craft), hospital staff, postal service staff, police. Together with their families all these reside in new or recently up-graded domiciles, sometimes in 'reserves' of their own behind barbed wire for protection against the people they are protecting from the old protectionist policies.

The Aboriginal population itself lives, by preference, in scattered wind-breaks and lean-tos dispersed over a wide area – sometimes setting up camp immediately outside their brand new house. (In answer to any questionnaire seeking to ascertain a Community's needs and wishes – 'housing' will always head the list, followed by 'a school'. In fact both items have zero priority in the present scheme of things.) Every settlement has rows of vacant houses that lie wrecked and befouled in *cumuna* abandonment.

About mid-morning the seemingly inanimate scene begins to show signs of life. Figures emerge from the camps and start converging in slow procession upon the store. As the doors open, the line of forms leaning upon them disappears suddenly from the bright sunlight into the exciting gloom of the building's interior. The game is on, and one of the kinkier aspects of our particular Third World reveals itself.

Eager but cautious hands self-service into freezers to extract their varied contents – rocky lumps of mince-meat, lamb chops, pork, bacon, steak, stone-hard pies, frost-white chickens. Long arms reach up for bags of flour, rice, spaghetti, potatoes, onions, sugar, tea, tins of jam, powdered milk, honey, fish, baked beans – a pyramid of wrapped, sliced bread, together with a shelf of Kimbies, disappears. A rotunda of cassettes and video books is stripped bare in minutes.

Swinging on the door of an upright refrigerator a black imp in a new red track suit makes grave decisions. In a corner more track suits are tried on small bodies to exclamations of delight from mothers to see their children so modishly got up. More conventional themselves they flip through racks of floral dresses and button-up cardigans while men look for their right size among a stack of trousers, shirts, fleecy-lined jackets and wind-cheaters … Yesterday the Social Service plane with the pension, unemployment, child-endowment cheques flew in from the nearest town – Alice Springs, or Darwin, or Katherine, Wyndham, Kalgoorlie or Port Augusta …

Tomorrow things will be quieter. Before the fortnight is out children will be rummaging again in the trash cans of the settlement's white employees and the lucky winners in the big gambling rings will have shot through to the nearest town in their new Toyotas or old jalopies.

~

Less than 50 years ago some of these big, stale, benighted desert settlements consisted of only a few drums of water, a few bags of flour, left, once a month, by a local Road Board truck on a corner of neutral tribal ground in a perishing drought. After the vehicle was well away the desert men would come out of hiding, drink the water and savour the *manna*. There were no ritual proceedings for sharing the latter as required with the scant bush foods. First come was first take. So some sat down then and there and waited for the truck's return. More followed suit. They were naked, quarrelling and unredeemed the Missionaries heard tell … and so tenuous points of neutral tribal territory became the places like Jigalong, Cunderlee, Warburton, Yuendumu, Yalata … (Hermannsberg, too, but its story is older).

When the desert men joined in the hymns they received trousers. Some cut their hair, gave their brow-bands to their uncles and took to wearing hats. Women, too, put on dresses to speak to the Book people and undefined arrangements to leave their children with them were made … These were the waste lands.

In the more productive areas of sheep and cattle stations contact between the races began earlier. Loose pacts, mutually useful and beneficial, were made between the Aboriginals and the pastoralists. Every station came, in time, to have its complement of still-tribal but co-operative groups, the men worked for half the year in the stock-camps while their families lived adjacent to the homesteads – a pattern set that lasted in places for 60 years. Then action, spearheaded by radical whites who surfaced after the War, forced the issue regarding the payment of wages to Aboriginal pastoral workers.

This was a reasonable enough idea for any group having an alternative such as the collection and sale of surface minerals, but reform proved a disaster for most station Aboriginals. Pastoralists simply divested themselves of all their Aboriginal workers together with their families. Camps, adjacent to the nearest bush town were set up to meet a temporary emergency which, over the years, became a permanent one.

Was it too optimistic then after ten years of the new enlightenment, the big U-turn in official policy from assimilation to separation and the joint national effort to make a reality of 'multi-culturalism', to have hoped to see some general improvement instead of an extraordinarily depressing botch of a Third World?

Anyone can ask questions but who can supply the answers? Do current policies aimed at re-identifying the Aboriginal gratify or bewilder? Do those in remote settlements see themselves as abandoned, used, or newly liberated? How, in fact, do they see themselves at all? How do they want to see themselves? How would they have themselves presented if asked?

Nearly white in well-tailored suit hurrying up the stairs of Parliament House in Canberra, brief-case in hand, vocal and televised? Savage and noble? Old and naked on the red ground at Yilpilli, Warakuna or Kintore long hair matted with mud – reincarnate from the pages of Spencer and Gillen? At the town store in Hall's Creek – pink stretch jeans, Stetson hat and neck ornament, (not teeth or finger bones but a sign of the Zodiac, silver, as the single earring is also silver), chatting loftily with a group of less sartorial young men? Astride a horse? (This in memory only now and nostalgically), swaying to Country and Western music at the Battle of the Bands for the great sports weekend at Yuendumu – dazzling in green satin weighed down with a gleaming instrument shaped like the jaws of a shark and trailing amplification cord?

In a bright red guernsey embracing a fellow player for kicking a goal? Asleep where he fell with the bottle beside him? (No. None of those, burn them! Burn the lot!) In a peaked cap – nonchalant, confident – at the wheel of a big new vehicle with plenty of torque?

Stop there, settle for that one …

And drive, drive on, out of the nightmare.

Could it be as simple as that?

They thought so in the ivory towers set among manicured gardens beside the manufactured waters of Lake Burley Griffin.

Essay: Land Wrongs: The Iconoclasm of Marc Gumbert (*Quadrant,* January-February 1985)[33]

> The central argument of this book is that classical anthropological conceptions of Aboriginal local organisation, and consequently, traditional land tenure are based on inadequate models. These render narrow and indeed distorted views of social reality. I offer here an alternative approach.
>
> Marc Gumbert

You're likely to run into them anywhere in the bush today: *French* men and women. Maybe one has just opened a Cordon Bleu restaurant in Todd Street, or a lingerie boutique (smile in your grave, John McDouall Stuart) in the Mall at Tennant Creek, more than one will be in Australia twice traversing on 'Aussie Passes', while another may be way out back of Central Mount Wedge on an ANU/Sorbonne exchange deep into resurrecting the old ritual carry-on of the *Kaititja*, and here's another – hyped on benzedrine and expounding to the world at large on a TV series *Sur le Coeur Mort Magnifique d'Australie*. And meet this one – she's married now and settled down here for good, has a fine repertoire of swear words but only a smattering of Strine. And, what have we here? (just pull up there, under that bottle tree will you), this is interesting! Another Françoise – you can pick them for that certain *Je ne sais quoi* – and this one is studious, wrapt, lost in thought, quite inspired, transported in fact and armpit deep into a Land Claim in some kangaroo court under the shade of a coolibah tree at Mudbura, Lake Amadeus, Uluru, Utopia – or where have you.

And wherever you do happen to strike any French men or women and whoever they are and however varied their occupations or preoccupations there is always the one underlining thread that connects them all: "How," they ask themselves, "did we, as a nation, come to miss out on all *this* – all this fun, all this sun, all this room, when, so easily, it could have been ours for the taking, could have become our very own, wide open, glorious *lieu désert lumineux* in the South Pacific, still containing what's more, what's *more,* the original model of Jean Jacques Rousseau's *Sauvage Noble*?"

"Why," they muse on, "did we end up with just a scatteration of seascaped pinnacles as our only foot-hold in this hemisphere?" Bougainville skirted it and left his name behind in a blaze of scarlet blossom and La Perouse – ah! La Perouse, he is still out there somewhere … and Western Australia's loveliest and most romantic coastal names are all French, as, too, is the name of its loveliest wild flower – Leschenaultia – called for the botanist who sailed our way with Baudin in 1801. Espérance and le Recherche Archipelago, Gulf Joseph Bonaparte, Cape Leveque, Gantheaume Point, Naturaliste Reef and Point D'Entrecasteaux … Just to see the names on the map is to savour the heady wine of that season and the after-taste of disappointment and regret. But it is with such dashed hopes that the path of history is strewn.

For there it was: after Waterloo the King Tide of France's expansive energies receded and dried back revealing only dry sand and an occasional rusting spade left behind from the hasty burial of treasure trove. Moreover, by then, France had Canada on her hands and a new goal *ensuite* after the Heights of Abraham – "the battle of the bassinette". By then, too, the West coast of Africa was stretching out before her in miles of steaming mud – ideal for her own penal extensions and much closer than Botany Bay.

So Australia, that great Kohinoor of the Pacific, was claimed finally, holus-bolus, lock, stock and barrel by Great Britain. And no amount of multi-cultural di-ssectioning, nor republican flagging-downing can ever or will ever refute that. It's ours! Eat your heart out France! Conjecture, contemplate, ruminate as you will, new migrants! Many of the latter, have, however, now settled for the next best thing: they hop right in here with us and *enjoin.*

There's nothing to stop them. Indeed there's welcome for new-migrant involvement and a deep respect for it at the level where we feel that we cop the credit end of the brain drain. (Old Aussies, like myself, and like the Aboriginals before us feel, always, that new-comers, automatically, know more about the things we are thoroughly conversant and familiar with than we do ourselves. So we set them up chairing panels, publish their books, ask their opinions and advice. We call this our 'cultural cringe'. You won't change us.)

Enjoinment is exactly what lawyer-anthropologist Dr Marc

Gumbert has done with his book *Neither Justice nor Reason* recently launched in Sydney. It will put him right in the foreground of our press and our TV screens for the sub-title of the book is that current hot potato: *Aboriginal Land Rights – a legal and anthropological analysis*.

This is a book of major significance and anyone even vaguely interested in the subject will have to read it. Personally I've been waiting for it ever since hearing the author speaking about his ideas and findings concerning Aboriginal society on an ABC radio program some months ago.

At the time I experienced something of that fellow feeling of the wondrous kind variety particularly as the speaker appeared to be one better able and better qualified than myself to express doubts concerning the narrow straitjacket that our traditional anthropologists had imposed upon that vaguest of all social entities: the primordial functioning structure of Aboriginal society, what held it together and what, really, was the attitude and relationship of these very first Australians to *the land*.

"Look!" we said to each other – i.e. my bush friends and I yarning away together, "there was so *much* land in the pre-European epoch when about 250,000 people were dispersed over some 777,000,000 hectares that land must have been like air – taken for granted – gratuitous and eternal."

In good seasons foraging areas might be quite small but during periods of drought a much wider range of movement was necessary for survival by surface skimming the hard earth. Making this possible was, of course, the extended family. In the old days this elaborate system of kith and kin consisted not only of direct relationships but minute degrees thereof (the 'little-bit' and the 'little-little-bit' uncles, aunts, cousins *et al*), which links gave access to terrain extending far and wide.

We knew this. We took this knowledge for granted. We observed and heard tell of examples of it. Enormous journeys were made right from the inland to the coast and back, cutting clean across 'tribal boundaries' and language differences. The intricacies of these remarkable excursions and how they were negotiated was a primary topic of conversation in the shade of the tank-stand and around the camp while old folk would delve deeper and ever deeper into genealogies of the far past with all the total recall of the illiterate memory – the one long ago destroyed in ourselves.

Now it appears that Marc Gumbert, out of the blue as it were, has alighted upon a similar assessment of the amorphous, contractable/expandable nature of Aboriginal society:

> "simplistic mini-states of permanent cell-like, autonomous 'hordes' conceived by Radcliffe-Brown were ethnocentric creations, they had no place in this land-abundant, class-less and fluid society of hunter-gatherers." (Part II, page 92)

This then is the theme of the book: disproving and debunking the old classical anthropological theories as first propounded by Radcliffe-Brown, followed faithfully by all his academic descendants, hallowed by time and enshrined as dogma. But make no mistake. This book, with its iconoclastic central contention, is not *anti* Land Rights.

Far from it. What Marc proposes is a much more liberal and inclusive Land Rights policy generally – one that would include all those sections of the Aboriginal population that, he argues, have been disadvantaged to date because the *lex prima* of Land Rights has been 'traditional ownership'. All the land made over to the Aboriginals in the Northern Territory and South Australia has been on this premise. Marc keeps hammering away at what he describes as an anthropological 'blind spot': the false assumption that to an Aboriginal his home was his castle, that place above all others dear to him and defend-worthy just as it was to Harold the Last of the Saxon Kings or as it is to Tommy Aitkins in his east-end Council duplex.

Marc sees the liberalisation and expansion of Land Rights as both necessary and desirable yet, at the same time, he teases away at its very essence. Can he not see (and is not this *his* blind spot?) that unless Land Rights *is* ethno-centricised the whole concept of it becomes null and void – *Terra Nullius*, in fact, of Square One *Anno Domini* 1788?

What is so interesting to me about this book is that a great deal of what Marc has to say parallels what my bush mates and I have been saying for a very long time but, of course, his language comes up much sharper and more scholarly than when we were nattering together in

Strine on the verandah, trying to catch that breath of air when the temperature was about 40 degrees in the waterbag. Had he been with us – we equipped only with our undisciplined empiricism but he with a vast epistemology – I feel sure we would have found some common ground and have had a darn good yarn.

We wanted to know. We wanted to understand. We loved anthropologists. (Naturally we had our private jokes about them — so, too, did the blacks.) Our old Dad took Elkin by the hand and led him through the Kimberleys in 1924. Phyllis Kaberry and my brother were vaguely in love during the time she stayed with us in the 1930s. (They would clear out together up the Soda Springs road of an evening. Once when my sister and I suggested we make a party of it and bring a jolly thermos of coffee we realised that we were *de trop*.)

I am reminded of these long ago happy days when Marc attempts to retrospect, for this is where he loses his way altogether. Here we would certainly have been able to help him. This Part I of his book seems, almost, to have been written by another person or someone with an ulterior motive.

Herein all the old Aunt Sallies come in for their now familiar battering: the pioneers, the establishment of a pastoral industry, the opening up of the map, the blazing of trails – anything, in fact, that has made Australia what Australia is including a land comfortable enough for a Frenchman of perception and scholarship to ease himself into and onto a swivel chair in an air-conditioned office in central Sydney.

Part II is the gist of the book. Here Marc hits form. Drawing from his own study, research and intuition he castigates the whole of classical anthropology and all the proponents thereof. Demolishing sacred cows and bulls with reckless abandon, he sweeps on towards the presentation of his own rectification.

Part III, which takes up more than half the book, examines actual Land Claim Cases in the Northern Territory and gives a valuable and concise account of six famous Cases over the past decade. Much of all this is richly spiced with Gilbertian situations as lawyers, anthropologists and Aboriginal men of High Degree all *dis*agree, while we observe the author himself diving in, clothes and all, in one rapturous plunge straight from the Seine to the Alligator River.

But just as Marc has no rear vision neither does he seem capable of looking forward to where his bonanza of a debunk is headed. He stands in one spot, spanner poised. Well, then, that is probably his particular role in the general scheme of things: he is a spanner thrower. He has thrown a spanner into the legality of 'traditional ownership', and he has thrown a spanner into the works of every anthropological factory in Australia.

His *coup* sure puts the cat among the pigeons of the old academic anthropologists, stiff with their own posturing – to say nothing of their set lectures and those eager-beaver students of theirs who can hardly wait to set up their plates in Alice Springs, Kununurra or Darwin as Land Claim Consultants. None of this mob is going to like Dr Marc Gumbert at all. But what with the anti-discriminatory laws they'll not dare to say what they might have a few years ago: "Who the hell is Marc Gumbert? Never heard of him. Never went through us. He's not even a Pom – he's a bloody Frog!"

OK. So what are the alternatives? If the Marc Gumbert model be accepted, there are only two:

Land Rights (i.e. free-hold title to land on the basis of restoring it to the 'traditional owners') is kicked through the bush gate for good and all;

Australia, bit by bit, is relinquished to a mini-minority group via a minority group that numbers about the same as the crowd in a Grand Final League Footy grandstand.

Patent absurdity.

Is, then, this book itself an absurdity?

Nearly, perhaps, but I don't really think so.

The title, however, is a hell of a one and what does it mean? Is it a quote from someone or somewhere?

Does it mean that Australia itself was established without Justice or Reason?

Perhaps, yet the author is at pains to explain, in Part I, the niceties of *Terra Nullius* and the 18th and 19th century attitudes regarding settlement in 'wilderness areas' of the world as differing from demarked and clearly delineated arable lands with their distinctive social structures and provisions of entry.

Does it mean that Land Rights themselves are neither just nor reasonable? Or, simply, that the handling of Land Rights to date lacks justice and reason but that from now on, post the Marc Gumbert Enlightenment, all can be rectified? Or what?

Why didn't he call it: *Towards fairer more inclusive Rights pour le Sauvage Noble* or, simply, *The Wrongs of Land Rights*.

Had he asked me, *I* would have suggested: *A Judicial Jungle and a Social Bungle*.

There are some aspects of this book however, concerning which one can be neither facetious nor tolerant.

So before the whole of our Australian civilisation as we have grown to know and love it, as it has grown to know and love us, (and not all of it, as regards the Aboriginals, was culture *clash,* there was culture *contact* too: mutual respect, reliance, admiration and love. God! Where's all that gone?) along with its origins, its motivations and, (dare we say it?) its brilliant social and technical achievements, is drowned in a deluge of Newspeak, blows off into the heat haze, crackles and goes up in smoke, is flushed down a blood drain or dispensed with by any other type of cultural purge some upstart may care to nominate – I'm buggered if a few words of defence are not warranted concerning just three or four of Marc Gumbert's arrogant and ignorant indictments. (The anthropologists can defend themselves.)

RESERVES

"Reserves came to be seen as the key 'management' solution to the 'Aboriginal problem'," says Gumbert and goes on to develop the theme of Reserves as "open goals" describing them as "the actual physical incarceration of thousands of human beings …" Reserves were "a vast Australian archipelago of camps for the internment of the country's original inhabitants", loose "labour pools" (page 34). This surely, is crude distortion of fact.

Certainly the Reserves were not located on prime river frontages but, be it realised, river frontages did not mean as much before the introduction of quadruped stock. Emus and kangaroos often 'beefed' better in the more arid and stony regions than in tall grass country which they would by-pass in favour of the easily cropped herbage that sprang up after desert rain. The huge Reserves were set aside so that the Aboriginals could there roam free, (by the way, the Table on page 39 doesn't list the Arnhem Land Reserve of 8,080,800 hectares at all – or is my eye-sight failing?) and be left alone to do all their own things undisturbed and unmolested. Whites were not allowed entry to these sequestrations. They never made forays upon them for labour. As if they could have *found* any Aboriginals had the latter chosen not to be seen – they are total masters of the art of camouflage and can disappear into the landscape more effectively than a chameleon. Moreover the Aboriginal has been uniquely successful at avoiding coercion to work. Those employed in the pastoral industry were there voluntarily. Occasionally on the reserves they may have followed a Health Patrol that visited them occasionally and have led it into the camp of someone with "the pig stick" – leprosy, or some such malady beyond the scope of primitive medicine.

That the Reserves didn't and couldn't work out quite as idealistically as was hoped is another story. Suffice it to say here that Aboriginal Reserves in Australia were benignly intended. (Just how benign for Australia at large the severance of these areas from our map and the establishment of them as sovereign Aboriginal Homelands and where such might lead is not for discussion here.)

MISSIONS

This repetitive present-day denigration of the Missions and the "massive control" exercised by them over the Aboriginals, this definition of Missions as "prison farms", as an arm of wholesale oppression is further crude distortion of fact but ever so popular in Newspeak.

The primary motivation of the Missions was simply Christ's directive: *Go, teach all …* (As well, in Australia, Missions didn't prosper economically as they did in the small Pacific Islands where *the Missions came to do good and did well.*)

Now Gumbert would have us accept the idea of Missions being

equivalent to Solzhenitsyn's *Gulag Archipelago* – instruments of oppression for an oppressive and monolithic State. How double-plus wide of reality can one get? Missions entered the Aboriginal societies of Australia as the waves of settlement broke in upon them – first among the thin coastal encampments, then as the hordes lost their old linkages, and scattered lost and bewildered – to tell them it was not the end, to show them another way and to give them hope.

That *this* idealism *has* borne fruit can be witnessed on all sides today as Mission-educated Aboriginals and half-castes take their places in the foreground of today's resurgence.

There is a dearth of recognition of the enormous contribution made by Missionaries to the sum of anthropological knowledge and linguistics over the years. Names like Strehlow, Worms, Love and Piele spring readily to mind yet in a recent publication, piously and rather misleadingly called *Aboriginal Religion*, the work of only two of the above even cracked a mention. The others were ignored.

Few of the old Missions are now nominated as such, the original location having become an autonomous Community with its own indigenous Council who are employers now themselves of an ever-growing staff of whites. Ever so many places seem to carry on in much the same way as 100 years ago and when this occurs it is because the Aboriginals want it that way. It is never fully appreciated just how many truly devout Christian Aboriginals there are. They are really, at present, a besieged minority as Christian Aboriginals are unfashionable – they are an affront to 'multi-culturalism'.

For any of the younger ones who feel that the old 'paternalism' is too restrictive, at least they can clear out with sufficient education to enable them to obtain a job in another environment – the Department of Aboriginal Affairs, for instance, or the National Aboriginal Council, or the Aboriginal Development Commission, or Aboriginal Liaison, or Aboriginal Sacred Site Authority, or the Aboriginal Arts and Craft, or Aboriginal Community Workers, Aboriginal Cultural Foundation, Aboriginal Development Foundation, Aboriginal Essential Services, Aboriginal and Islander Medical Services, the Aboriginal Land Commission, Aboriginal Legal Aid, Aboriginal Special Works, Aboriginal

Education, Aboriginal Housing and Hostels etc. All these organisations are bursting at the seams with white staff and are ready and eager for any possible Aboriginals to share the weight of their burdens.

QUEENSLAND

The extent to which Marc Gumbert reveals himself as one of the New Men, *cool as spreading fern* (I quote from the immortal Ern Malley), is the stridently arrogant manner in which he berates this state's Aboriginal policies. Of all the states in Australia, at least they have been consistent and that, alone, is a singular virtue today and one that must be sincerely appreciated by the Aboriginals themselves. Queensland's policies may yet prove to be the soundest and the most far-sighted of any in Australia.

Has Marc Gumbert ever been to Queensland? Ever visited Aurukun or the Wellesley Islands, ever heard the split voting in any of these places between those in favour of the status quo and the pressure-group stack?

The Queensland blacks and part-blacks, and Islanders and Kanakas and part this, that and the other, know full well that they are streets ahead of many of their counterparts in other States. This has historical reasons as well as political. Even the most land-locked of the original varied people in this part of the continent have always been – because of the nature of the terrain, and because of their external contacts with Papua New Guinea and Melanesia – more *with it*, more genetically diverse, lively and adaptable.

HALF-CASTE CHILDREN

They are repeatedly reckoned today as having been snatched from their mother's arms by the cruel and evil Protectionist policies of yester-year – a misguided film was made on the subject.

Sad as it was for both mother and child, most, if not all Aboriginal women, were resigned to the idea of their half-caste children being taken from them and brought into the white man's world. Many came forward with them as babies or youngsters and tearfully presented them to the Mission or to the recruiting parties that went through the stations and out-back towns collecting pale-skinned infants and placing them either with white foster parents or in Church orphanages. Aboriginal women were well aware of all this. That was why they had half-caste children. That was what they used, as opportunity arose, their bodies *for*. (Be under no illusion, knowledge of contraception was general – it was part of their survival kit.) But they had their half-caste children in order to give them a chance in life – the chance to assimilate. They called it: "grow'm up white fella way".

This is nothing new – it is as old as history: women of a subjected, displaced, or conquered people have always, either by coercion or choice, mated with the males of the new regime.

> What do fond and dear old crones talk to me about as we sit in the shade – beside the Elvira River, on a clay pan near Gregory's Great Salt Sea, out the back of the Lake Darlot, in the Robinson Ranges, on the edge of the Gibson at Kintore, in the Eastern Goldfields camps, Granite Peak, Cosmo Newbery, in out-camps behind Yuendumu, Hartz Bluff, Ringer's Soak, Fork Creek – or on more familiar ground at Bandicoot Bar near Lake Argyle? We're quite on our own. The men have all gone off somewhere in their new Toyotas to the endless meetings with the endless anthropologists and lawyers who are matching up the endless unmatchable 'traditional owners' with untraditional claimants …
>
> Like women together anywhere conversation reverts to children. But do they talk of their black children? Seldom. But finger by finger they count off for me the one, two, three, sometimes four half-caste children that they succeeded in bringing into the world way back in their youth: "My little yella fella kid where I bin sit down longa Brock Creek …"
>
> "You know my little Georgie, Missus, you bin see 'm that time … that time mob sit down longa Tanami – minein' mob. Well that time … 'nother time I have 'm my little girl – man call 'm, Yellarose – Yellarosatexas – you know 'm …?"
>
> "Yeh, you know 'm alright. You see 'm when 'm baby that time you comin' there with Heddy [Eddie Connellan] … long time now … 'm on'y little fella …" (Their memories are scalpel sharp.) And at the mention of each half-caste child they wait for my nod of recognition and approval.
>
> What they are trying to tell me, (and how bloody old hat and *mat*-ernalistic it sounds, yet again it was only last year) what they are trying to convey to me as they rummage through my hand-bag, not for money, what's the good of that? but out of curiosity concerning what I carry in my tilla-bag – and have I a spare comb or mirror?, as they try to rub off the polish on my nails and as they examine, thoughtfully, the soles of my

> shoes, what they are trying to tell me is – we took things as far along as we could while we could … "My little Rosatexas goberman grow'm up. She porget now her old mummy – close up binish now …"

But *retourner à nos moutons*:

It remains to be emphasised that, daring as Marc Gumbert has been with his *coup d'iconoclast*, the fact of the matter is, *he does not go far enough*. Even more important than the realisation of the Aboriginal's non-Euro-centricity in their attitude towards land is their non-Homo-centricity as well.

It is only our conditioning, our cultural background that made Man the measure of all things, a separate special creature that a God-made-man died-for-to-save and all that. In contrast to our Homo-centricity the Aboriginal inter-twined and inter-related with the entire animal and plant world in that totem brotherhood of a wholly shared and mutually en-bonded habitat.

So animals and plants, too, will need to be taken into account and must be included in any widened picture frame of their human brothers' rights to land. What about the long-eared bandicoot, the nail-tailed wallaby, the shaky-paw lizard, the bamboo-grass women, the fresh-water croc, the stink lily, the hairy-nosed wombat, the emu-tucker horange, that boab-nut man, that shit-weed wattle, that noisy scrub-bird, you blood-wood pungle-man, you fig-heatin' flyin' fox, your wedge-tailed high flyer, your quandon sisters, your spider look-out owl, your spectacled-hare-wallaby, your miss'em me mopoke etc. etc. etc. These were real. Real brothers – not simply pretty similes and myths upon which Euro-centric artists might extend their imaginations and their Windsor and Newtons, but dinkum mates with whom was shared a pre-eternally close and mutual dependence – a kinship closer even than that of blood brother. *Protection of a totem brother was a sacred trust. Along with this personal commitment, and as part of it, went habitat.*

So are not all these creatures, together with those men and women which Marc maintains have so unfairly missed out in Land Claim cases, even though they held both *Indaringinya* and *Ingwalilanima* rights and sometimes *Kurtingarla* and *Kirda* claimancy as well – are not all these hairy, scaly, furry, feathery, leafy and flowery creatures being equally overlooked and most unfairly disadvantaged?

Animal Liberationists arise!

Arise spirit of *Illapurinja*!

You have nothing to lose for you have all been undone. No one has anything to lose but we do have a whole continent to hold and to share as our mutual home. The loser is the credibility of Land Rights.

Essay: Artes Australis Percepta – An Overview[34]

Peering from the bow of the brigantine *Geelvink*, Willem de Vlamingh could just discern a landfall. Then, coming in as close as he dared, he observed the western coast of the fabled South Land. In the mist of early morning the shoreline lay stretched out away to the north and south. Looking intently at it he drew what he saw. Later he painted over the outlines with blue and yellow aquatints and inscribed them *Terra Australis Percepta*.

Nearly 300 years on from then we look at these first Australian landscapes – lent to us by courtesy of the Dutch government – in the required subdued light of the West Australian Maritime Museum and, with the aid of a modern map, we note with what accuracy de Vlamingh defined the bays, the inlets, the low sandy dunes.

Do they belong to a Museum or to an Art Gallery?

Until these first recordings from direct observation the presence, let alone the shape of a South Land, had been largely theoretical. The mapmakers of the day – heads down in Dieppe –prognosticated that 'the weight' of Europe and Asia necessitated a counter-balancing landmass in the southern hemisphere. Vague confirmation of this had come in via Magellan and Anson but nothing definitive. Thus Vlamingh's actual *percepta* represented a significant advance. Certainly everything moved on from there.

By degrees, perception was to lead on to possession – the declared possession by Great Britain of the whole of *Terra Nullius* now defined, since Cook's journey, between degrees of longitude 112 and 153 – but still unmapped. It was as yet not known whether this new found land was a solid mass or just a rugged atoll enclosing a great inland sea. It was the latter theory that, for half a century after settlement, seemed the most plausible.

Possession and exploration merge as one.

Australian art has followed much the same progression: the slow transition that moves from finding and seeing to claiming and possession; the first degree, then the second – as of burns. There is a third; we have yet to come to that.

At first the goal was information for which there was an insatiable demand. A fire of seeing and recording ensued and an explosion of drawing and painting. It is the latter that fetch the high prices at Sotheby's today.

But were these early informers artists or visual hunters? Or are the two the same?

No one questioned at the time, provided the required commodity kept on rolling in – gist for the Knowledge Mills at home. The British Museum, established not long before the Colony, was a great open maw while the Royal Society that had sent Cook on his investigative way felt justified in claiming first findings.

ART as such, however, was seen in Australia in those days to be about something else than simply trove and FINE ART was always some*where* else – far away in London, Paris, Rome. The commissioned paintings for the new rich in the new colonies that depicted their new houses, new estates and new selves were seen less as ART than as a form of personal reassurance and to reassure or crow over others. Provided the painter could depict with competence and could flatter as well, he fulfilled the requirement of his patron. Let Art Galleries house ART. Australians wanted paintings for the record, for private reasons. Early on they *knew what they liked*.

What belongs, then, to a Museum and what to an Art Gallery? Well, for a start, Aboriginal 'daubings' on rock and wood, tool, weapon and stone and other 'scratchings of the troglodytes' (we quote Twice-Traverser Ernest Giles viewing the latter in 1872 around just discovered Ayers Rock) belonged, if they belonged anywhere, in a Museum.

The Germans realised this early on as collections in Liepzig attest to this day and Pitt-Rivers [the English ethnologist and archaeologist] was not far behind. Then the camera with Spencer and Gillen moved in – too late for the coastal and grassland regions but just in time in and around the Centre. About the same time, the now famous letter of November 1885 was being written:

To: The Curator of Paintings	From: The Curator of Paintings
The Art Gallery	The Art Gallery, Sydney
Manchester, England	New South Wales, Australia

> Dear Sir
> The cultural life of this Colony has made considerable strides of late. We now have an ART Gallery in this city but, to date, not very much to put in it. If you could please send as many paintings from your collection there as you can spare …

The response to this request was swift, warm and generous to a fault, the evidence of which can be seen right to this day. As the doors of the new Art Gallery opened, a reverent public filed past rows of gold encrusted frames surrounding thickly pigmented landscapes – *after* Old Masters – and, even more deeply reverent, past great big story-picture paintings depicting themes from the Bible and from Greek and Roman legend. Two generations of Australians grew up seeing this as the apogee of ART.

Meanwhile, the day of the artist simply as informant, as image-maker, as commissioned importee in response to the gold boom, was waning. Now and then small bonfires broke out ignited by especial talent but these were ignored for the most part by the ART Galleries. Photography was on the ascent, particularly as portraits became suddenly available for all through the democratic lens of the camera.

Even so the concept of Art for Art's sake was deeply entrenched and, emerging from the various art teaching academies of the day, there were by now – the latter part of the 19th century – a number of ART aspirants.

In order to promote oneself, personal contact with the Motherland – that source and font of all ART – was mandatory. This led to a restless, but not unrewarding, seesawing between the hemispheres. An artist could dine out in London simply by being Australian and could reverse the process on his return to Melbourne or Sydney. This social quirk came to be known as 'the great Aussie cultural cringe'. It was not confined to the 19th century. Let an artist flout it to his/her peril!

As things turned out, some of those early mobile artists succeeded in breaking through the subtle barrier that lies between description and interpretation and their paintings took on a new found confidence and assurance. They came to see the Australian landscape very clearly and with the love of pride and possession. In short, they had graduated to that *second degree* – as of burns.

By the end of the 19th century, in the new art galleries of the growing cities, there – for all to see – hung wide canvases that carried now the proud inscription: *Australian School.*

We look back nostalgically at those faraway days of golden fleece and golden season. It was all so simple then *the way we were* … Into the bargain it is damn competent painting and, *sotto voce,* are we moving backwards now when paucity of ideas and blatant lack of basic skills is often no impediment to advancement?

Which question leads on to the complex subject of the Art Dealer and Promoter and the Patron as Speculator that has become such a salient aspect of the Australian art scene over recent decades.

And, while so much has been going on in the ART coiteries of the in-growing urban centres, what about *out there*, out of ear-reach of the hubbub, outback, back of beyond, out *Where the Pelican builds her Nest*, out *Beyond the Rim of our brittle and disintegrating world … Out where the Dead Men lie* …? Look up and see how the *Lightning Brothers* and the *Wandjina*, *Bungudmana*, *Ingaladdi*, *Bremera* and the *Grey Owl Dreaming* are fading away from the rock ledges. Why does no one come any more to delineate us afresh and breathe back life and shape to fish and wallaby, snake, bird-men and flightless bird as we all lie here stretched out waiting across the sandstone rock-face slanting in the lee of the streaming monsoon? Or further out again in the dry country and the red lands where the hooves of the driven herds have churned to dust the sand maps whereby we charted and chanted the pathways back to *Altcheringa* … ?

Then suddenly, so it seems, we have arrived at the present day. Time, for 'Australia', is wrapped up in parcels of roughly twenty years each. So what do we find as we untie the tenth?

Not so much has changed as one might have thought it would 100 years ago but now there is more of everything and everything is bigger – more artists, bigger galleries. The former still seesaw between Australia and Europe but much more frequently and they all do so now on *Grants* of one form or another. Support for 'the yarts' is catered for in the national budget. Eligibility for that support has become a new kind of lucky dip. Artists are still 'coming to terms' with themselves and their environment, with the weight of their talent and with 'stress' of one form or another. Some are in pursuit of 'the universal', others of that elusive individual and/or national idiom. Tell me, now: is 'regionalism' in or out?

The *Australian School*, if such a discipline ever existed, now trails such clouds of eclecticism as to bamboozle even the most tenacious and the most earnest student of Contemporary Australian Art.

As for the ART buying public, it has become more brow-beaten and more subject than ever to the manipulation of the Art Dealer, and even more ready to accept paintings it may secretly think are awful because they are presented in the light of their re-sale value or as Art not understood by the Philistine. Some, valiantly, stick to their guns declaring they *know what they like* and being prepared for the consequences.

But what *is* new in Australian Art today is that which is the oldest.

Due to an ironic twist of poetic justice, the 'troglodytes' of yesteryear – those furtive casualties of history – live on and, of late, have really lifted their game. Quite literally lifted the whole box and dice of the Art game off the ground and positioned it firmly into *the third degree*. I mentioned a while back that I would come to this and now we have, and so I shall recap: The *first degree* – to perceive with the senses, to see – the contribution of de Vlamingh *et al*; then the *second degree* – as of burns – the feeling for, the possession of the beloved – the classic Australian School of the late 19th century. And, finally, a *third degree* – as of torture – being possessed as of *a daemon*, as dementia.

The desert artists of Australia now armed with prime primed canvases, some as big as a Queen size bed and with gallons of acrylic paint, Windsor and Newton brushes if they like – although they'd prefer a chewed stick – and with Australia Council Visual Arts Board cheques burning holes in their pockets, have succeeded in creating nothing short of an Art Renaissance.

Old men, dredging deep into the thalamus of memory and minds' eye, have recalled and reawakened the ancient thought-lost songlines and symbolic ground maps of the past. Once drawn out upon the sand or incised on wood, these arcane charts have somehow survived the dust and ravages of recent times and now live again to spell out their powerful message.

Since the Papunya Tula paintings of Central Australia took the international Art world by storm no one asks any more: where do these belong – in a Museum? in an Art Gallery? They are hanging in the Tate, in the Pompidou, in MOMA in New York, and the Australian National Gallery in Canberra has several hundred of them.

Because the artists have been helped financially and with the display, promotion and marketing of the work, sceptics declare that the phenomenon is "all politics", that it will not last or that it will continue in a cheapened and bowdlerised form after the present generation passes on. This however is irrelevant, for these paintings are themselves bowdlerisations while yet remaining a very beautiful, uniquely Australian and genuine evolvement from an earlier form and medium.

Thus we have in Australia today two distinct and parallel modes of Art expression. While one, for the main, tends to become more dependant and derivative, the other has become more deeply and more manifestly indigenous.

It would be a brave seer who would predict of what the Great Australian Tri-centennial Art Exhibition will be composed but it is safe enough to bet that the Papunya Tula paintings will be a part of it accompanied, perhaps, by a few such artists who, between this and then, may also have graduated to that third degree – as being possessed by *a daemon* – within or out of Australia.

1990s

I always had the Tendency What tendency? What tendency? To take off, of course …[35]

One evening, in early January 1990, I called in to '47'. Mother was preparing an evening meal. The phone rang. I answered it. I didn't recognise the male voice. He assumed that I was Elizabeth. He then identified himself wondering how he might contact 'Perpetua'. David Ledger, an old beau from the 1960s, had been chatting that afternoon with cousin Andy [Miller] at Broome's Conti bar.

Within a few months I flew to Broome. The wet season was over. The town was booming. It had been transformed under the guiding hand and eye of Lord McAlpine.[36] There was now a five-star resort, a world-class zoo, even an art gallery – a gallery that was doing so well it was about to move to a larger premises. Caught with a serious bout of 'Broome Fever' I saw an opportunity to take over the space about to be vacated. It was an original Broome-style building – two rooms and verandahs on which to show work, with some basic living accommodation in the rear.

Durack Gallery | Kimberley Fine Art opened in January 1992. It exhibited historic prints of Kimberley together with contemporary artists working in the region and beyond. Over the decade many solo and mixed exhibitions were held – also an occasional Travelling Exhibition from the National Gallery of Australia. Locals, interstate and international visitors all frequented the gallery in Robinson Street, especially during the cooler 'high season' months.

PDC

Essay: Confess and Conceal – On Political Correctness in the Art World[37]

In the short space of time since Robert Manne wrote "On Political Correctness" (*Quadrant*, Jan–Feb 1993) and so wittingly described and located the provenance of Political Correctness for those of us who are even later developers than he declared himself to be, the phenomenon has become more evident and appears to be gathering momentum. Its career has been aided too by the recent elections, which, as it turned out, proved sheer serendipity for all adherents, devotees and Friends of PC generally.

Nowhere more so than in the Art world has Political Correctness become assertively rampant. Covert for some time, it is currently operating quite openly and from being, previously, a single thread among many, it now threatens to overtake and, at the same time, down-grade all other Art activity thus to become the only worth-while, worth funding, worth viewing Art expression in Australia today.

If an artist fails to grasp this and if he/she cannot succeed in becoming a part of it then he/she is up the proverbial creek without the proverbial paddle and might as well give up.

While Political Correctness, as Manne points out, derived from the academies of the US, in Australia the starting point for the Art take-over was the establishment of the Australia Council for the Arts in the early 1970s. Since then Art as a centralised arm of government has become sturdily entrenched and analogous to the prickly pear or the rabbit while the great wide vacant expanse that is the Australian mind offers limitless space and ideal conditions for propagation on a grand scale.

We now propose to proffer some advice to aspirant artists on how to deal with this development, to point out some of the hazards with which the road to qualifying as a PC artist is strewn and to demark certain advantages under the circumstances.

1 As a short cut into PC Art, it is a plus not to have been born in Australia. To be ethnic and from southern Europe, say, is quite good but to be Asian is even better. Best of all, and to really shine as a pulsating star of Political Correctness, is to be loudly and declaratorily Aboriginal. Reference to even the vaguest and most attenuated link with Aboriginality is all that is necessary. (It needs

to be said that we are not here referring to Aboriginal artists of the calibre and lineage of, for instance, the Papunya-Tula school – the sheer quality of whose work sets them apart from the theme of this critique.)

2 In contrast to all other periods in history it can now be actually beneficial to be a *woman*, preferably a very young one and one partnered by an active PC male. It is advisable for an aspiring woman artist to acquire some degree – a failed degree is OK – and if the subjects chosen contain a unit or two of Anthropology, Psychology and Cultural Studies, with the latter served up in trendy PC mode, all to the good. A Fine Arts Diploma from Open Learning or some such Academy can help but is not of much value because a natural gift for drawing or the acquisition of this skill is a disadvantage and, in fact, something to be avoided.

3 An artist who can neither draw nor paint but who enjoys a close relationship with a teacher or mentor in the Art limelight – a taste twister of repute – can also expect to be admitted into the ranks of the Chosen. To be young and malleable – to be *new* – is always an advantage. A *discovery* properly presented and supported is acceptable to sponsors and decision makers alike and is in direct line for a Major Grant of indefinite duration.

4 By and large the advantages of possessing no talent, skill or originality cannot be too strongly emphasised. Maturity, perseverance, a long record of productive and consistent work are all serious handicaps and all such baggage should, if possible, be discarded or kept dark. An additional drawback is ever to have been stimulated to produce work that derives from a direct visual response to sight or scene. Worse still is to produce anything that stems from an opposite conceptual viewpoint or one that has never been wot of in Australian art except by the ancient ones. Paradoxically this can be viewed as Politically *In*correct.

However, should perchance an artist happen to be both young and talented but to have already fallen into one of the above pitfalls, he/she should not despair. They can still qualify provided he/she is prepared to recant and to radically change his/her style so that any vestige of good drawing or technique is stripped away and the resulting product made ugly, lumpy, big (big is important) and invested with a Politically Correct Message – a Green statement, a Royal Monarchy send-up would be good. Commitment to PC is all that matters. This is the passport to Beulah Land and to all good things including, very likely, representation in the National Gallery of Australia.

5 It is an advantage if an artist does not happen to be a several generation Anglo-Celtic Australian. Such types, one way or another, are currently suspect and tend to be associated with Australia's dark and awful past as so felicitously exposed for us by an ever-growing number of PC historians rewriting the books and burning the old ones.

6 The PC artist never operates in isolation but is always enveloped in a protective sheath which ensures he is free from financial stress. Exhibitions are held quite independent of any commercial aspect. For the PC artist support and recognition come effortlessly from celestial regions aseptically removed from grubby Bugis Street. Thus the PC artist can completely ignore the general public who, as we should know by now, is without either taste or understanding and in dire need of re-education. (Is it ever revealed what happens to all the 1500cm x 1700cm paintings? and all the huge fragile installations?)

An artist who makes a commercial success of things will find it virtually impossible to ever attain true PC status. This is one of the more curious aspects of the PC Art Happening and no satisfactory explanation has yet come to light. It is better for successful but rejected artists to forget about it all and just continue to go on quietly crying all their way to the bank.

7 It should be remembered that single isolated Applications dispatched to the desk of the Visual Arts section of the Australia Council from artists of any ilk or gender carry no weight what-so-ever and if the mandatory referees, for all their eminence, should happen to exude Political *In*correctness it would have been as well not to have bothered in the first place.

On the other hand a group of aspirant artists with an Application put together by some astute Art Advisor who knows the ropes can often be assured of an affirmative response. Success with Applications is an art in itself – something one needs to have been born with rather than learned.

We will pass now from generalisations to the particular and to a particular exhibition which was, in fact, the fiat for this essay.

Entitled *CONFESS & CONCEAL – Eleven insights from Contemporary Australia and South-East Asia*, this exhibition is a fine example of Political Correctness in full flight and is by far the most impressive show ever initiated in and mounted by the Art Gallery of Western Australia. It represents a triumph for the present gallery directorship with its US originated policy: "to educate and to draw (the benighted population of WA one presumes) into a global and wider art perception and comprehension."

This spectacle has been funded by the Australia Council via the International Promotions Committee of the Visual Arts. It has also received the blessing of the Australian Government's Cultural Relations Branch, Department of Foreign Affairs and Trade. It *is* political so it would have to be correct. Together with official government support the exhibition has also a corporate sponsor, for good measure, in the form of a leading West Australian legal firm with its sights set on an extension of its professional services into trendy Southeast Asia.

The Opening was a glittering social occasion and was performed by the newly elected State Premier – Richard Court – somewhat incongruously Carmen Lawrence, the former Labor Premier, having missed out in this recent hurly-burly. Several long speeches made reference to the good news that the exhibition would bring to the regions beyond our northern shores and to all the Art conscious (and, presumably, unconscious) people of the zone. Applause.

Initially, the sight of 50 paintings – some of them very large – is impressive. It is on closer inspection that one experiences a feeling of let-down as the depressingly uniform and largely minimal content of the work itself comes through. Nor could one escape the feeling of having seen it all before – in magazines, in catalogues and in galleries here and overseas for at least the past twenty years. Almost without exception the underlying thread of the paintings themselves was that of variations on the themes of self-portraiture, autobiography, the sub-conscious, women's issues along with the obligatory injection of aboriginality.

It was not surprising then, with so much uniformity, that there was no telling which were the Australian paintings, which were by naturalised Asian artists living in Australia and which were the ones painted in Southeast Asia itself. With only one exception all the artists were completely new names – fresh Discoveries. As to what they were *confessing* and what *concealing* was anyone's guess. Answers were left hanging in mid air.

The catalogue essays are gems of esoterica and, as well, reveal something of the larger aims of Political Correctness as it proceeds on its way to further enmesh and obfuscate the Art world generally. It would appear that "an international and a transnational meta-mega culture" is foreshadowed. In this nebulous world, "artists transcend hierarchical ordering" by "anchoring their work to the exploration of self-centrality" and "the validity of exploring and exploiting inner perspectives over externally prescribed agendas."

These artists have no time for areas where "form is confused with content" but "where notions of identity, sexuality and gender are involved artists need not be mere reflectors of cultural conditioning but can become activists and fabricators not simply passive documenters ..." Read on. Artists, at the same time, must find "a new optimism for Art based on the validity of Self." And so on and so on. There are some twenty odd pages of this. All the various organising personalities have their say.

We are led on to believe that it is through introspection and, seemingly, an ever conscientious contemplation of one's navel, that we will find the right and Politically Correct path to a glorious all-embracing, transcendental, international mega-culture.

But what if Art proceeding along these lines were to have the effect of contracting rather than expanding? Might we not then be in danger of getting stuck with a world shrunk to a global village and ruled over by a Politically Correct but naked Emperor and his similarly attired Consort and retinue?

Having taken in the *CONFESS & CONCEAL* exhibition this becomes more than just a remote possibility.

Diary: 8 September 1994 at '47'

I have turned on my Random Access Apple Mac to see if I can operate it with one hand only, while the other hangs a dead weight in a great lump of plaster.

It would seem I have entered a phase in my life when I am in a state of continual conflict with the forces of gravity. In the course of the last month I have fallen down three times yet on each occasion it has been a distinct accident. Try as I did, all the time I was in Sydney, to outsmart this negative opponent – I took the hand-rail on steps and stairs, I waited for the little Green Man, I did not reject a proffered arm on slopes and at corners but in the end, somehow, it managed to gain the upper hand and brought me crashing on to the pavement in front of the Art Gallery of NSW.

The Doric columns that frame the view westward from the sloping green lawns of the Botanic Gardens were suddenly soaring above me, deeply fluted skywards – but not for long. Within minutes, they were blotted-out by a sea of faces. First Paddy and Kate[38] who had come to pick me up from the gallery and take me to the airport and then the faces of strangers taking over authoritatively and bombarding me with questions. A buxom young woman in a firm-fitting uniform lifted my head on to a pillow – of all things to materialise suddenly in Domain Road. When I looked at my left hand I saw that it was turned completely around. It is broken, I thought, but I felt nothing.

"Did you black out?"

"No, I tripped, I missed the step …" She was jotting down all my answers on a sheet of white paper.

"And who are you?" I asked the man in a crisp blue shirt. He said he was First Aid and had seen me from the roof. What a funny thing to have been doing on a fine Sunday afternoon, looking for trouble from the roof of the State Gallery – and finding it.

An ambulance came and they lifted me on to a stretcher and into it like a doll, as though I was as little and light as a doll. Everyone around seemed young and strong and fit. Inside the ambulance it was quite fun, like a cubby-house. The buxom young woman was still beside me, still asking personal questions and writing down the answers busily.

It wasn't far from Domain Road to the Sydney Hospital in Macquarie Street.

I think it has taken me nearly an hour to write those few paragraphs, but it shows it is not impossible to write a brief letter with the right hand only. I have used the forefinger of my left hand to do the caps while the plaster-cast is resting on the desk but it is very tiring.

Dr Hodby [family doctor of many years] said it may be possible to replace this big heavy plaster with something lighter in a couple of weeks. Nothing in the whole range of medical science, he said, could hasten the process of the bones re-knitting. Where will the patience come from? I am worn out already after only four days and four nights.

The first night was the worst in that big, old, ancient, grey hospital. There were eight beds, as far as I could make out, in Ward 4. Four women, including me, and four men – a uni-sex ward. By the time I was conveyed up to this section from the emergency area where I was first deposited, it was dusk – dusk in an old, grey, hospital on a Sunday evening with an arm that felt as though it was having red-hot pokers driven into it. All through the long time since 2.30pm which was the appointed hour that Paddy was to pick me up from the gallery, he and Kate had hung in, steadfastly, sitting in the corridor there through the long waits between all the various stages. The atmosphere in the emergency area was quite relaxed – no horrors – and the attendants chatted away on a wide variety of topics until the radiologist showed up and I was taken to another section. Another long wait and a young doctor materialised. I told him I was due to catch the plane back to WA at 7.00pm.

"You won't be catching a plane to anywhere tonight," he said. "The wrist bones are both broken." And in the meantime Patrick had apparently been making various phone calls, to Ansett and other points around. From being in control of everything and of my life generally I now felt all personal authority slipping from my grasp. Furthermore, I was being quietly, systematically and literally stripped. Theft was a problem in the hospital, I was told. "So take the very minimum with you up to the ward." I already had only the minimum as I had packed up from the RAC in Macquarie Street and had only a handbag. Into it now went my shoes, my stockings, my skirt, my blouse, my jacket, my earrings, my rings, my watch. Hanging on to my pants I was eased into a white cotton garment that tied at the back. I retrieved my notebook, a small cosmetic bag and the watch. I had to know the time although it seemed by now to be mattering less and less. Paddy took charge of the lot – of my life, as it were – and Kate took care of the post-cards that I'd written from the gallery.

Two of the women in Ward 4 were large, white-haired in pink nighties and bed jackets, with a stack of toiletries beside them on their lockers. One had had two kneecap replacements and the other a hipbone. The third woman was little and dark. Then some time later I heard a male nurse say in a cross voice to a man who came to her bed-side: "You've got all day, yet you come in after hours. And I can smell liquor."

I was wide awake, sitting up in bed wide awake, clutching my arm that had a tightening bandage around it. Chimes sounded on the hour – from the Greenway? church nearby – and a concert of snores. I was given an injection, the upper part of my thigh. Two nurses supervised this, checking and signing a paper. Any drug administered was checked and re-checked and so was blood. A doctor said if the bones could not be manipulated an incision would need to be made and a small plate inserted, blood tests were made with this contingency in mind.

Two young doctors came and talked to me, one called Stening and the other Bye.

Another older doctor came at some time. All this was, I guess, happening within quite a short space of time but thinking back it seems to have been over a period of days. This older man was an anaesthetist. All of them asked a great many questions particularly with regard to smoking and drinking. I was told they would operate at noon the next day and that I could have an early breakfast which turned up, I think, about 6.00am. I was given papers to sign. I suppose I should have read them but by this time I had passed into a state of almost complete passivity. The nurse helped me take a shower. The shower and w.c. area was also uni-sex. A couple of men were shaving. The floor was dark red cement and the fittings very old but there was plenty of room. Through the windows I could see the people down in Macquarie Street starting up a perfectly normal new week as though nothing had happened.

After breakfast the jug of water was taken from beside my bed which caused me to instantly develop an acute thirst. Meanwhile Pacific Islander women were mopping and dusting the ward with graceful swaying motions and wheeling tea trolleys along under the tall coconut palms with sweet smiling faces and tall-standing hair. We never see such in Western Australia, or hear such soft singing voices: "No tea? No coffee? Oh, oh, ah sorry for you."

The male nurse who had reprimanded the visitor from Redfern the night before was quick, efficient, kind and strong and something of a character to boot with his blond hair and gold earing. I said I couldn't get any sound from the radio on the patient's hand gadget. It was a trivial complaint and one that a busy nurse could easily have ignored. However a little time later when things had quietened down for the night he reappeared beside my bed with a radio and listening cord. "There you are, Luv," he said. "No one need know where it came from."

It was the same too with any of the women nurses, continually kind and good-natured, to a total stranger who really had no right to be there at all and who had come in off the street without even a nightdress or a sponge bag.

It is now nearly 3.00pm on Tuesday, 13th Sept 1994 – Noni's birthday. She phoned on Sunday last. This document seems now to be stored on both Claris Works and 'Jeremy' – the latter at the suggestion of Nigel Dolan [IT support] who I phoned to help me find this text which had disappeared when I tried to retrieve it on Sunday. I spent over two hours looking for it. I thought it would show up straight away as I had done no other work. It is exasperating things like this that nearly drive me mad about this computer racket. I mean, a letter left on top of a desk is still there when next required, one doesn't have to search high and low for it.

The man who wheeled me down long corridors – along balconies, through temporary doors and wind-breaks made of plastic, in and out of lifts, on a rocky road, all the way from the ward up to the operating theatre – was called Frank. He had the look of someone who had been doing this same work, with the exception, perhaps, of a brief break during the War, for over 40 years and who was now viewing the prospect of retirement with mixed feelings. He wore the thoughtful expression of one pondering a mathematical problem – calculating, perhaps, how the distance he must have traversed with his trolley of human cargo would compare with that of the length of a piece of string stretched between the earth and the moon.

"And that's the lot for today," he said, when we finally reached our destination. "Least ways as far as my instructions to date." And the theatre sister said: "Thank you, Frank," in a tone of voice both affectionate and familiar but also with a touch of hauteur that reminded me of cousin Edith Horrocks who was Matron of the hospital in Alexandria and whose presence there in the 1940s, as part of the elite Queen Alexander Empire Military Nursing Service, was the real reason for Rommel's retreat.

As it turned out Sister Margaret Hall had recently been in Broome. There, she said, she had come, unexpectedly, upon a charming little gallery in a quiet street. It was run by "Perpetua …? Perpetua …" she was trying to recall the name. "Hobcroft," I said, "Perpetua Hobcroft is my daughter."[39]

Dr Boffa, the anaesthetist, turned up looking quite different in a white cassock and neat fitting biretta. I thought he was about to bless me but he started tapping the back of my right hand in search of a vein. "We'll look after you," he said, noticing that, although completely passive, I was also stiff with apprehension.

"I am still fully conscious," I said defensively, and looked to the Sister for support.

"It's just for a drip," she explained and I relaxed.

Then, suddenly, a section of time was completely excised from the total time of my life just after noon on 5 September 1994. What became of it? Where did it go? Is it an addition, perhaps, rather than a subtraction? A little credit somewhere on some arcane account?

I have been back in Perth now for over a week but the passage of days and nights for me is still out of kilter.

Early in the morning of 17 December 1994 I received the news that Aunt Mary, mother's beloved sister, had died in Perth. I needed to be with mother urgently and so booked a flight and closed the Broome gallery for two weeks.

A few days after Christmas, mother said: "Come and have a look at what I've been doing." She spread perhaps 15 paintings out on the big courtyard table. The work contained much that was familiar – figures, creatures, landscape, all within the signature sense of movement. She was calling them "morphological" paintings. Initially I saw the work as another stage – a freer, more abstract stage, of her long-running series The Rim … the rim of our brittle and disintegrating world. *On closer inspection layers of distinct images appeared – not unlike the way they can gradually emerge on ancient rock surfaces or within moving clouds.*

Who can ever pinpoint the impetus behind creativity? One explanation for the new "morphological" paintings was that, barred from visiting Mary in the months before her death [the aftermath of a family dispute], Elizabeth found an outlet for her grief in producing powerful new work. Although new, strong and free it was closely aligned with all that had gone before.

In summary: over three hectic days, 28–30 December 1994, Elizabeth, in collusion with me, embarked upon an experiment that from the start was precarious: three paintings by 'Eddie Burrup', a Karrajarri man, were to be added to a mixed January/wet season exhibition at the Durack Gallery in Broome. Unlike other works on show, the Burrups were not for sale. The purpose in hanging them was simply to garner response from the public. However, in the space of barely a week, the persona of Eddie Burrup – his experience, his imagination, his concerns, his knowledge – began to take hold of Elizabeth herself. Paintings poured out. It was only a matter of time before Burrup/Durack was keen to receive informed opinion on the work. An idea grew to contact the director of Australia's leading commercial gallery specialising in Aboriginal art.

PDC

Letter: Elizabeth Durack from '47' to Perpetua in Broome, 12 January 1995

Dear Perpetua

As Eddie [Burrup] draws me deeper and deeper into his world I find myself becoming not only reluctant but actually resentful of putting him on the back-burner – or, worse, of having to turn off the jet altogether, while I drag myself back to old ED and all the involvements ahead,[40] and none of which is the real art world of Australia or art world of the intellect. *She* is so boring; *he* is so interesting …

Also I keep thinking of refinements as to *first moves* from your point of view and it occurs to me: how would it be to involve Jimmy Pike or *a* Jimmy Pike in a casual first exposure? By 'involve' I mean only to unwrap a couple of EBs and ask him if he knows this artist …

If a Jimmy Pike should say: *Black pella no more make'm dis one*, it would be v v interesting – and of course, discouraging. But if a Jimmy Pike should look at the paintings with attention and then attempt to unravel the images and identify them and so forth – and was prepared, under say, your interest, to proceed – I think it would be a good first ploy. But it is up to you there and circumstances there in Broome generally. I mean Broome is so assimilated that I doubt there would be any dinkum black there of the type I am thinking of in this general context. Derby probably better …

I'll post this for what it is worth. On my way out now.

love,

mummmmm

PS This would be a Fax. I have made prime moves today for a Smart Fax 2000 to be installed. I gather a separate number means another line required – and another fee?

Letter: Perpetua in Broome to Gabrielle Pizzi,[41] Melbourne, 23 January 1995

Dear Gabrielle Pizzi

It was helpful speaking with you last week and to learn of your interest in viewing new work.

As discussed, I am sending a few photographs of recent paintings by Eddie Burrup.

I first met Eddie Burrup when he called in here late last year. He is a *Karajarri* man, born about 1925 in the Bidyjadanga (La Grange) area south of Broome. Says he has lived all over the north and worked from time to time for mining companies in the Pilbara.

Referring apparently to Aboriginal totem relationships he says of his work: *'im pella my brother. Chinging out all day longa me.*

It seems to me the work is sufficiently different to warrant some special presentation or introduction – preferably in a larger, more informed centre than Broome.

I would be interested in any suggestions you may be good enough to make.

Yours sincerely

Perpetua Hobcroft

Encl: photos of six paintings by Eddie Burrup and pre-paid envelope for return of photos in due course.

Letter: Perpetua in Broome to Elizabeth Durack at '47', 23 January 1995

Dearest Mother

As I'll be telling you by phone 'off-peak' hours later today: Eddie Burrup is on his first flight as I write. Photos of six of his paintings will probably arrive at Gallery Gabrielle Pizzi, Melbourne, about the same time as you receive this. How will he appear? How will he be received when he turns up there at #141 Flinders Lane? …

God, it's nerve-wracking. I have spasms of terribly cold feet. Just as well there are several things on the boil as well.

Copy of my note to GP follows.

lots of love,

Perpetua

Letter Elizabeth Durack at '47' to Perpetua in Broome, 24 January 1995

Dear Perpetua

Just back from PICA [Perth Institute of Contemporary Art]. The exhibition: *Aboriginal and Torres Straits Islanders Raise the Flag*. Revolting

– yet I gather it has been touring internationally … ? … ? … ? Australia …? Whither?

I just get the strongest feeling that far from wishing to engage with the Australian art scene, I want to completely distance myself from it …

Cheers now, this just might catch the post if he's late collecting from teddy bear's box.

love, Mummm

2 March 1995: At 10.16am Gabrielle Pizzi (in Melbourne) faxed me (in Broome) saying she found the photos of Eddie Burrup's paintings "very exciting", and asking to see the actual paintings.

PDC

Fax: Perpetua in Broome to Elizabeth Durack at '47', 10.30am 2 March 1995

Look at what has just come through!

Will have to reply. Tomorrow, Friday 3rd will do.

I will want to take Eddie's paintings personally to Melbourne.

Let's talk tonight.

love, P

Fax: Elizabeth Durack from '47' to Perpetua in Broome, 10.59am 2 March 1995

Sketch of a fish hooked on a long line by a figure at the end of a jetty.

Caption: *I am thinking – but the fact the bait has been taken (although a long way to the jetty) is a gigantic leap. I think Melbourne in person. I am going on thinking*

mummmmm

Fax: Perpetua in Broome to Elizabeth Durack at '47', 11.05am 2 March 1995

A lovely reply! E/P/EB on the jetty with the fish.

Now the thing is about fishing –

Interruptions ……. thick and fast at that point.

Fax: Perpetua in Broome to Gabrielle Pizzi in Melbourne, 7.00am 3 March 1995

Dear Gabrielle

Thank you for your reply by fax yesterday.

Your response to the Eddie Burrup paintings is encouraging.

Now I need to visit Alice Springs and the eastern states later this month, planning to be in Melbourne 28–30 March. I could bring some Burrup originals with me and leave them with you for say a day or overnight. Would this be convenient?

Yours sincerely

Perpetua Hobcroft

Fax: Perpetua in Broome to Elizabeth Durack, 11.15am 3 March 1995

Another busy morning here. Three 'meetings' already and off to another – in a minute.

Message just received on answering machine:

"Hello, it's Gabrielle Pizzi speaking. I received your fax and umm I look forward very much to seeing you at the end of this month. Perhaps nearer the time if you'd like to give a call we can fix up a time that is convenient for both of us. Thanks very much, bye …"

So – state of play to date.

P

Fax: Perpetua in Broome to Gabrielle Pizzi in Melbourne, 16 March 1995

Dear Gabrielle

Thank you for yesterday's facsimile and phone message.

Your suggestion to meet at 6.00pm on 2nd April in your Gallery sounds ideal.

Should you need to contact me in Melbourne I plan to stay at the Victoria Hotel in Little Collins Street. Tel 03 653 0441.

Yours sincerely

Perpetua

Fax: Perpetua in Broome to Elizabeth Durack at '47', 27 March 1995

Dearest Mother

Gradually returning to normal here while still receiving a few (favourable) comments re Friday's performance[42] – but at last some time to think again about Eddie B.

This is what I am thinking and I wonder if you are thinking the same way:

The paintings still belong to Eddie. I and/or Kimberley Fine Art have not bought them from him.

As gallery director and agent I believe the works that Eddie first started bringing in a few months ago are outstanding and different and at this stage I am simply seeking a range of informed opinions about them.

I will not sell the paintings on Eddie's behalf to GP or to anyone else as yet.

Eddie is quite ambitious. He of course knows Rover Thomas, David Downs, Peter Skipper, Paddy Carlton (all relatively old-timers up around this part of Australia and painting for the past 8 to 10 years and all of whom command/receive big prices for their works). Eddie is quite philosophical – not too hungry or eager for fame and fortune.

If Gabrielle Pizzi wants to hold some of EB's paintings – perhaps to seek another 'informed' opinion – then she may hold *five only for a week to ten days*, which should be sufficient time for her to come up with an offer which I then need, in turn, to relay to Eddie.

If the offer is acceptable, say it is a one or two man show at Gallery GP later this year (Sept/Oct?) then she may hold on to the works.

But if her offer is not acceptable, or if she is not interested, or if she sees through the experiment/device/ruse/stratagem/trick/ploy/hoax/cunning manoeuvre … oh oh oh – then she should return the paintings forthwith.

We have to be careful now for *the truth will come out* you know, sooner or later. This you have to face.

We don't want to make utter fools of the art gurus. We'd suffer a backlash if so – and at all costs we must avoid criminal allegations, let alone criminal charges. Oh, oh, what a tangled web.

"Eddie doesn't like being photographed." OK but will try and send one to GP, probably after Easter.

If GP and/or other gurus want actually to sight Eddie – if there are some doubting Thomases among them – then the story is that Elizabeth Durack herself *becomes* Eddie when she paints these morphological paintings? And this is actually true. Let's say Eddie Burrup is Performance Art.

Surely there's nothing criminal about this.

Well, what do you think of these current *pensées*?

We are in this now for long term, the long haul.

love, Perpetua

Fax: Elizabeth Durack at '47' to Perpetua in Broome, 27 March 1995

Dear Perpetua

Well, by this time next week we will know a bit more than we do at present.

And now, cutting across a lot of other topics and even though we spoke last evening, I thought I would jot down a few of the musings as they have come to mind over the past couple of weeks and set out a rough agenda of what may lie ahead and what your meeting with GP may entail and – render.

So much will depend on the chemistry between you and the interview will either go well or the opposite. We need to be prepared for the latter for with Eddie B we are following the Groucho Marx directive: *If at first you don't succeed. Quit!* By this I don't mean we are not prepared to be patient, even persevering to a point, but always with a goal clearly in mind:

> a Melbourne exhibition, or two-man exhibition at a prestigious and appropriate gallery; press attention, critical appraisal – acclaim, ideally – though a bit of good comment, space, a photo (of the work) would do; acquisition of even one work by a leading Australian gallery or purchase by a private collector of repute OK. (But here is where the patience bit may come in for if, say, GP should say: "Let me take a

> few pieces to a contact of mine in Roma, Milano." OK that would be OK because of the cultural cringe, which as ever is still alive and kicking and it could be OK for Eddie to do the time-honoured *loop* – without which not one of the leading names in Australian Art would ever have emerged.)

Over the above, a time limit has been imposed – that is, one year from the date of Eddie's birth which, according to my record, was 28 December 1994. If nought affirmative has emerged by then or if we run into difficulties, unforeseen troubles and complications then Eddie just disappears under a rock up the tippy end of the Burrup Peninsula and is never heard of again. Pity, after all we did for him; all we were prepared to do for him. But how typical – *they show no gratitude*.

Let us be fairly clear in our own minds just who Eddie Burrup is and what he is on about and, at the risk of being repetitious, note the following:

Yes, he is, as per your letter to GP of 23 January 1995, pars 3, 4, 5 all OK but also, for an Aboriginal, Eddie is something of a loner. He has been in and out of gaol a few times which is probably why he doesn't like being photographed …

It was when in gaol that he became interested in art and received some basic tuition.

As per letter of 23 January, Eddie has found his theme. He continually expresses concern for the old Aboriginal totemic affiliations and feels they are being ignored by other artists who seem almost exclusively pre-occupied with the translation of *Country* – thus, his oft repeated assertion: *'im pella all day chingin' out longa me* … By this, he seems to mean that his totemic brothers call to him to put them in to his paintings. He is proud of being Rock Crab which with his mother, who was Nail-tail Wallaby, gives him the run and access to both the littoral and the inland – and to re-position and re-assert that time when the universe consisted of a shared partnership between all living creatures and life-forms: an equilibrium of total interdependence, self-governing and self-guarding. (Note how closely Eddie's philosophy, that is, original Aboriginal philosophy, enlines with current trends – the Greens et al.)

Eddie has not a lot of time for today's blackfellas and yellafellas: *'im all day want'm money, want'm motor car, Toyota. 'im all day talkin' land claimin'. No good talk'm claimin' land, land claimin'. Leave'm Brother behind. That not right way.*

Eddie worked for most of his life on stations and later, in the 1960s and 70s, he had a job with BHP with a team of surveyors marking out the rail line from Newman to Port Hedland. He saw plenty blackfella art at that time: *plenty long'a rock, eberywhere – dat the burst time I hear'm ol'man chingin' out b'la me.*

Eddie had an accident on the rail line and walks with a bit of a limp. He received some compensation money. This, along with the pension, has helped to shape his present life-style.

Eddie trusts P Why? Is it because of some early link when he worked for a while on her uncle's station, *Kildurk,* just over the NT border? Was this why, when he came to Broome he – "See'm same name longa calico," and walked into the Durack Gallery with some of his paintings?

Eddie's work has picked up since receiving encouragement from P and since being supplied with decent quality materials. Previously he had worked on brown paper and tea towels pilfered from clotheslines. P has not influenced Eddie in any way other than responding to what she could make out he was trying to say through his paintings.

Eddie, while not prolific is presently working steadily. P would not want to see this pattern disturbed by untimely exposure. At the same time, Eddie is quite well aware of what is going on with regard to Aboriginal painting and he knows, or knows of other Aboriginal artists who have 'made it'. For example, Jimmy Pike and Rover Thomas. He knows little of the artists of Central Australia other than what he has seen in the Durack Gallery. Most of this he dismissed with: *'im all day talkin' Country.* But he liked paintings of the Namatjira style. He would like to have his own work known and understood by *Wadjila mob, longa sous country.*

P has/has not? told him that she was taking a few of his works with her on her present visit to Brisbane, Sydney, Melbourne. She feels sure he could put on a burst of work if given a date to work towards – say, 4, 6, 8 moons hence.

Now Perpetua the knotty problem raised by you last evening …

I paused here at about 2.45pm to have a bite of lunch and then, just as I finished, your telephone alert and your fax came through. I have it beside me now as I write this and I find it quite amazing how, essentially we are thinking along the same lines.

Your fax covers most of the points I was going to raise. I shall need to sleep on the contents of this communication so won't reply in any detail here. By and large though I am in agreement and I can see that you have really bent your full concentration to the matter which is impressive seeing the psychic stress (?) strain (?) hugger-mugger, fun (?) within which you have been embroiled for the last two weeks leading up to the Regal Opening.

I think I was going to say before this fax came that something has to *give* somewhere, sometime. And I think I was going to say: let GP buy say 4 or 5 for a more or less give-away price – 250–400 dollars on the basis of the remembered scene at Laverton years ago when the price asked for the boomerang dropped from: "Five quid to three quid, ten bob, two bob …" as we continued to drive quietly out of town. But mainly P I would defer to you being a lot closer to the whole world of Aboriginal art generally and the commercial scene than I am and as I read your plan of procedure I think it is sound. I, too, have given a lot of thought to *how and when the story breaks* – but this is a long way ahead. Meanwhile Stet! Stet! and we won't raise the topic of the *alter ego* at this stage.

love – mummmmmm

Fax: Elizabeth Durack from '47' to Perpetua in Broome, 28 March 1995

Dear Perpetua

Yes, it is an *experiment* – not a hoax – not a crime.

Think Professor Higgins and Eliza Doolittle – not Ern Malley – not Macbeth.

Professor Higgins did not set out to send up the shallowness and hypocrisy of London High Society, he was simply engrossed in the concept of *Voice* as the arbiter of all standards. He proved what he set out to prove. In the end everyone was happy and no one felt deceived, put-down or outraged, and the professor himself went on to live happily ever after with the tangible evidence of his successful experiment. It has never been even mooted that he lost all credibility and all his work was rejected by the academic world.

I'll send this as a fast letter as well. I looked at the enclosed three photos of Eddie under a mag[nifying] glass. I think you could have these in your handbag, just as is? It is all very well for me to talk, I guess, because I am not at the cutting edge of this turnout, at present anyway, but I haven't got cold feet at all. I feel quite confident and excited although I am ready and watchful for the pin that can prick the balloon.

Who knows what lies ahead for Eddie – he might never be exposed – who knows.

Your week there will fly past. Here too. I got the last, I hope, of the stuff to Mark [Art Presentations, framers] yesterday. He takes the lot down to the Stafford Studios on Tuesday 4th [April]. Marlene is in Hong Kong. They are going to hang in her absence. I'll have a say in this. Looks like some 70 pieces going up.

I feel a bit happier about this modified version of yesterday's fax [from you] which really took the wind out of my sails. I can't really live without Eddie B now. He has become a part of me – *Me* – in fact. I can't go on, or get on, without him. I know he is an antiquated version of Aboriginality and that the Albert Barungas & Co now lie in the past, yet I hoped this ilk could live on: *gidgi-gidgi – h'arm-in-h'arm, blackfella–whitefella – that the right way*.

Yes, think: Lawrence of Arabia and Richard Burton – and Wongar – and Lin Onus for that matter. I was very interested to learn that Gabrielle Pizzi had shown him. Interested, too, to learn that Pat Hutchings still vocal. Yes, he loved the art milieu, a relief, I think, from Philosophy.

I'll just pop this in a fast letter although nothing urgent about it. Could stay in your box for that matter until your return from Melbourne.

Bon Voyage,

love, m~~~~~~

The meeting with Gabrielle Pizzi went ahead on 2 April. GP was interested in the work and wanted to see more. It was agreed that Perpetua send further paintings on her return to Broome. Soon after the Melbourne expedition Elizabeth joined Perpetua in Broome for ten days over Easter. This was when P took photographs of Elizabeth/Eddie alongside a number of Burrup/Durack paintings. In Broome Elizabeth also began a monologue of Eddie Burrup talking about his life. A week after return to Perth, 24 April 1995, Elizabeth commenced a Journal on her computer that she titled: Reinvent – How I reinvented myself in my 80th year *(*'Reinvent' *for short). She kept up this Journal, with some breaks, for the rest of her life. Note: for the sake of clarity,* Reinvent *is identified here as* Diary.

PDC

Diary: 24 April 1995

My great fear now is that Eddie will be lost to me. I have had no chance to get back to him since my return from Broome a week ago at Easter where we were together so happily. How I loved sitting under the mango tree with him in the dappled shade with the brilliant sunshine splashing over the fresh buffel grass and on to the red ground while he told me of his life before we met – every moment drawing closer as we shared so much of past experiences and life in the north when it was still a closed secret.

Where is he now? Is he still there in Broome? Or has he taken off somewhere over the Leopolds meeting up with all his friends? They'll see him coming and sing out to him from the high rocky summits of the range, and then he will forget all about me. When and how dare I call him up? So many other matters have intruded on my time since we parted. So much here demands my attention and is keeping us apart …

Monologue: Extracts from *The Art of Eddie Burrup, text commenced in Broome, April 1995*

Preface

Well now, I tell'm you.
My old uncle, 'e kite hawk,
'e got'm eye for readin' country
where old pella bin make'm first time.
'm bin learn'm me.
We two pella gissa-gissa,
rock crab 'n kitehawk.
We follow'm up all t'em oldenday track
place where Dreamin' mob
bin put'm birst time.

Alright, by'n'by 'e an' all-about knock up
'e go underneat' for sleep.

Place where'm go down
'e leave'm mark b'la rock.
You see 'm?
'im there alright!
'e t'one t'at all day
chingin' out, chingin' out b'la me.

Same now, I put'm b'la picture.

Well, alright,
I tell'm you now
I tell'm you b'la
all t'em olden time
where we bin sit down
long time, looong time
b'longa t'is country.

Nothin' *gudea* t'at time,
nothin' *wadjila*, *balander*,
nothin'.

On'y all t'is country
'im on'y we got 'm
we pella, blackpella.
Everywhere t'is country where we bin mak'm
we 'n old-pella bin make'm
first time, olden time.

Gudea call'm *Dreamin'*
desert mob, 'im talk *Tjukurrpa*
plenty 'nother name:
Gooning, Djumangani, Ngarangani–
(t'at Ord river way)
Lalai longa *Gooniyandi,*
Borunga – 'e 'nother one.
What you reckon?

A'right, now
you know that one
where 'm double up
b'la me 'n allabout?
all t'em kangaroo,
emu
all t'em bird mob –
big mob, bird mob –
all t'em fish,
lizard, bandicoot,
hinsect – pig mob insect

plenty 'nother one too …

You see'm morning star?
sun-go-down star?
you feel'm wind,
east from desert?
you smell'm north-west wind
where 'e come
longa wet weather time?

you see'm t'under cloud?
rain
lightnin'
fire
chmoke
dust.

You know'm t'at willy-willy wind?
t'at one woman
'e gota watch out –
might be 'm go h'inside –
come out piccaninny.

You know 'm little one turtle
swimmin' about
swimmin' about?
'm wanta look out
might be heagle 'awk,
might be sea-gull, catch'm …

B'longa my Dreamin' place
big salt water comin' in
cover 'm up land
t'at 'igh tide now
t'en 'e go out long way,
long way … low tide now
t'at same my Dreamin' …

My mummy an' 'im mummy –
my old granny –
'im two pella nail-tail wallaby.
'im straight b'la me, two pella.

We can go up river
up river long way – b'la 'ead-water
where 'm start b'longa 'igh ground.

Gudea call'm Hamersley Range
'm put'm longa map

"Hamersley Range."
Blackfella no got 'm map longa paper
'im on'y got 'm map h'inside,
b'longa head.
T'at way can't lose'm …

My ol' uncle, 'e bin learn'm me
right way for read'n country –
oldenday, Dreamin' time.
'im 'nother one uncle (no more turtle)
'm kite'awk –
'e got'm eye for read'm country
where old fella bin make'm first time.

A'right –
we follow'm up
follow'm up
all t'em old tracks
olden day, Dreamin' track now.
All t'at country l'a top-end Yule river
'm bin leave'm mark l'a rock
where 'e go down …

A'right!
You know that big ol' man kangaroo?
where'm stand up straight
close on six feet?

Wal, t'at my mummy daddy
true fella!
on'y long time now
'm no more talk like t'at.

No one talkin' like ol' Eddie now
'e on'y one for keep'm olden day longa head
can't lose 'm.
Young fella, 'm know nothin' now
'm don' listen – don'care less.

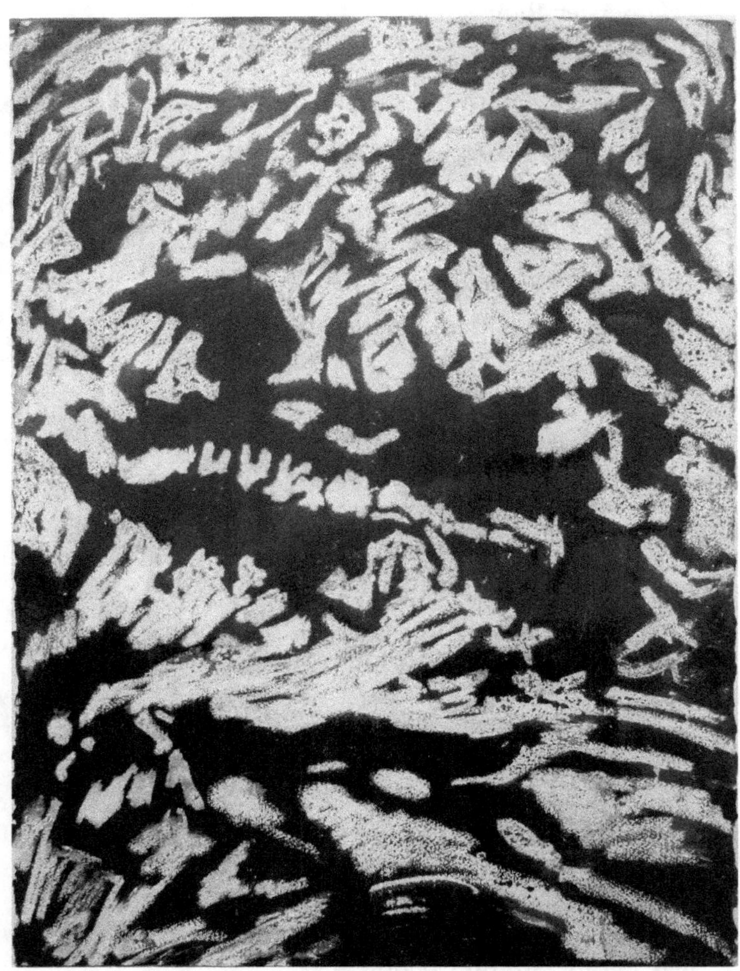

Kangaroo rat 'im go lead. All the rest follow 'em now 1994
from the series *The Art of Eddie Burrup*
mixed media on paper 76 x 56 cm, estate of ED

Old Eddie 'e *on'y one* left now for talk up
b'longa me 'n ol' fella
all t'em totem –
(*Gudea* name 'totem')
all dem olden time
Dreamin'

Gudea call'm Dreamin'
on'y Gudea got no Dreamin'.

A'right!
Turn'm off now.
I come back 'nother day.

Diary: 24 April 1995 continued

… Perpetua was looking at these paintings, the morphological works, down in the rear studio early one morning a few days after Christmas.

They must have emitted a potency or charge of some sort for she became very quiet as she studied them. Then it wasn't long before quietude turned into exasperation, although it was not as if the images had sprung out of the blue. She was familiar enough with their derivation, 30 years of it in a direct line and earlier again back to the wanderings with the Goanna men when the *Cord to Altcheringa* was still intact although hanging by a thread and further back again when the faded *Wandjina* leaped at me off the cave ceiling over 60 years ago.

The drift of P's exasperation seemed to run: why do this mad 'morphological' stuff when you must know you'll never be able to exhibit it and even if you did, it wouldn't be looked at, let alone receive any intelligent comment, let alone be understood, let alone sell?

But, she paused for breath, then ran on quite angry and looking at them intently: if these had been painted by a man, the galleries would be clambering for them.

There was a pregnant pause: if they had been painted by an Aboriginal man the National Gallery would have them hanging on their walls. The trouble is, you have always played things so straight and above board you'd never come at signing them with another name.

We went for a walk around the river on that gold and silver morning and we talked of other things – of grief, of effort, of hope. A pelican floated on the water, two little ducks quarreled in the seaweed by the retaining wall. A kurrajong tree was coming into pale pink flower and as I stopped under it, rather to my surprise, I heard myself saying: "I am not totally opposed to the idea of presenting those morphological works under a pseudonym."

The shadow of Eddie Burrup, hat and all, fell on the ground between us.

The game was on and time was of the essence. P was catching the plane back to Broome on New Year's Day.

The Eddie Burrup originals she was now taking with her had to be sorted, photographed, catalogued and signed. A biography required composition.

More important still, a photograph of the artist would have to accompany the above.[43]

We searched the Yellow Pages under Fancy Dress. *Silly Nonsense* in Subiaco, the nearest suburb, had gone out of business due to a fire. We were told by answering machine to re-contact them in a few months' time. *Apparitions* had three premises, one in Kalgoorlie. (I could see Paddy Hannan masquerading as Claude de Benarles.) *Apparitions* in Claremont, the next nearest suburb, was closed for the long holiday. *Stepping Ou*t was a long way out and so too was *The Fun Room* and *Copy Cat.* P opted for *Jingles* over the Causeway in Victoria Park.

"You get on with the biog. I'll be back as soon as I can." But she returned with very little – some glues and solvents, some frizzy hair – eyebrows, perhaps, but useless otherwise.

Our options were narrowing and the whole day was nearly gone. However, guided providentially, we were getting closer all the time to *Doyle's Fancy Costumes* in Scarborough Beach Road, Osborne Park. Now my heart always sinks at the prospect of entering upon this part of the city. Back in the 1920s a sand track overlaid with jarrah planks set end to end was the only access from Perth to the glorious rolling surf of Scarborough Beach. Sometimes of a Sunday, when Dad was down from the north we would undertake this hazardous adventure in the Dodge with a picnic basket. It was a whole day's outing.

Since that time Scarborough Beach Road has become a huge major artery down which traffic of all descriptions thunders night and day. From where all the vehicles come and to where they go no one knows – what with the desert to the east and the ocean to the west.

There was a serious, almost reverential, atmosphere within the walls of *Doyle's Fancy Costumes*. Oh! And what walls! From floor to high ceiling they were lined with a phantasmagoria of every article of apparel and every object to disguise ever devised by man or woman to camouflage and conceal, to deceive and belie, to falsify and to misrepresent, to inspire laughter and merriment, to evoke tears, fears, horror or dismay.

Doyle's have been in the serious business of make-believe for three generations. Mr Doyle was courteous and helpful. What was it we were after?

"Something for a bushman, an old bushman, the old style of bushman – not the Reg Williams, not the Tamworth Country-and-Western bushman."

And my eyes were combing the shelves.

"Something more along the lines of Waltzing Matilda?"

"Yes. More like that – like *that*." And I pointed to Eddie Burrup's hat on the second row from the top.

The long retrieving pole required an extension but eventually a soft furry object with a battered brim and a hole in the crown landed on the counter. From a long row of wigs and beards one intuitively found its way beside the hat.

We walked out of the shop with Eddie Burrup's materializing shadow in hand.

Early the next morning up on the flat roof over the west studio at 47 Browne Avenue – the idea was to have only sky as background – a first set of photographs was taken.

"It's hopeless, it's hopeless," said P. "The light's all wrong. It doesn't even vaguely look like the tropics."

Then we shall have to take some more in Broome later on.

Diary: 27 April 1995

This is an attempt to put the script into some order. It is all over the place.

I shall leaf through the pages of this Eddie Burrup file and see what it tells us of his history from the beginning. No, not from the beginning as that lies, for both of us, too far back in the misty past but just as far back as a bright summer morning when he first emerged with neither name nor persona and yet fully formed like a classical mythic creature all ready to go.

Eddie was not conceived for such would entail slow gestation, growth, birth. He just arrived – not so different on that first day – 28 December 1994 – than in the photos of him taken in Broome at Easter time – April 1995.

But first I must digress about the *morphological* works:

> [Text copied from *Diary*, 1 December 1994]
> These morphological works – what are they about? From where do they stem?
>
> I suppose they are actually about what I am about – what I have always been about, all my life, I guess, but only now coming out in this particular form – quite quickly too, daily in fact – daily for a number of years – 15? or 20 years? – in sketch and small form (find in the red folders on sheets of A4) but now sizing up to larger proportions – about 3' x 2'– vertical mostly although earlier, in direct line of provenance from the wild *Flightless Birds* … and the wilder still *The Rim, the rim of our brittle and disintegrating world* … all of which were, almost invariably, horizontal like laid back sprawling Australia – but thinking about it – or about anything, is always vertical.
>
> These morphological works are any way up and they are very private. They are removed from the work I might exhibit or be asked for or the work I guess with which I am associated.
>
> These are creatures and stuff – an essence of – animal

vegetable mineral – not separate but all interchangeable.

When I was small – perhaps three or four years old – I looked down at my two feet – heels together and toes out – and saw the tail of a fish.

I was somewhat older when I stretched out my arm and felt the membrane between the fingers of my hand – bone matching bone. So fish and bats are continually in mind. I see them where the shadows of leaves are thrown against a wall and sometimes hints of how they came about – accident? blind chance? deliberate action?

I am concerned with form and structure – rock faces – pre-Darwinian classification – the similarities of fundamental characteristics – forms, relationships, metamorphoses – the phylogenic development of organs quite apart from their function although function is crucial – but there can be too much of it and it is a relief to escape back into rocks, particularly erosional and corroding forms and shapes which cross over into the sentient world – geomorphology and the androgynous.

Do rocks feel? If not why should they have gone through so many traumatic convulsions before coming to present themselves to us – you and me – as static, fixed in time and fixing time – conveniently for us – so cute, so smart, to reckon with. I wonder. Take another look at the Gondwanan Dispersion and think again.

I shall spare the reader and myself more of these meanderings on what I was then calling my *morphological works* (just before the personal tumult of the next few weeks)[44] and before they emerged into the trauma of the Totemic Tumult, the totemic ideograms, wherein they found a focus through the eye and hand of Eddie Burrup.

Diary: 28 April 1995

Perpetua must have phoned four or five times today. She is very apprehensive and nervous about the whole carry-on but eventually she packed up the five original Eddie Burrups and sent them on their way. It was the covering letter to the Gallery Gabrielle Pizzi that has caused her so much anxiety. She has worked in a sentence about there being more to Eddie Burrup than meets the eye: his name, for instance, could be a 'pen' or rather a 'brush' name. She feels this gives her a let-out but I am doubtful. It introduces a hint of duplicity where none existed before.

P's anxiety has infected me now and I was seriously thinking at one stage today of going to Melbourne, seeing GP myself, telling her the exact situation and enlisting her support. But what would I be asking her to support?

Why should I ask support for an artistic and social experiment which, though so interesting, important and exciting to me, would not be of the least interest or importance to her. Rather the opposite. I think she would drop Eddie Burrup like a hot potato. There is really nothing for it. Either Eddie Burrup dies, and disappears forever, or we proceed along the lines as originally planned.

Diary: 30 April 1995

A call from P in Broome first thing. She is all but a nervous wreck over Eddie. Says she has had a sleepless night and that if GP gets back to her she is going to expose Eddie: "There is no way I'll get into that story about his being in trouble with the police. How someone as bright as you can be so incredibly stupid."

She was really angry. I could feel the satellite bouncing around in space with her agitation. I pleaded with her to let Eddie Burrup live a little longer as a personality in his own right, to let the initiative and the challenge to him come from the other end, not to jump the gun, or worse, turn on poor defenseless old Eddie.

Diary: 13 May 1995

We have run into an unforeseen contingent. Silence. A wall of complete silence around Melbourne and the Gallery GP since the dispatch of the Eddie Burrup originals, the transcript from his tape/monologue as delivered by him to P over Easter in Broome and her covering letter sent on 28 April 1995. That's 15 days ago now. GP said she would let P know when the originals arrived.

What's happened? What is happening? The ball is definitely in the Melbourne court so P is refraining from making any contact until midweek. Meanwhile she is cracking under the strain of it all now and I must say, for all my bravura, I am feeling the tension too. As well as sleepless nights P says dreams come to haunt her: "There was a party, a gathering, a lot of people around. Eddie was there – someone knocked into him and his hat fell off and then his beard and there you were with nothing on. I said to you: don't go around like that – you can be seen through the lattice. And you said, they'd never know it was me. Then I woke up but it was really a longer dream and more worrying."

I refrained from asking how she could have long dreams and a sleepless night at one and the same time. P is past banter and jollying.

Diary: 9 June 1995

8.30pm. At Easter time this year there was a partial eclipse of the moon. I have made a miniature of this with flying foxes in the foreground. I sent some little ones up to P a week or so ago – nothing can be too small to meet the tourist market. P has little patience for the average tourist but as this is 90% of her visitors there at the gallery I think they should be catered for. Kimberley Fine Art is far too elusive and ethereal. That is why I have evoked the spirit of Sir Walter Scott and am busying myself, through the hailstorms, with the miniatures.

The amusing part of it is that Eddie is quite intrigued with this carry-on. He watches me quietly looking over my shoulder and exclaims from time to time: "By Cris', alla same photo!"

He works on every day with his drawings and is adding titles to them, fragments of "old blackfella stories" or enigmatic jottings, a mixture of ancient myths and his own reminiscence. He hasn't tackled a bigger painting for a while. Perhaps he will over the weekend. And this depends somewhat on what the weekend will reveal in contact between P there in Broome and GP down in Melbourne. He has the idea that he will be having an exhibition at the latter's gallery in September.

Diary: 11 June 1995

8.30pm. Quite suddenly this afternoon Eddie must have got fed up with the miniatures that previously he had been quite interested in for he turned round and swiped them clean off my drawing board and I found myself receding into the background as he went into action.

But what a surprise when I saw what emerged! It was not part of either of his main themes – the Totemic Ideograms or the Pilbara railway line continuum, but a Bible story as taught to him years ago by Sister Philomena in the Broome convent school.

He elaborated: "This one for Sister Bilomena. 'e learn'm me plenty Piple story – I mak'm pig mob picture b'la Sister Bilomena. She bin sit me back b'la class room – 'm reckon: You can mak'm picture Eddie – never min' too much ABCD – I sit t'ere all day. Sometime, s'pose'm I got'm plenty paper, I stop back when school binish."

The composition itself was in his recognisable style. In this case a threatening *Wandjina* type figure dominated the upper and central area with an elliptical shape below and the form of a serpent on the right hand side.

"We call'm," said Eddie, excited with his creation, "Look out now! That 'n God! 'm comin' down brom 'igh place, proper sulky fella. 'e ching out: I can see you had'am an' you woman h'eve – you bin steal'm my bruit!

"That had'am 'n h'eve now – see'm flat out la deep shade? an' that chinake b'la tree? – 'im mak'm pig trouble la garden h'eden. Sister Bilomena reckon dat true story – Might be *gudea* dreamin' eh?"

The silence from the Gabrielle Pizzi Gallery in Melbourne has been deafening. I persuaded P to fax her. This went off on the 17th and the reply came the next day:

Due to the shift in direction of the Gallery program at Gallery Gabrielle Pizzi I suggest you contact the following galleries regarding Eddie Burrup's work …

Diary: 27 September 1995

… That is now over two months ago. In that time I have travelled thousands of kilometres while Eddie B has remained stationary, immobilized. There was a flicker of excitement while I was in Kununurra the second time (August 2 – 10) when P phoned to say that Ray Hughes [art dealer] and Joseph Furlonger [painter] from Sydney, had visited the gallery and shown interest in Eddie B's work. There was another flicker of excitement on August 29th when Paula Latos-Valier[45] and her husband Byron were in the gallery and P was showing them varied work including a few by Eddie. "I like the Burrups," said Paula and it was at that very moment that I came in with my camera and broke the thread.

But when I say Eddie B has remained stationary that is not really correct. My Day Book is littered with his drawings, incongruous among graphic sketches of the eternal road, sights and scenes and crazy Race meetings, and since my return I have done several large paintings and have redrafted *Eddie Burrup's Story in his own words …*

He is making it harder and harder, if not impossible, for me to do any other work than his.

Nothing seems to hold my interest – every other form of expression seems dull and simplistic compared with the persistently intriguing ideas that Eddie keeps coming up with. But how can one go on working in a complete vacuum? If ever any one has painted him or herself into a corner it is surely I.

Diary: 8 October 1995

9.00pm: Whither Eddie Burrup? God only knows.

I have been working with him all day down in the rear studio. We completed a new composition relating to *Grasshopper* and then named most of the paintings and signed them with Eddie's mark – a little rock crab – on the back. There must be about forty pieces there now. Some better than others but some very good. Then P would have ten or more in Broome. Altogether quite enough for the exhibition which I foresaw a while back would occur some time in September. September has come and gone.

The work I have been doing, apart from Eddie, seems so tame and insipid. Scenes of the eternal road and *Veduti di Roaming* generally. I feel closer than ever now to Piranesi.[46] Eddie Burrup is the ultimate in a prison of the imagination.

Diary: 22 October 1995

Too late again to be opening this up. I got carried away by Alan Rumsey: *Language and Territoriality in Aboriginal Australia* and the new insights that the Mabo investigation into traditional land ownership is bringing to light.

The primordial 'traditional owners' of the land were the anthropomorphised creatures/animals/totems. It was – is? – *they* who map territorial boundaries that coincide linguistically with their peregrinations which, actually, have almost nothing to do with a human concept/construct of 'my place'.

If this sounds complicated it is really a simplification of Rumsey.

Diary: 7 November 1995

Melbourne Cup day which I watched on TV and now to try to update this before another month slips by.

Today, Eddie, I posted off your Christmas card ideas and paintings the preparation of which has been very very absorbing and I am not sure quite when we started in on this or what triggered it off.

I think it was P in Broome who said she wanted a Christmas card to send around the world to all the people who had come to the gallery during the year. I said I had no ideas at all, that I was tired of doing Christmas cards and was going to use some old ones and some of the ones that Hamersley Iron brought out as cards from selections of the Marandoo Collection.

It was then, I think, that you cut across saying that you had a few ideas and that you thought some of Sister Philomena's Bible stories that you had illustrated for her years and years ago in the old convent school in Broome might be resurrected. You were remembering how Sister Philomena loved your drawings and let you do them in preference to schoolwork.

There was one that she particularly liked and that you called: *Two fella angel – 'e ching out for lovelybaby Jesus l'a hay trough*. So you set to and did this again.

Then there was another one. It was entitled: *Stockman 'e leave'm nannygoat l'a yard – 'e go look out lovelybaby Jesus l'a hay trough*; and another: *Three fella Maban 'e got'm present for lovelybaby Jesus*. So these three compositions came to light – all on the Nativity theme.

Diary: 8 November 1995

10.00pm: The weather has reverted to winter and it is colder and wetter than it has been all the time since my return from the north. As I write the rain is streaming down. There is a drip in the rear studio right beside my drawing board. I have lost my secateurs and think I must have thrown them in the bin with the cuttings. I feel too low-spirited to go on just now. Nothing is coming together or progressing even a fraction of an inch.

Diary: 15 November 1995

9.00pm: I have left it a bit late having got caught up in Quantum and the Galileo probe of Jupiter on TV. I rarely watch TV. Mainly it is either soporific or boring but the picture of that odd shaped little toy caught up in the orbit of Venus and company gallantly sending messages back to earth the while got me in.

My original intention for making an entry here this evening was to report on the progress and non-progress of Eddie's Christmas card. It

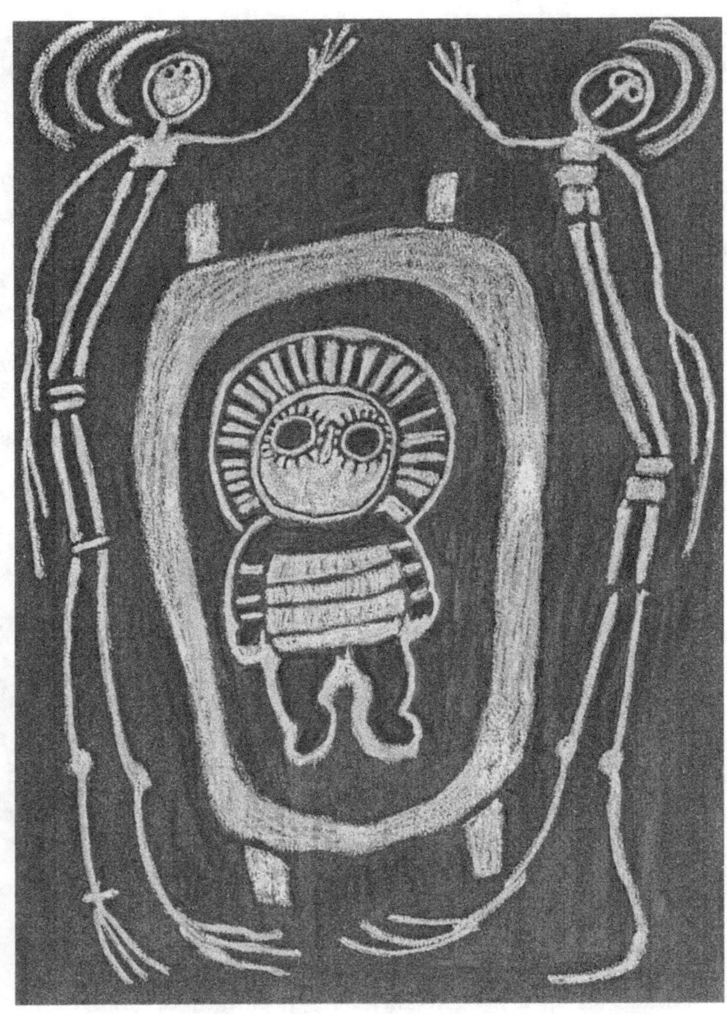

Two fella angel 'e singin' out for lovlybaby Jesus 'la haytrough 1995
Durack Gallery Christmas card,
from the series *The Art of Eddie Burrup*
mixed media on paper 76 x 56 cm, estate of ED

would be hard to imagine how many variations the few words of text accompanying this card were capable of being rendered in by someone like P who has processed and re-processed them with '*a meticulosity bordering on the insane*'[47] and which has entailed an endless number of telephone calls and innumerable 'guaranteed next day delivery' letters between here and Broome.

However today I eventually got Eddie's 'art work' back to MacDougalls and any time after 8.00 tomorrow morning I shall be able to collect 200 copies of his rendition of the Nativity: *Two fella angel 'e singin' out for lovelybaby Jesus l'a hay trough.*

I don't suppose anyone will ever know what it was like for Eddie and me to break through the iconography of the past 2000 years in order to arrive at this particular image of that great world turning event: *And the Word became flesh and dwelt amongst us.* Certainly not P who simply fastened on to the accompanying words on the back of the card and insisted on reducing them to something so minute that one needs a magnifying glass to read them at all:

> *Two fella angel 'e singin' out for lovelybaby Jesus l'a hay trough.* from a series: *Sister Philomena's Bible stories* by Eddie Burrup b.1925 Yarraloola reproduced here by permission the artist Christmas 1995 KFA Durack Gallery – PO Box 2168 Broome Western Australia 6725

So much for Eddie's first exposure to the great wide world.
How I (tried) to reinvent myself in my 81st year and nobody ever knew.

Diary: 19 November 1995

8.00pm: However his Christmas card was finally completed and I sent 50 of them up to P by fast post two days ago. She immediately phoned to say she wants a heap more.

I'll send some more next week although the whole edition is only 200. I won't be able to use it myself but want some for my records etc this being the first time that Eddie's name appears in print.

I might develop *The Adoration of the Magi: Three fella maban 'e got'm present for lovelybaby Jesus l'a hay trough.* The figures for this are adapted from the petroglyphs in Father Ernest Worms' first paper about them in *Oceania* in 1952 and Bruce Wright's *Rock Art of the Pilbara Region, North-West Australia* in 1963. I am seeing the world though these symbols now.

Diary: 3 December 1995

It will be a year on December 28 since Eddie Burrup entered my life. And where in all that time have we got? The answer is – Nowhere. In fact, far from *joyous liberation*, the relationship has brought about a situation in which I am now trapped, hoisted by my own petard, frustrated, thwarted. I did not think that, this time, it was going to be so slow, so hidden, so meandering. Both Eddie and I foresaw an exhibition in Melbourne in September with things moving from there. I really don't think I can face another *s l o g*.

It would not be so bad if all my previous modes of activity had not now become so dull, depressing and tedious. It is not so long ago that I derived a lot of gentle pleasure out of producing a whole series of *Bett-bett's wonderful lonely palace,* and works of this ilk. I really enjoyed doing the big *Dreaming up the Victoria* set of 25 and the trip to Timber Creek that preceded this. I was functioning quite well on the two levels, the graphic and nostalgic together, while quietly progressing with the *morphological works* at a discrete pace.

Now I can no longer operate this way. Eddie is too demanding and too interesting. Yet can anyone go on indefinitely operating in a vacuum?

When people ask what I am doing, in a pleasant and polite way, leading in with the inevitable question: *Are you still …*? I reply weakly: "Not very much." Or I say I have been involved with a number of the Benefit exhibitions – true enough. Or sometimes I say: "No. I've retired. Or: I'm hibernating." *Will no one rid me of this tedious priest?*

Diary: 19 December 1995

9.30am: This morning first thing I re-established contact with P after the silence of the last week since she left Broome for Balgo in company with Bob Juniper. As it turned out it had rained heavily and when they got to Halls Creek the road south-east was 'closed to all traffic' so they looped up to Turkey Creek and looked in on the Warmun Community. This is the home of Rover Thomas and Queenie McKenzie and others who have just had a big exhibition at the Mora Gallery in Melbourne which, according to Larry Foley [friend and art patron] who saw it and to the press that applauded it, was very successful. Bob also had an exhibition in Melbourne this year. It was ignored by the press and sales were minimal.

In his gentle and respectful way Bob was, according to P, pretty dismissive of the formula paintings coming out of Warmun. To her amusement, he said: "I think I'll knock out a few in a similar mode, sign them 'Bobbie Djunapur' and you can sell them for me in your gallery."

Eddie Burrup's first Christmas card (1995) received much favourable response. The most significant for future developments, was that from Doreen Mellor, Director of Adelaide's Tandanya National Aboriginal Cultural Institute, who had been one of many visitors to the Durack gallery. In January 1996 Mellor phoned Perpetua to ask if Eddie Burrup would consider entering work in a forthcoming exhibition Native Titled Now *scheduled for the Adelaide Festival in April. Perpetua soon called back to say Eddie Burrup would be pleased to be part of the exhibition. In due course three Burrup works were included in* Native Titled Now. *The distinctive works elicited heart-felt response from Tandanya staff and the public. Subsequently they were selected for a two-year Touring Exhibition of eastern Australia.*

PDC

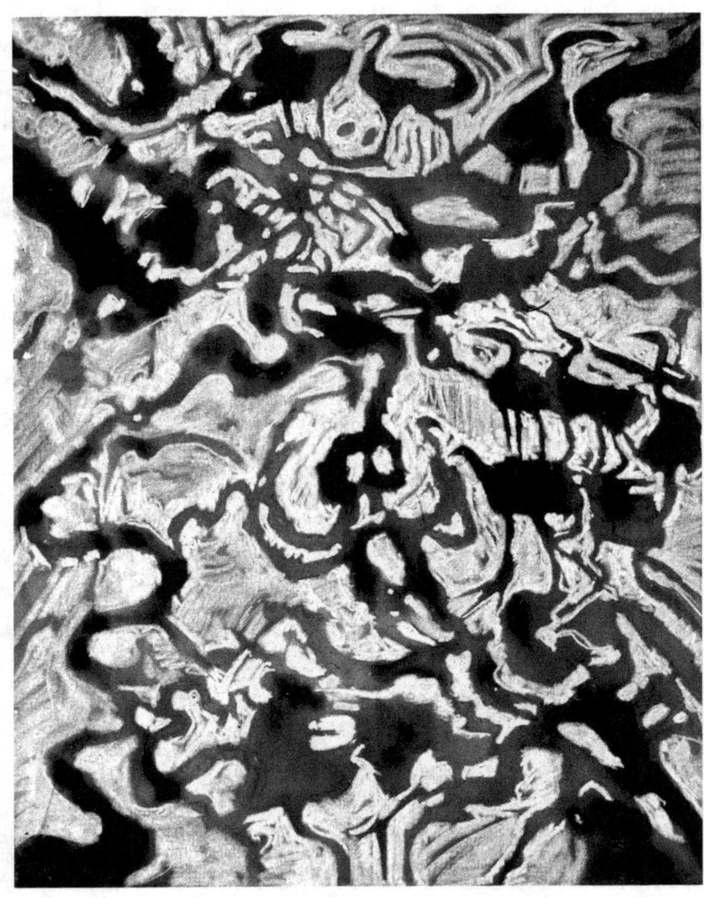

Jinnaweibinna Pool on the Yule River 1996
from the series *The Art of Eddie Burrup*
mixed media on linen 106 x 57 cm, private collection

Diary: 23 May 1996

The thing is to think very positively and optimistically about all this [loan arrangements with the ANZ Bank] and regard it as an extra stimulus rather than an added burden. In the same way as Eddie Burrup has been an incredible psychic stimulus to me and opened a whole Pandora's Box, not of evil spirits but, rather, a host of imprisoned and benign ones who were, previously, locked up in the dark confinement of my very personal thalamus, my personal radiant relay station where all those somatic, sensory and optic paths connect with my cerebral cortex.

Eddie Burrup does a drawing a day, title and all. He has done two paintings for the Telstra National Aboriginal and Torres Strait Art Award 1996. They are among his best works to date. Oil resiste on canvas they are within the stipulated size limits measuring 106 by 57 cm. The theme is the creation of the Yule River. The *gudea* title is *The headwaters of the Yule River.*

Aboriginal cartography has the Yule River, and all the rivers, divided into sections commemorating the creation myth and the path of the serpentine ancestors. Encounters, conversations, exchanges – contentions, duels and cobber-cobbers punctuate the way and prescribe language variations.

I owe this to my visit to Yandeearra and yarning with the old women there.

Eddie's other painting is the same size and medium. Its title: *Jinnaweibinna Pool – Yule River* and Eddie's title:

> *Wal, you know that one*
> *where 'e got'm*
> *per'ment water – all-year-roun'?*
> *We call'm Jinna wei binna pool –*
> *same b'la gudea map.*

This permanent waterhole marked on all the maps was originally a meeting place and site for initiation ceremonies.

I don't know which one to enter for the Competition. I am going to leave it to P to decide. In either case I am suggesting that which ever she chooses the other one is referred to as a companion piece and that

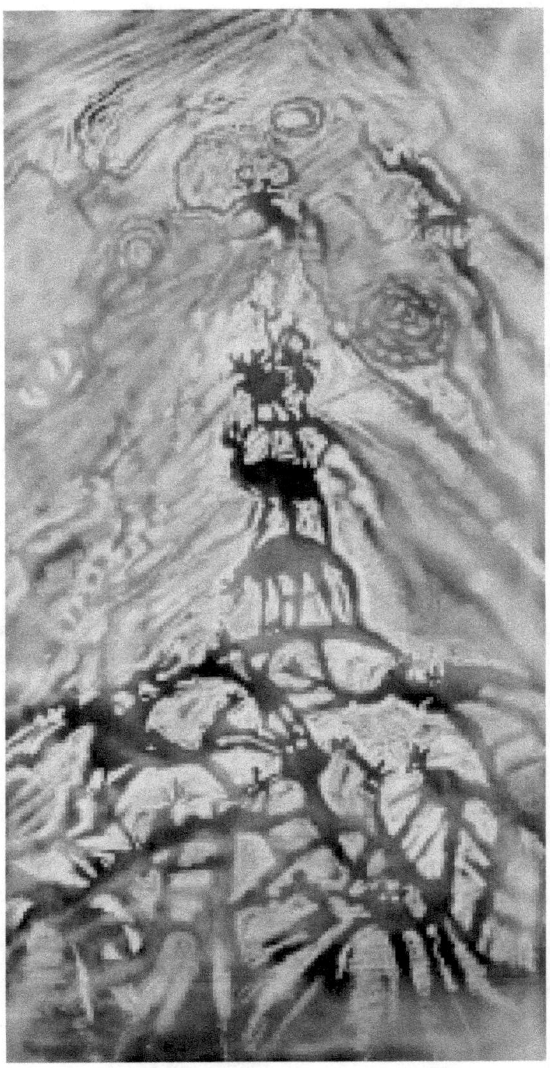

Ladder to the Sky 1996
from the series *The Art of Eddie Burrup*
mixed media on linen 184 x 92 cm, estate of ED

a slide and photo along with the title be included when P sends off the Entry Form to reach Darwin mid June. There is a selection set-up and this is the first hurdle that has to be overcome.

Diary: 5 June 1996

On the radio this morning there was an Arts program about two women artists, Nora Heysen and Jean Appleton, who are having an exhibition at Mossvale in the southern highlands of NSW. A Bruce James was speaking and questioning why two such senior women with a lifetime of work behind them should be so little known and yet a woman like Emily Kngwarreye can spring to national fame overnight as an Aboriginal artist apparently simply because her work derives from an ancient culture. But, Bruce went on to say, so too does the art of Nora H and Jean A derive from antiquity, in the direct line with European culture from the Renaissance and further back than that.

He ran on in this vein and I was very surprised to hear him. It is the first time that such apostasy has ever been voiced publicly.

Diary: 9 July 1996

Yesterday the sun came out and Eddie took the opportunity of doing a painting – *Ladder to the Sky*. This is the first time, ever, that he has used *blue*. The piece measures 183 by 94 cm, oil resist on canvas. We have no one to show it to or to talk about it to. Working on like this, forever in the dark, is just about killing us both.

I went down to the Fremantle Arts Centre in Finnerty Street at 5pm to see the *Sub Urban* exhibition – *with particular focus on survival despite racism, child theft and assimilation policies*. Hardly anyone there, a few young women, a few children …

I saw Ferry yesterday afternoon, he has gone down a lot since being in hospital and since the summer time when he might call sometimes twice a day with figs and leave his hat behind. There is someone with him in the house all the time now.

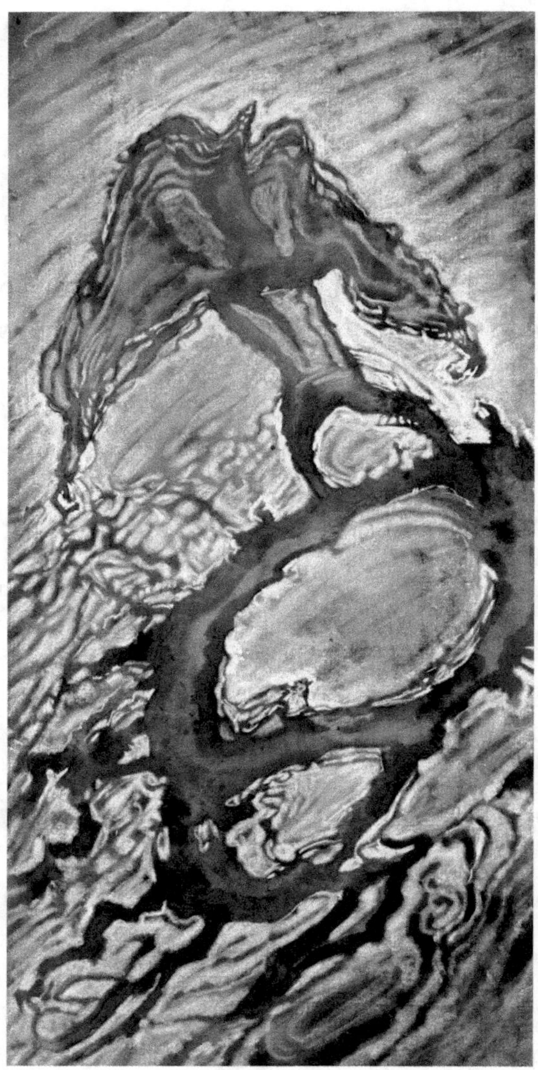

Djanba! 1996
from the series *The Art of Eddie Burrup*
mixed media on linen 200 x 100 cm, the estate of ED

Diary: July 11 1996

8.00pm: The coldest morning this season, 3 degrees. Except for a few very determined and tenacious ones all the leaves have fallen from the liquid amber.

Eddie stretched out a big canvas on the courtyard table just before it got too dark this evening. Unlike most of his works that have long discursive titles this one is simply called *Djanba!*

Diary: 12 July 1996

9.30pm: *Djanba!* is now stretched out in the courtyard.

The big looming shape at the top of the composition reminds me of a painting by Goya but I can't find it in any of the books – it might be by another artist. Daumier perhaps. But of course *Djanba*'s derivation has nothing to do with either Spain or France. Eddie knows about *Djanba* – the cult? the creature? the ceremony? the ancestor? being a part of his own experience and relationships.

Djanba is not tied to one place – he can appear anywhere at any time. He first emerged from a waterhole in Queensland. He travels around. He could have passed through Yandeearra en route north. I remember Mundi [Ivanhoe stockman] saying that he often showed up at Bandicoot Bar on the Ord. Mundi believed he came from Queensland and that he circulated south and west and north from there following the stock routes. Father Worms sought to align him and his movements with a Christ-like manifestation but others believe he is more recent and that he is the personification or the reincarnation of Argyle Boxer who was also noted for his sudden and unexpected appearances and who didn't die in Darwin as reported but simply goes on living and moving from place to place in the same unpredictable way as on that morning when we first met on the verandah at Argyle and he looked me in the eye and asked: *Which way Ol' Man?*

Some say *Djanba* is not a Being at all but a number of different songs about Being.

Where he came from the other day I don't know or how I came to do the painting.

Diary: 24 July 1996

The collapse of the kitchen ceiling is the stuff of nightmare except that it doesn't dissolve on waking.

I am now into the 2nd day of all this. 8.30am and the young man has just come and is setting up trestles etc. His off-sider hasn't turned up as yet so I don't know how far things will progress today.

I managed to get into the AGWA to hear Julie Lewis' talk on Kate O'Connor. It was an excellent talk and the theatre was full. I also saw Janda [Gooding, Curator of Australian Art, AGWA] and we have set up a tentative arrangement to meet here on Friday.

Keith Mattingly [journalist, businessman, art patron] was collecting a drawing by Streeton that he had lent to the Gallery and we had an interesting talk over a cup of coffee about the time, back in the early 1960s, when he was in London as a special Menzies' appointment at Australia House and about the Society of Australian Artists in London at that time of which he was President: "I thought the Art world would be a pleasant relief from the rough and tumble of politics and journalism but I discovered that it was much worse – rivalries and jealousies and friction – you wouldn't believe …"

> *There was enormous media interest after Elizabeth Durack's revelation of her* alter ego *to art historian Robert Smith was published in* Art Monthly Australia.[48] *The editor of the magazine, Peter Timms, blitzed the media with a sensational publicity release about Smith's article, 'The Incarnations of Eddie Burrup'. Elizabeth's intention had been to see the story in print and to let it unravel quietly, slowly.*
>
> PDC

Diary: 7 March 1997

8.30pm: The storm broke without warning. Except for a couple of peals of thunder yesterday afternoon as when an Ava Hubble from the ABC phoned and a John McNamara also from the ABC called down here.

The intensity of the unseasonal disturbance came as both a surprise and a shock. So much so that I am completely wrung out. I have repeated so many times that I have nothing to say and that I definitely do not want to appear on TV. By the afternoon I let the phone and the fax ring and beep their heads off and cleared out with Eddie down to the river.

There are some scribbled notes of all this in my Day Book which I won't recap here.

At 5 o'clock Rex came over to report that P and Michael had been trying to contact me to see if I was alright because P had been having a comparable drenching there in Broome and, apparently, Bob Smith in Geelong also. I phoned the latter and heard some of the background to the radio talks that he had given today. I had only heard a brief one over Radio National at 8 this morning.

There was something in *The West Australian* on page 2 that I'd better cut out.

Not all the calls were difficult and a number positively heart-warming including a number of messages passed on to me from various artists including the SA potter Milton Moon, old friends John Wilson, Robert Juniper, Leon Pericles, RWD, nephew Doug. As well, there was a fax from cousin Tom Stephens [Member of the WA Legislative Council]:

> … I also wanted you to know that I read the piece in *The West* in ref to 'Eddie Burrup' and I am sure there will be many Aboriginal people, friends and others, who will understand entirely. I feel that I do. Of course your long years of friendship will have impacted on you enormously (my short 25 years or so in close contact with Aboriginal people has). For the artist to find in that friendship and contact a sense of 'alter ego' is understandable and explicable and wonderful. Particularly wonderful that it still finds new artistic expression. I am confident that so many of your Aboriginal family and friends will know that. Others will choose neither to understand nor to tolerate.

Which is better than an angry mob howling for my blood, talking of suing me and stripping poor old Eddie's paintings off the walls of a gallery – as seen on the ABC television news tonight.[49]

I have to be up early if I am to do at least some of the Saturday morning chores and get to the UWA by 8.30am in time for the Seminar on *Aboriginal Rock Art* as arranged by the Kimberley Society. Spoke to Cathie Clement [historian and founder of the KS] and she is very pleased with the response to this. It is to run all day and wind up at 5.30 but I doubt I shall stay the distance.

P will be down from Broome on the night flight arriving about 11.00pm.

Diary: 8-9 March 1997

9.00pm: *And all day long the noise of battle roll'd*

Non stop – P fielding most of the incessant phone calls, the fax and callers. Now, at last, things are quiet. P has gone out and I can see the day in perspective. On the whole I think it has been a satisfactory one. So just extracting the most important item from the pile:

Tom Stephens contacted Ernie Bridge[50] for me and I had a talk to him. He will compose a piece about me, my work, my relationship with the Aboriginal people that, we hope, will placate or silence the most strident voices arising out of the general pandemonium. This document has then to be got through to Bob Smith so that he can arrange for it to get to all the main media simultaneously. There is to be effort, too, to contact Jeff Chunuma in Kununurra but no one is sure if he is there. If we can succeed with this contact it would be the second time that I have turned to my classificatory son for help, the first being when the exhibition at the AGWA in 1995 *Derivations and Directions – the work of ED 1930s to 1950s* – was brought to a stand-still in a similar way.[51]

Letter: Elizabeth Durack from '47' to Jan Mayman[52] in Nedlands, 10 March 1997

Dear Jan,

Thank you for your letter just received – apropos the current 'furore' regarding the Elizabeth Durack/Eddie Burrup crossover.

I was assured that by taking the initiative in this matter I would be safe from the chance of being 'exposed' by possibly antagonistic or ignorant outsiders.

As things have turned out the story that appeared in the March issue of *Art Monthly* has not protected me from the latter.

Under these circumstances I intend to remain silent and to let what my whole life – both as regards my Art and human relationships generally – has stood for, to speak for itself.

Elizabeth Durack and Eddie Burrup have no intention of going on the defensive about what has occurred between them. It is a private matter.

We may change this course of action over the ensuing weeks but for the present we plan to ride out this unseasonal storm. It will die down.

Life is short – media interest likewise – Art is long.

Affectionately,

Elizabeth

Diary: 26 March 1997

… Eddie took up most of the day and a 6' x 3' composition is drying out on the courtyard table. He finds it hard to work much smaller than this.

Title: *An underground ladder*

Alternative title:

Old black-fella story – allabout make'm ladder – put'm underground

Bye' n bye 'e gonna come out b'la China –

Old Argyle Boxer run'm that one – On'y I reckon might be hum-bug.

Diary: 12 December 1997

… Went to the ANZ Christmas party at the King's Park Function Centre with Ruth. I was nearly not going but then changed my mind and now I'm glad I went. I gained the impression that many of those there were strongly supportive of both old ED and EB – quite a number came up to me to say so.

Then very quietly Ruth and I started to exit – in the direction of the Wishing Well. By this time, the throng having spilled out on to the open-air section, this was relatively easy to do. As we walked along we heard the strains of a didgeridoo and there in a little amphitheatre a fat man with some mud smeared over his body was performing.

"You'd better take your name tag off, Auntie Bet," said Ruth. Around stood a small gathering of people – a few of mixed descent though mostly *wadjila* – eating canapes a plate of which was arranged in the colours of the Aboriginal flag. We watched this scene for a little while and were about to move off when a young blond woman came up to me and said: "Would you be Elizabeth Durack?"

And so by this strange coincidence I met Rebecca Hossack.[53] She and her companion [writer Matthew Sturgiss] had just arrived from London. Apparently they had gone straight to the AGWA to see the art of ED and she spoke of a painting – I don't know which one it would have been – that impressed her greatly and: "Would Eddie Burrup ever consider showing at the Rebecca Hossack Gallery?"

Rebecca first came into the picture way back in March this year at the time of the storm. I can't quite remember the circumstances but she had apparently been asked by some galleries and by Australia House whether the art of Eddie Burrup would affect Aboriginal paintings. I can't recall what her response was at the time. Anyway she is now going up to Broome, staying at the Cable Beach Club and intends to visit the Durack Gallery when there. I told P about this in an early morning call.

The previous evening the French Ambassador and his wife had also been to the AGWA and also seen a painting by ED and also expressed appreciation both of it and of *The Art of Eddie Burrup*. M. Girard told me the story of a French artist (I can't remember the name) who likewise had, in later life, worked under a *nom de plume* and of how the French people and art circles had simply congratulated him on his creativity and M. Girard contrasted this reaction to that of my experience.

Meeting French people at that party I was struck with the depths of their civilization, their sophistication, their artistic comprehension. For a short hour I breathed free fresh air in a layer above the fetid fumes rising from the political morass in which the art of poor ED and EB is floundering.

More phone calls from Peter David and from his 'pop' Uncle Andy Ebro (one of the Elders and signees of the document). It is all wheels within wheels. This group headed by the three Uncles is trying to dislodge Robert Eggington [an executive officer of Perth's Dumbartung Aboriginal Corporation] and they speak very disparagingly – not to say slanderously – of him and his activities.

But now the Kimberley Land Council are putting in their spoke too and the Uncles are trying to make me contact my family in Kununurra to get their support. But alas, 'my family' – the old Argyle and Ivanhoe mob – are in the manipulative hands of the very powerful legal world as well as that of local exploitation. Chunuma and co will be torn between loyalties and the dollar with which they are being baited. The Uncles now see a chance of using me to further their ends – I got a whiff, too, of: *we did you a favour now it's up to you to reciprocate*.[54]

It is really all too much – but in the telephone conversations I didn't cut them short or decline emphatically but said: "Look, let's put everything on *hold* until after the holidays and then let us all have a re-think."

Into the bargain the Uncles are proposing that we all go north together, confront the Kimberley Land Council head on and clear the air for good and all. "That is an expensive proposition," I rejoined, "Broome and Kununurra are a long way away." "Oh, don't worry," they replied. "We can get the money."

Meanwhile vital energy is being squandered, nerves are being frayed, imperative trains of thought are being sidetracked. Eddie, as usual, simply clears out. It's alright for him over in the Leopolds – over in the limestone. He has the *Ngarangani* into which to immerse himself and escape. It is I who is left carrying the can – of writhing worms.

Diary: 12 July 1998

9.15pm: I am feeling somewhat relieved to gather from P in various phone conversations today that her meeting with Ted Ryan [director of Gallery Link International, Sydney] there in Broome went well and I feel it has had the effect of bringing more rationality into her attitude to this curious (and worrying) liaison. I do not want to dwell on the very great strain that P's extremely negative attitude has been to me for some months now – made all the greater by the fact that I am really in agreement about the many unanswered questions regarding this strange turn of fate.

However I intend to proceed and right now will not get too analytical.

In defiance Eddie Burrup took over yesterday and produced a painting on paper entitled *Vantage point (1)* wherein Wonditch, standing on the back of his brethren views the extended landscape. There will not be time before I leave on Tuesday morning to follow this up with *Vantage point (2)* which shows Spider casting a net high in the branches of a river gum. I say "in defiance" because Ted is swooping on all and anything of the work done 50 and 60 years ago. While I am able to recall any amount of this work, and did so with the *Transcontinental* drawings last week, it is a going backwards not forward – the view through the rear window.

Diary: 13 July 1998

6.00pm: I am in the grip of a terrible desperation and am doing things and making moves against my better judgment and that, certainly, if anyone should ask my advice if so situated, I would tell them firmly to stop. I am looking for a way out of Gallery Link International before it squeezes me to death.

The escape point is *The Art of Eddie Burrup* – the publication of the manuscript and the exhibition of the paintings (in London?) so this morning I phoned Allen & Unwin again and was not able to get on to either Emily O'Connell or Sophie Cunningham but I left a message with 'John' to say I would be in Sydney and was hoping I might have the chance of meeting Emily and asking her advice (or words to that effect). Then I had to go out to do some shopping. When I got back, there at the front door, the MS returned from Allen & Unwin:

> Dear Elizabeth
> Thank you for enquiring about Allen & Unwin's potential interest in your manuscript – *The Art of Eddie Burrup.* While we read your submission with interest, I am afraid it would not be right for the list our trade publisher is developing, so we are unable to make you an offer of publication.
> Thank you for thinking of Allen & Unwin.
> With best wishes

One might have thought that this was enough to slow me down but it had the opposite effect – it exacerbated my desperation. I phoned Random House and got through to Jody Lee who is mentioned in the credits of Paul Sheehan's *Among the Barbarians.* I said who I was and she said she knew the name. I said I had a manuscript that was something in the nature of an artistic corroboration of *the Barbarians* – in an oblique way. I outlined the plot. I was talking to someone who could speak good English. I said I would be in Sydney briefly for a Film Australia promotion and as I would be staying in North Sydney I would not be very far from Milsons Point and it would be great if I could meet someone from Random House and obtain their advice (or words to that effect). "Look," said Jody, "I think I have the picture and I shall run it before our team here and get back to you."

Less than two hours later she phoned back to say much the same as Allen & Unwin: We do not think it would fit into any of the lists that our trade publisher is developing.

So that's it. *The Art of EB* [the Monologue and Comment by Leon Deutsch] is un-publishable. I have to face it. This is now the fourth rejection: Queensland University Press, HarperCollins (long delayed reply came in from Helen Littleton last week), then Allen & Unwin and now Random House. Try Pan McMillan, said Jody. But they are in Melbourne and I won't pursue this just now – if ever.

Some of my present desperation is a result of having read the QAG catalogue of *Emily Kame Kngwarreye – Al halkere – Paintings from Utopia.* This publication itself is a work of considerable art and of high quality professionalism. Compared with it the Catalogue produced by Gallery Link International on ED is pathetic.

The Art World both in Australia and internationally has come together to lift the work of Emily Kngwarreye from its beginning, less than ten years ago, aloft, high and flying on the vertical banners of fame, what a dream run. Eddie Burrup eat your heart out.

In the midst of this entry Rex phoned and gave me an account of his recent visit to Moscow as one of a panel of judges for the Tchaikovsky Piano Competition, very, very interesting. It is Rex's fourth visit to Russia over the last 30 years and this has given him a unique opportunity to participate in the cultural heart of the musical world.

"And coming back to Australia after such a marvellous experience – does it seem like the end of the world?"

"No, no. Australia is absolute Paradise," said Rex.

Yet some of us living in it still create our own Purgatory.

Diary: 20 July 1998 …

8.30pm: I phoned Dan Maddock at 9 this morning and he came this evening and has solved the problems. Dan is a young Canadian now living permanently in Australia. He is head of the Cygnus internet operations at UWA. He divided this text at page 400 and it should be OK now to tap on. As well, a thorough backup has been made on to two disks and these I have set aside.

Posted off ten small Eddie Burrups to Broome and then settled into the rear studio and doing the *Whirlwinds.* I'm working on all five at the one time leaving sections to dry out as I move from one to the other but I am missing a good purple purple and shall have to get over to Jacksons in the morning. I'll need some caneite too for backing for some medium sized EBs as it is only a week now before Evie Ferrier [arts writer for *The West Australian*] will be here with a photographer. I don't know how this will go or, rather, how I shall handle it. I don't really want another boring personal rigmarole but on the other hand don't feel I should give Evie *The Art of Eddie Burrup* manifesto or perhaps I shall give it to her to read but not to print and I hope she will come up with some breezy comment of her own reactions – but not, of course, flippant.

Essay: Background to *The Art of Eddie Burrup* (1998).[55]

> The central theme of *The Art of Eddie Burrup* is the totemic tumult that has been engendered in the arcane depths of the *Ngarangani* as a result of the radical decrees of the High Court of Australia over the past five years. It is concern for his Totemic kin and the manner in which they have been ignored by the Judges of the High Court of Australia in their Mabo 2 (1992) and Wik (1996) decisions that weighs upon the heart of Eddie Burrup and manifests itself through his Art.

The situation regarding the anthropomorphised creatures of the *Ngarangani*, their union with the world and their role in its continuum, was overlooked by the Mabo 2 ruling and even more acutely by the inventors of 'Native Title'.

While the High Court verdict stretched contemporary wisdom and extended contemporary conscience further than had previously been legally attempted, it nevertheless imposed a Eurocentric view of land tenure and turned a restricted tunnel vision upon the pre-historic Aboriginal situation.

The Mabo verdict was deeply flawed – applicable as it might have been to the tiny garden-culture oriented island of Mer. It would appear that the Judges were unaware of the original situation vis-a-vis the land and the unique ontology of its inhabitants.

The land in pre-contact Australia was a *shared* staple – shared indivisibly between the creative ancestors and their substitutes in alternating human, animal and physical manifestations.

No accommodation for the *shared* occupancy of the land appears ever to have been brought into the judicial deliberations and because of this the seeds of all the subsequent problems were sown — together with the sheer impracticality of implementing a 'native title' that neither did nor does exist.

With settlement and the introduction of alien unrelated species the closed circuit of what was, till then, a secluded archaism surviving in isolation from the rest of the world, was abruptly shattered.

On January 26th 1788, precisely, elliptical time was replaced by that of linear time and from then on events were no longer sustainable –

intact and circuitous by supernatural agency – but became sequential and mundane.

Pre-contact Aboriginals did not own land – they were *the land – its incarnation – an intimacy infinitely more binding and chimerical than mere tenure and one that predates by millennia even the earliest historic epoch.*

The concept of Gods/God emerged a mere 8 to 10 thousand years ago. The idea of Adam *naming every living creature* or of *Man as the measure of all things* belongs to a relatively modern world.

The High Court invoked Common Law to support its decision and although this perception pre-dates more formal renderings, it too, is recent compared with the antiquity of the Man/Land relationship such as survived, *uniquely,* in Australia right up to the end of the 18th century after which date its extinction was rapid and inevitable.

The pastoral industry, predominant among the despoilers, shattered the old ontology and the old way of life completely – more so in some places than in others.

So minimal was obstruction to the settler and his rapacious quadrupeds that for all intents and purposes, it was as though the continent was uninhabited.

Missionaries, active from the beginning, kept plentiful records, so too did the Government but apart from these official accounts and some fragmentary literature along with copious letters 'home', it would be over 100 years before there was even a backward glance at what relics lay in the wake of the tidal wave of European expansion in Australia.

Anthropology itself was a new discipline and of the late 19th century – *A study of a Stone Age People* by Spencer and Gillen came out in 1879, *Ethnological studies among the Queensland Aborigines – the Roth Report* in 1896 and *Australian Legendary Tales,* as collected by Langloh Parker, also in 1896.

(To find any reference to 'Aboriginal resistance' one needs to come forward another 100 years and to undergo a complete attitudinal change. There is no dearth of literature today in this regard and a leading proponent of this construct had the ear of the High Court throughout its deliberations.)

But swift as destruction was in south-eastern Australia, the process slowed down as the map extended, and pastoral and agricultural activity spread to utilise nearly all potential areas no matter how marginal and, where the latter let up, mineral operations filled in the gaps – or vice-versa – with the still-uncommitted areas being classified as Crown Land and Aboriginal Reserves.

Only around the Top End and the Centre was there any leisure to observe the final scenes of the same all-over drama. About 30 years ago these locations were to become the happy hunting grounds for exotic philosophers and the apologists of 'new historicism' *et al.* As a consequence and coupled with an activist High Court, Australia's 200 year stable land tenure has been shifted from firm ground to morass.

Out of this on-going psychotic and political turmoil, *The Art of Eddie Burrup* emerged as an additional stake in the implausible edifice upon which was mounted a National Reconciliation Program formalised ceremoniously in May 1997.

If Eddie Burrup had not existed it would have been necessary to invent him.

Diary: 16 January 1999

11.30am: Too many things on too many different levels, as Mary used to say – e.g. the Maureen Smith[56]/Eddie Burrup conjunction, the Gallery Link International partnership split, *Signals from Howling Dog Rock.* I think it is fairly good but am not sure. It is this uncertainty and the sense of confidence wavering that is my greatest worry – new too. Previously there were no doubts or misgivings about the work itself but going into the 5th year now without any encouragement, the opposite in fact, and increasing silence and sense of isolation. I have not heard back from [UWA] Chancellor Alec Cohen but this does not really matter much as Maureen's letter has altered priorities.

Contact with Bill Bunbury of ABC Radio National *Hindsight.* He called me about a theme he has in mind on MDM. I said I had an unpublished MS, *The Time of our Lives,* with a lot of references to MDM. He was interested in this and is coming here on Monday morning. I may show him *The Survivor* also. It is the best thing I've written, I think, and really the way I have used the bush vernacular with old Maurie Foley speaking has a distinct link with old Eddie Burrup telling his story in kriol. It never struck me before until I re-read it. Talk about dinkum Aussie voices.

Then on Tuesday morning the Department of Transport is calling to ask me about my ideas for safe driving for the elderly. Ohh.

Fax: From Elizabeth Durack at '47' to Rebecca Hossack in London, 28 March 1999

Dear Rebecca

I was most interested to receive your letter and enclosures of March 24th. Thank you. As the 'few other options' that you mention come to hand we will be better able then to decide upon a plan of procedure.

In doing so the aims and objects of holding a London exhibition of *The Art of Eddie Burrup* will need to be kept clearly in mind. As I see it there are several such objectives and they all concern important rights and ones that have so far gone undeclared:

> the right to have Eddie Burrup's art assessed aesthetically and independently and separate from social and political issues; the right of an artist to the use of a pseudonym for whatever reason he ordains – and that without fear of attack or censure; the right to gain a legitimate place for Eddie Burrup in the extremely complex and inter-wed world of contemporary 'Aboriginal Art' (see Ian McLean, *White Aborigines – Identity Politics in Australian Art* Cambridge U Press 1998); the right to air the voice of Eddie Burrup as representative of *Aboriginal cooperation* — this voice has been silenced by the much louder contemporary one that would emphasise only the victim/oppressor rendering of Australian history; (On the theme of collaboration, see Henry Reynolds *With the White People: The Role of Aboriginals in Australian exploration and development*, Penguin, 1990; and Bill McGregor *Nyibayarra: Kimberley Tracker*, Aboriginal Studies Press, Canberra, 1995, and various other publications not easily come by as they, too, seem to be censored.)

Eddie Burrup asserts his right to his place in the scheme of things via an intellectual and psychic connection with this country's ancient culture and via knowledge which has been donated first-hand and accumulated over a life-time of learning. (The theme of the old men in the bush camp at the Ivanhoe Crossing having 'sung' ED and to which the latter's bush sisters refer whenever we meet, need not, I think, be noted although it has possibilities for the press if handled discretely.)

Now, as regards The Gallery in Cork Street, yes, that is certainly a steep fee particularly with the present pound/dollar relationship but if by engaging with such an obviously prestigious address it achieved the above aims and objects then, perhaps, it could be considered.

We would need to know and, if possible, receive some supportive evidence of the value of the gallery from previous persons who used it, artists particularly.

It is good, I think that the gallery gives the lessee a completely free hand to operate even though this would mean that everything with regard to the proposed exhibition would need to be in hand and set up well ahead.

A list of questions could run on and on and of course there is the crucial one: who presents the exhibition? *The Art of Eddie Burrup presented by Elizabeth Durack*? (The combined shoulders of these two octogenarians are not, I fear, strong enough.)

Earlier an exhibition under an official umbrella was foreseen, the Australia House venue, but as this fell through the question now re-looms somewhat ominously and I can hardly expect, nor would I ask you Rebecca, to play Zola to my Dreyfus, if this is what things have come to in this particular day and age.

I note on the brochure that HRH Princess Sibilla of Luxembourg is a director of The Gallery in Cork Street. Does she, I wonder, have a London address? Might she present the exhibition? There are deep German and French links here with the old people and their early missionaries.

I'll leave this now,
wishing you and Matthew a Happy Easter.
Elizabeth D

> *Soon after receiving this fax Rebecca Hossack phoned proposing that the exhibition go ahead as:* The Art of Eddie Burrup presented by the Rebecca Hossack Gallery together with Elizabeth Durack. *Mother agreed and arrangements proceeded to show at The Gallery in Cork Street, London, the following year.*
>
> PDC

Diary: 22 April 1999

2.30pm: I can feel the censor cinch tightening. Every day now it seems to get that little bit tighter.

We are working on the only door, and that a creaky one, ajar: the Ros Sadler[57] story in *Modern Painters* scheduled, we think, for the Summer edition.

Diary: 23 April 1999

3.00pm: Kathryn H called this morning and Colleen W yesterday evening re ED/EB and the Lesmurdie College Art exhibition respectively, all time and energy consuming. I feel put out, put about, put upon, put other-where than where I want to be. And there may be worse to come. The whole thing is a sort of conspiracy to stop me spending long uninterrupted days in communion with Eddie Burrup. I don't think people would do it to a man, or rather, a man would have some more than cooperative woman screening him from it all.

Diary: 25 April 1999, Anzac Day

Yesterday's *Weekend Australian* was bristling with interest, the Rosemary Neill story in the Focus section: "The debate we don't dare have" on whither Aboriginal self-determination. I can answer that one: self-determination and the 'enlightened' and dollar intensive policies of the past 30 years have proved a disaster. No one is facing up to the fact that the new order ushered in with so much fan-fare and congratulations is, in fact, proving to be the final *coup de grace* for the old people. Meanwhile however, the ideologues are holding power and ready to swipe right, left and centre if anyone dare to say so, in so many words.

Diary: 2 May 1999

12.30pm: My head is clearing and I am beginning to see a bit of a track ahead now through the dense brigalow. My mind has been working overtime since Rebecca's letter came in last Tuesday, and today, for the first time, it has settled down to a more normal pace.

A beautiful day here, bright sunshine after light rain in the night. P says the season has changed in Broome, the South Easterly is in and the days of heaven are back after all the dense and oppressive months of the Wet during which hardly visible winged creatures inject near lethal doses into the blood stream of humans.

Before the week is out I shall contact Rebecca and ask her to close on the Cork Street Gallery as the venue. We won't do better and clearly Rebecca likes the place. I shall tell her to try for a date, two weeks from November 1 or from October 1. The former would be better for P with her commitments there in Broome. The letter to Rod Eddington at Ansett goes off today.

Diary: 14th May 1999

10.30pm: It's not a triptych but three paintings about how: *Warrabuda* walked straight out of the fire – he was *Smoke*.

Worked all day on this with the phone off the hook – fax from P at 6 pm and another from CARE soliciting donations for the release of Pratt and Wallace? [Australian aid workers imprisoned in Yugoslavia.]

Diary: 23 August 1999

9.15pm: Went into the ABC for the interview with Liam Bartlett. They arranged a taxi for me, to and from. It was an easy non-demanding chat more than anything else and will go over the air tomorrow morning at 10.00am. Liam B is a wonderful young man and very good at his important job of communication. Ten minutes before this chat with old Granny he had been in the thick of the controversy over the disposal of nuclear waste with Pangea aiming to involve WA.

The Mount Hospital phoned to confirm the appointment with Dr Mark Buck for Wednesday next. It is hard to keep track of all these various appointments.

Diary: 25 August 1999

3.00pm: "The unbearable lightness of being" would seem to describe the trance-like state in which I now find myself.

Diary: 28 August 1999

6.00pm: Matt Galligan came and took photos of ten Eddie Bs. This made for a much better day with emphasis on something other than the physical. What a relief. I chose some from a small pile that I had not looked at for some time and was struck with the quality and variety of the works and their titles. *Smoke*, which measures about 122 x 92 cm, looks particularly good.

The ever-changing landscape of the human heart, mind, circumstance.

Diary: 13 September 1999

8.00pm: I can manage no more than the briefest outline: went into Hollywood Hospital on the evening of Friday 10th (this was the evening that Robert Juniper's exhibition opened and for which it was planned that Michael and I went together). Severe pain on right side.

M has taken over here so I don't know when I shall ever get to this page to outline the sudden alteration in my entire life. A time will come when there may be a chance to develop this – but meanwhile, also, M has been working out, in detail, the space within The Gallery in Cork Street and he sent off a fax to Caroline Edwards this evening asking for verification of certain measurements etc.

Michael cooked a roast dinner and have just had that. The same efficiency in the kitchen as at the drawing board. The weather is cold and bleak. A wind, not from the southwest but direct from the Antarctic.

Diary: 16 September 1999

9.30pm: *I have always tried to live in an ivory tower, but a tide* (now) *is beating at its walls, threatening to undermine it.* Gustave Flaubert, in a letter to Turgenev – November 13th 1872.[58] That about sums it up.

Diary: 21 November 1999

8.00am: Anniversary of a death

All we were needing
was a quiet farewell –
But no –
You wrenched
the Hour Glass
from the hand of Time
and smashed it –
glass slivers
flying everywhere
– oh –
I am bleeding.

Returned from Broome yesterday afternoon but rather than embark on things there which, in fact, to do justice to them could only be done by a Chekhov or a Joyce Cary, I shall get right on to the letter to Rebecca Hossack.

Letter: Elizabeth Durack at '47' to Rebecca Hossack in London, 22 November 1999

Dear Rebecca

As regards your request for some sort of a statement from me (your letter October 14th last) I might refer you to a letter of mine of 28th March (copy enclosed) and in which are set out some of the objectives that I have in mind for our exhibition.

Things have moved along since then of course but the sentence: 'the need for Eddie Burrup's work to be assessed aesthetically and independent of social and political issues' still holds and this I hope will be forthcoming.

It needs to be appreciated that this artist and his particular frame of reference is a resource – one untapped until his work emerged, fully formed, late in 1994.

The Art of Eddie Burrup is visionary although not in the sense of visionary as prophet or demiurge – he is far too pragmatic for that – but rather as a visionary medium who facilitates entry into an arcane and enigmatic world.

His visions are wildly eclectic – they range from Totemic Tumult (his central theme) enmeshed within the *Ngarangani* (the Dreaming), to random incident within historical times (the impact of the hoof upon the precinct of the paw being ever in mind), to fragments from the lives of the creation ancestors and the lives of old stock-men – identities of both races, current events, the ancient maps and their making, increase ceremonies, yards, fences, stock routes, devils, apparitions – even Bible stories.

The visions of Eddie Burrup are unpredictable, often inconsistent always precipitant. They are unified by a coda of their own and by the artist's unique therianthropic ideography. The titles accompanying the paintings are sometimes statements in themselves. The artist uses the bush vernacular as invented by the Aboriginals when the dislocated bands, all speaking different languages and dialects, created an Esperanto of their own. As Dante used colloquial speech rather than Latin for his *Comedia* so too do Eddie Burrup's titles lend endorsement to this form of communication.

Rebecca, will this be enough for your purpose there? I could enlarge but am reminded of Matisse's admonition to artists to speak only with their brushes and, of course, none of the above is consciously in mind when the images swim up to me out of the silt of the past or when I hear the old voices re-echoing from what is now another and a lost world.

Elizabeth D

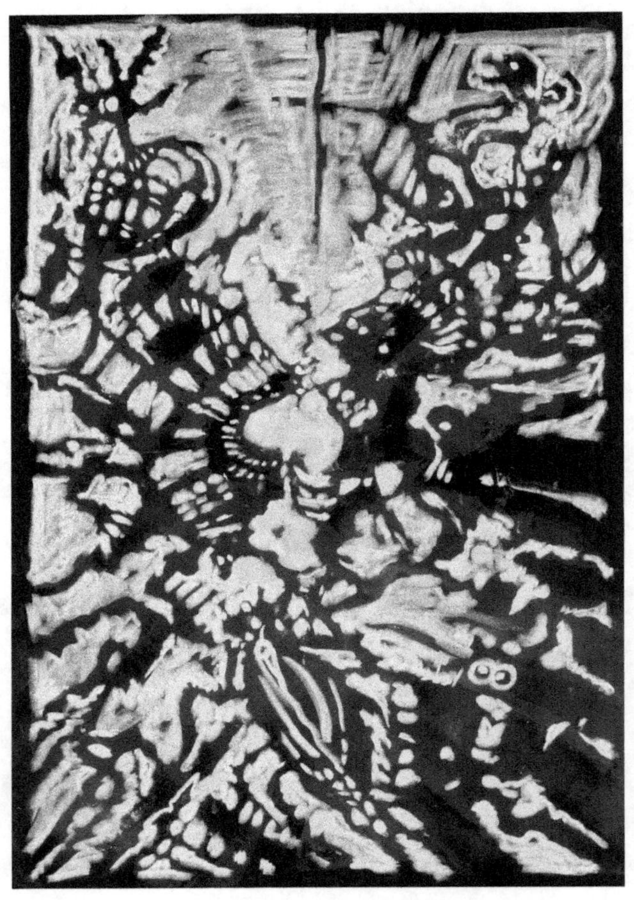

Crested Ibis landed at low tide on Karacumbi bar. The mission boat picked him up April 2000
from the series *The Art of Eddie Burrup*
mixed media on linen 133 x 92 cm, estate of ED

2000

E PUR SI MUOVE

The words – but still it moves – attributed to Galileo Galilei in 1633 at the end of his long trial on charges of heresy for holding the belief, contrary to Church orthodoxy, that the earth moved around the sun are expressive of courage, scepticism, perseverance and Faith. With some temerity, Michael and I chose e pur si muove *for our mother's headstone.*

It must have been towards the end of 1997 – or perhaps it was in 1998? – that I received a phone call about 8 o'clock one evening. I was in the kitchen at the rear of my Broome Gallery unwinding after a busy day. It was cousin Anne, Dr Anne Durack, calling from Perth.

In a calm voice Anne told me that mother had been taken by ambulance that afternoon to the nearby Hollywood Hospital. There she was undergoing 'tests'. She was expected home within a few days. I don't remember whether the word cancer came up. It probably did.

I spoke to mother the next day. She was reassuring, making light of it all, impatient to be home. She positively did not want me to drop everything and be with her in Perth. Looking back now, that was the first of countless calls from Anne to me over the next few years. I continued in regular touch with mother. She came north and stayed with me on several occasions.

We were in London together meeting Rebecca Hossack in November 1998; in Kununurra in June 1999 with Aunt Enid and family for the internment of Reg's ashes alongside those of Mary's at the Argyle Homestead Museum; and for ten heart-aching days in Broome in early May 2000. Mother's positive outlook, her endeavours to continue as normal – indeed her good humour most of the time, belied how sick she was. I wanted to close the gallery and be with her but she insisted it was not necessary. I think also that she might have preferred Anne's equanimity to my more emotional nature. Whatever it was, despite growing sons, her own elderly parents and a demanding husband, cousin Anne was in almost daily attendance on her Auntie Bet until very near the end when I was with her all the time.

PDC

Diary: 3 January 2000

Midnight: Three days now into the first century of a brand new millennium, but too late to more than note. Later I will try to describe the unbearable sadness of seeing them all flying away, through the rear mirror, further and further, out of sight now, but oh! not out of mind.

Only the frightened cattle see them –
See the dead men go by!
Cloven hoofs beating out one measure,
Bidding the stockmen know no leisure –
That's when the dead men take their pleasure!
That's when the dead men fly! [59]

Diary: 5 January 2000

I can't get back to this but must press on with the mad Application to ARTS WA.

Diary: 7 January 2000

A sense of urgency is gripping me. I thought it might be the Bonair cooler that I had serviced yesterday and that is blowing on to me as I write this and bringing some relief to the heat settling in now for the day but when I turned it off it made no difference to the current imperative.

Yesterday I broke through the hiatus and there suddenly before me almost unbeknown to me – almost as if I had not painted it – lay a new

6' x 3' composition: *Argyle Daylight's lost Thaloo*[60] – *the fence between Flying Fox yard and Smoke Creek effectively dissected the Thaloo place for Jabiru.*

And then today: *The Devil that can split itself in two* has shown up in drawings – I can't wait to get on to them. I could send these to P in Broome for her Horse exhibition.[61] But back to the turn of the century, the turn of the millennium, I kept to myself the really deep sadness of the occasion, the sense of loss and regret felt as I saw the old calendar fly past and along with it everything and everyone who had shaped what ever I was and what ever I became. There will be no more shaping for me. I am simply now what I am. Incidents that lie ahead will be only an unravelling not any more shaping. All my shapers are all in the past now, in another century.

In the pell-mell of my lost and loved all flying backwards, memory was completely random and eclectic. I thought of May and of Nurse Stevens simultaneously with Joe the fish-man; with Itchitara Sigura the Japanese cook at Ivanhoe in 1932; the very first visit of Kim to Ivanhoe and Mary, Reg and I waving down the little plane flown by Robby who landed it right beside the west verandah on wet ground to the whooping joy of all the blacks. There was a young man attached to the Ag. Dept of WA, David Wilcox. He gave up his seat to me on the plane back to Perth from Wiluna in 1952.

But even as one starts putting things into words order asserts itself. On New Year's Eve it wasn't like that. With words each incident or person recalled opens up a file of related persons and incidents but in the order-less kaleidoscope unwhirling all objects were of the same rank whether minor or major or – if they belonged to different times and different places, random higgledy-piggledy helter-skelter. It could be a way of doing one's biography with little various groupings holding hands, which they would never have done in life, flying backward flying backwards faster and faster. Now after only six days they are already out of sight – *don't start up on the Bimera file and lead on in sequence because it would be the opposite to New Year's Day 2000.*

Diary: 14 January 2000

5.30pm: Breakfast this morning at the Indiana Cafe on Cottesloe Beach with M and M and Fr Gerald Brennan,[62] a cool grey day and a thunder storm blew up when we were at the framers talking to Mark and Peter about the presentation of the smaller Eddie Burrups.

After the framers we ran on to Shenton Park Rehabilitation Centre and saw Ben Ward. His wife Mary, who is Sheba's[63] daughter, was with him and one of his children. They will be staying at the hospital for the next five weeks or so. I have missed Jeff Chunuma who returned to Kununurra yesterday.

Diary: 5 February 2000

9.30pm: Div [David][64] flew in from Baltimore, London, Singapore and was here for several hours giving generously of his time and thought to the, surely, tiny world of his ancient aunt. The Adelaide trip[65] has taken on another aspect since P turned up on the net an 'abstract' of a talk that Dr Christine Nicholls will be giving at a Conference in Canberra in a few days' time: *Masquerades and Identities – the Colonisation of the Soul?* She had said nothing to P of her involvement with this activity, as well as the Adelaide one, in all the time they have been in touch since last August and both P and I are feeling we have been hoodwinked into accepting the invitation to participate in the Adelaide show in view of the fact Christine Nicholls' paper:

> "will examine how the linguistic construction of 'Eddie' has been a necessary, indeed essential, accompaniment of the Eddie paintings, serving not only to 'authenticate' his art by commodifying the artist as an individual, but also as a discourse acting in the service of the salvation and redemption of a particularly unremarkable artist. My main focus will be on the symbiotic relationship between this linguistically-constructed 'Eddie' and the artistic works that have been the subject of such controversy."

In the face of this Div was inclined to argue in favour of our scrubbing the Adelaide trip altogether but this is not so simple for ARTSWA has paid $500 towards my Perth-Adelaide airfare (a first, ever, affirmative to an Arts Application from me) and also that I am deep into the Application for the new *Widening Horizons Fellowship* to help raise the wind for the London expedition. I've been working all afternoon on the COSTS for London and a Robin Ho is coming down on Monday afternoon to go over the forms with me which is part of the provisions for the entry.

But now the thought of going headfirst into a *melee* of demented women blue stockings is far from attractive to either P or me. Also we have already paid for the accommodation in Adelaide although had we known what we do now we would certainly not have paid out any money for the pleasure of being made Aunt Sallys of and sitting shots to boot.

It is really very worrying, although I must say when I first read Christine Nicholl's 'abstract' I could not help laughing.

Diary: 18 February 2000

8.30pm: Back from Hollywood Hospital this morning, went in on Wednesday 16th after speaking to Dr Craig Waters and telling him I was feeling good for nothing and pain on the right side. On Thursday at 1pm a 'cat' scan and at 5.00pm I was in the operating theatre waiting area on a trolley, looking at the low ceiling and trying to recite *sotto voce*: *Out where the dead men lie* … Another general anaesthetic and the right hand stent has been replaced with a bigger one – the first one only lasted two weeks whereas I thought the things were meant to last six months.

Craig saw me yesterday evening, he didn't say much and I didn't ask much either. It was a relief to be back here after all the rush and noise of the hospital.

Diary: 25 February 2000

P came down from Broome a few days ago. We plan to leave early Friday morning for Adelaide which is turning out to be a fiasco of an expedition as the Panel discussion at Flinders University, *From Appreciation to Appropriation,* seems to have turned out to be almost entirely a witch hunt against ED/EB, all too complex to more than note here. It has turned very hot again.

Diary: 8 March 2000

4.30pm: Trying to pack a small case to take to Adelaide for early morning lift-off tomorrow. Neither P nor I have any heart for this expedition since hearing about the antagonistic tone of the speakers on the panel for *From Appreciation to Appropriation.* Very hot oppressive day and working on the brochure for Scott 4 Colour or, rather, as it is now called Scott Print. Edward Stephenson came down yesterday morning and we went through things together. Maureen Smith, back from a visit to Vietnam, phoned and was also concerned for me. She said she wished I were not going to Adelaide.

Diary: 14 March 2000

8.00pm: The Adelaide expedition is now behind us. To a large extent the foreboding concerning this was the worst part of it. As things turned out P and I have returned to Perth with feelings of relief and some satisfaction. In the end I attended only one session, the last, on Sunday evening 12 March. P went to the one on the Friday evening and after this saw the whole situation in better perspective and with more a sense of where to go or, rather, how to proceed.

The following is what she said in her turn as we lined up on the panel:

> As most here would be aware much of the focus of the public forums over the past week has been on the Eddie Burrup Affair, not on the Art of Eddie Burrup but on the persona of Eddie Burrup, or, more directly on the person, Elizabeth Durack.

In effect, a kind of informal trial has been taking place during which one side, one point of view only, has been put forward.

To that extent, there being no real debate, the forums have failed in the original stated intention to be 'entirely educational'.

Elizabeth, as a highly creative artist is not here to defend herself; nor for that matter am I. At this stage I have just one point to make: Elizabeth did what she did, entered paintings in two Aboriginal shows, in order to get the work out and noticed on its own merits. And in this she succeeded.

As the work of Eddie Burrup the paintings were applauded and hailed as those of a genius, as the work of Elizabeth Durack the work was, and continues to be, vilified, maligned, defamed. Despite this and most remarkably under the circumstances Elizabeth has continued to work on.

At times, when I myself have almost despaired at the turn of events she has said, hold on, the story is not over yet. And that, I now know, to be true.

The above had the effect, for the first time, of putting Christine Nicholls on the defensive and, to a certain extent, Doreen Mellor as well.

All the proceedings have been recorded and we have already caught up with the earlier sessions that so upset and worried young Matthew Durack [grandson of brother Bill] and others who had attended the crowded ones prior to our arrival.

Diary: 19 April 2000 5.30pm

Note today as a change – a turning point.[66]

P came in at 8 pm having been met at the airport by Doug and the days have been flying, so much to do now, the 'Acquittal' i.e. the accounting for the Adelaide expedition went off to ARTSWA yesterday with P's help.

We decided to keep it very bland with really no reference to the malice behind the forums towards that old sitting duck of core-culture Australia – ED/EB.

Diary: 25 April 2000, Anzac Day 9.00pm
Pity about 'a great tide threatening to engulf my precious ivory tower.' It is developing into a virtual tsunami. P is here. Liam arrived from Brisbane. Michael *and* I think, [granddaughter] Julie will be here by Friday. Meanwhile the piece for *The Australian* is awaiting a brief cover note and then dispatch. Tomorrow I trust.[67]

Anzac Day has now come and gone. Liam went to the Dawn Service in Kings Park. Together P, L and I went to the Windsor Theatre to see *Topsy-Turvy,* an absolutely faultless piece of art, theatre, history, and really can't remember when I have enjoyed a film so much.

The Palliative Care Sisters are in almost daily attendance upon me but, of course, I am *far* from bed or housebound and between everything I am continuing to work. *Signals …* is nearly finished and also another very good composition for which, strange to say, I have not, to date, got a title.[68] I must leave this now. P found my book, *Tin Mosques*[69] and my Claddagh ring.

In the end I bought rosemary rather than lavender from the Dalkeith Garden Centre (Swee's place now and looking well-cared for) to go in the pots by the gate. The marigolds that P planted when she came down from Broome on the 14th April are doing well. I don't know whether to lie down now and wait for *my Garry come back from the Indies …*[70] in bed or to keep sitting up. It is getting harder to sit up too long because of some shortage of breath.

Bill's plane is due in [from Toowoomba], I think, at 1.00am.

Mother died at home around 11.00am on Thursday 25th May. Michael was there, Ruth was phoning from Philadelphia, other cousins and neighbours and friends were in and out.

Two days previously Scott Print delivered the London catalogue designed by Elizabeth, and the local ANZ bank manager called in, at mother's request, to attend to the transfer to us of financial matters.

The next day Elizabeth received the Sacrament of Extreme Unction from both Father Gerald Brennan and Monseigneur James Nestor. Soon after they left she made the last entry in her Day Book.

In a just legible hand she wrote:

The beginning
the beginning to the end
there is no end
but a loop
Mary and Elizabeth together
it is not so hard …

~

The Art of Eddie Burrup – *28 paintings – opened in London three months later. Michael and I were there to assist. The show went well. It served to confirm Elizabeth's earlier assertion: "the story is not over yet."*

Selected Chronology
Elizabeth Durack (1915–2000)

Exhibitions

1946-47	*Time & Tide*	Museum & Art Gallery of WA Perth; Athenaeum, Melbourne; David Jones Gallery Sydney.
1954	*Love Magic*	Anthony Hordens Gallery, Sydney.
1961	*Recent Australian Painting*	Whitechapel Gallery London.
1964	*Retrospective*	AGWA.
1979	*Discoverers & Explorers*	World Trade Centre, New York NY.
1981	*Kimberley Calls*	RFDS Benefit exhibition Melbourne.
1989	*Out of Australia*	Australia–Ireland Conference Dublin & Galway.
1991	*Out of Sight–Out of Mind*	Perth Cultural Centre.
1995	*Derivations & Directions*	AGWA.
1997	*The Art of Eddie Burrup*	Durack Gallery Broome.
2000	*The Art of Eddie Burrup*	*presented by* the Rebecca Hossack Gallery at The Gallery in Cork Street, London.

Murals, painting series, commissions

1950	*Coastline*	Darwin Club/Museums & Art Galleries of the NT.
1953	*The Cord to Altcheringa*	UWA.
1954	*Love Magic*	Private collections.
1955	*Chant for Kurdaitcha*	AGWA.
1956	*The Legend of the Black Swan*	Sir Charles Gairdner Hospital Perth.
1960	*Shearing – its Practice and Poetry*	Australian Wool Board Melbourne.
1961-65	*Look at the state we're in!*	Geraldton Regional Gallery and Private collections.
1963-64	*The Argyle*, *Ivanhoe*, *Auvergne*, *Moola Bulla*, *Cunderlee*, *Mulga Queen* and *Wiluna* scrolls	AIATSIS Canberra.
1969	*Bougainville Island*	Rio Tinto Melbourne.
1969	*Background to Hamersley Iron*	CRA Tom Price/Melbourne.
1971	*The Nigerian scrolls*	Estate of ED.
1975	*Flightless birds achieve lift-off*	Private collection.
1975-94	*The Rim, the rim of our brittle and disintegrating world …*	Private collections.
1994	*Dreaming up the Victoria*	Estate of ED.
1994-2000	*The Art of Eddie Burrup*	Private collections and the Estate of ED.

Awards

CMG 1983, OBE 1966, Hon D Litt (UWA) 1996, Hon D Litt (Murdoch U) 1994

Bibliography

Co-productions: Mary & Elizabeth Durack

Allabout, Sydney, 1935.
Chunuma – Little-bit King, Sydney, 1936.
Son of Djaro, Perth, 1940.
The Way of the Whirlwind, Sydney, 1941.

Illustrated books (selected)

Australian Legendary Tales K Langloh Parker and H Drake-Brockman (eds), Sydney, 1953.
An Attempt to Eat the Moon and other stories recounted from the Aborigines, Deborah Buller Murphy (ed), Melbourne, 1958.

Books written & illustrated by Elizabeth Durack

Seeing—through Papua New Guinea, Melbourne, 1968.
Face Value: Women of Papua New Guinea, Sydney, 1969.
Seeing—through the Philippines, Melbourne, 1971.
Seeing—through Indonesia, Melbourne, 1977.

Unpublished manuscripts (selected)

The House that Took Off (1963)
Seeing—through New York (1967 & 1979)
Seeing—through Nigeria (1971)
The Survivor (1982)
The Time of Our Lives (1987)
Eddie Burrup talks about himself (1995)
Reinvent … how I reinvented myself in my 80th year (1995–2000)

Books and articles by other authors (selected)

Hutchings, PAE (ed), *The Art of Elizabeth Durack*, Sydney, 1982.
Niall, Brenda, *True North: The Story of Mary and Elizabeth Durack*, Melbourne, 2012.

McDonald, John, "Let's Look at the Big Picture", *Sydney Morning Herald*, 12 March 1997.
McCulloch, Susan, "What's the Fuss?" *Weekend Australian Magazine*, 5 July, 1997.
Douglas, Elena, "An overlooked Australian artist and author", *Australian Financial Review*, 17 March 2015.

Website

www.elizabethdurack.com

Endnotes

1 "A work of art is a corner of nature seen through a temperament", Emile Zola.
2 Elizabeth Durack, *The Time of Our Lives,* an unpublished memoir (1987).
3 Ibid.
4 Elizabeth's brothers were Reg, Kim, Bill and David.
5 ED in London, writing to Reg on Argyle, October 1936.
6 Extract from video recording *Australian Biography*, a series profiling influential Australians of the 20th century produced and directed by Robin Hughes and Linda Kruger. Film Australia in association with SBS TV Lindfield, NSW, 1997.
7 Father John McGrath was the person who famously radioed Darwin about the Japanese bombers flying towards the port in February 1942 – a warning that went unheeded.
8 ED on Ivanhoe, writing to Mary in Perth, 22 May 1947.
9 From Bernard Smith's opening speech – ED personal archives.
10 Possibly from cartoonist George Finey – friend and best man at the wedding of ED and Frank Clancy.
11 Bill had married the writer, Noni Braham, soon after the War.
12 It was a long held ambition to build a gracious home in the north in harmony with the landscape.
13 Mary Durack, "Johnny Walker–O", *Pilgrimage – A journey through the life and writings of Mary Durack*, edited by Patsy and Naomi Millett, Bantam Books, Sydney, 2000.
14 Michael Patrick Durack (MPD), a 'first-footer', arrived in Kimberley from Thylungra, Queensland, at the age of 21 in 1886.
15 Near the end of his life MPD was determined to sell the stations. His children, with the exception of Reg who it was agreed should receive a block of country excised from Auvergne in the Northern Territory, were all opposed to the sale. In March 1950 the CD&D properties were sold. Six months later MPD was dead.
16 ED in Perth writing to Ida Mann, 3 November 1954.
17 Ida Mann (1893-1983). Ophthalmologist, Graduate, London School of Medicine and Oxford University, settled Perth, 1949. As a Consultant with the WA Health Department, Dr Mann travelled widely to remote regions. She was the first to record widespread incidence of trachoma among aborigines.
18 Salomon (Salek) Minc, Polish born medical practitioner. Settled Perth, 1939. Art patron.
19 The anniversary of Tom Naughton's death in 1937.
20 ED in Melbourne writing to Melbourne art critics, 24 June 1961.
21 *Paintings*, Elizabeth Durack, Athenaeum Gallery, 19 June – 1 July 1961.
22 Sam and Phyll Male, prominent, long-time residents of Broome. Their 17 year-old son, Richard, had drowned when swimming at Cottesloe beach a month earlier.
23 Jack Wherra was a West Kimberley artist. Early in March 1963 ED initiated moves, through the local Shire and Crown Law Department, for Wherra to receive a Royal Pardon. This was granted soon after the Queen's visit. On release, Jack Wherra went to live amongst his people on the Mowanjum Community, Derby, where he was renowned for his boab nut carvings and traditional stories.
24 To mark the occasion, students from St Mary's School, run by the Sisters of St John of God, had produced almost 30 paintings depicting aspects of present-day Broome for display during the Royal Visit. The works, preserved by Elizabeth, are now held by Broome's SSJG

Heritage Centre where they are exhibited from time to time.

25 Marianna and Ferdinand (Ferry) Korwill, refugees from Austria, patrons of the arts; friends of Mary and Elizabeth; had settled in Dalkeith c1940.

26 Russell Dumas, head of the WA Public Works Department.

27 Christiani Nielsen, the Danish engineering company in joint venture with Perth-based Clough Engineering, successfully tendered for the Diversion Dam, completed 1963, and the Ord River 'Top Dam', completed in 1972.

28 Charles Court, subsequently WA Premier, at the time was Minister for Industrial Development.

29 The Sydney based company, Northern Developments, had extended its focus – with State government sanction – from West to East Kimberley by 1960.

30 Quoting Ward Jackson of the Solomon R Guggenheim Museum, New York, November 1979.

31 Elizabeth Durack, *Seeing—through Nigeria, An artist's impressions of the Federation*, illustrated unpublished manuscript (1971).

32 ED writing to Robert and Janet Holmes à Court, November 1981.

33 *Essay/Review* in *Quadrant* – Marc Gumbert, *Neither Justice Nor Reason: A Legal and Anthropological Analysis of Aboriginal Land Rights* (UQP, St Lucia) 1984.

34 Elizabeth Durack, "Artes Australis Percepta", unpublished essay (1988).

35 Elizabeth Durack, *The House that Took Off*, illustrated unpublished manuscript (1963).

36 Alistair McAlpine of West Green. Businessman, politician, catalyst for change, inveterate collector visited Broome in the early 1980s, saw its potential as a major tourist destination, invested heavily and changed Broome forever.

37 Elizabeth Durack, "On political correctness in the art world", unpublished essay (1993).

38 Patrick Durack, fourth son of ED's brother Bill and Patrick's niece, Kate.

39 Perpetua formally added 'Durack Clancy' to her name after divorce from Rex Hobcroft in 1998.

40 ED is referring to a March-April partial retrospective, *Derivations & Directions*, at the Art Gallery of WA and a simultaneous commercial exhibition at the Stafford Studios, Cottesloe.

41 Gabrielle Pizzi, Australian art dealer, leading promoter of Aboriginal art at home and abroad. Established Gallery Gabrielle Pizzi in Flinders Lane, Melbourne, 1987.

42 The reference is to the opening of an exhibition *Putting Ourselves in the Picture* coinciding with the 20th Anniversary of International Women's Year.

43 When presenting Aboriginal art in the 1990s it was customary to have a photograph of the artist alongside his/her paintings.

44 The reference is to the imminent death of ED's sister, Mary.

45 Paula Latos-Valier has held a number of senior Art Director appointments in Australia.

46 Giovanni Battista Piranesi (1720–1778). Known for his study of the ruins of ancient Rome and his imaginative etchings of them as 'prisons'. Piranesi's *Le Carceri d'Invenzione* were in part a *memento mori* of Rome's Golden Age. ED felt instant rapport with Piranesi's work when she first came across it in the mid-1970s.

47 James Joyce, *Finnegan's Wake* 137.33–36: 'unconsciously explaining for inkstands, *with a meticulosity bordering on the insane*, the various meanings of all the different foreign parts of speech he misused'. For over 50 years ED had been at one with Joyce's enjoyment of 'misusing' and playing around with various foreign words to create new views of the world.

48 Robert Smith, "The Incarnations of Eddie Burrup", *Art Monthly Australia*, March 1997, No 97.

49 The reference is to three Burrup paintings touring with Tandanya's *Native Titled Now* exhibition being pulled from the walls of Victoria's Shepparton Regional Gallery.

50 Ernie Bridge pastoralist, businessman, country music singer, Labor Independent MP.

51 The reference is to objections raised by the AGWA's Curator of Aboriginal art to showing paintings from ED's 1954 series *The Cord to Alcheringa* in a 1995 retrospective. Jeff Chunuma Rainyerri was consulted about the paintings. He confirmed they represented a synthesis of two worlds and could be seen by the general public.

52 Jan Mayman, journalist and friend.

53 Rebecca Hossack, Australian-born director of the Rebecca Hossack Gallery, London.

54 This refers to an incident over a Christmas display window in BankWest, Perth, where an Eddie Burrup painting featured. Robert Eggington organised a demonstration against the inclusion of the Burrup work. BankWest and Perth City Council caved in and removed the painting. Peter David and 'The Uncles' sent a statement to *The West Australian* in support of the painting remaining on show.

55 Elizabeth Durack, unpublished manuscript, 1998.

56 Director Maureen Smith & Associates, Independent Human Resources Professional, art and literary critic.

57 Rosalin Sadler, "Is there no-one to untie us?", *Modern Painters* Vol 12, No 2, London, 1999.

58 Actual quote: "I have always tried to live in an ivory tower, but a tide of shit is beating at its walls, threatening to undermine it … it's not a question of politics but of the mental state of France", Gustave Flaubert.

59 Barcroft Boake, *Where the Dead Men Lie.*

60 *Thaloo* a general term for a sacred place where Rites of Increase were performed.

61 An exhibition *Salute the Horse* being prepared at Durack Gallery to coincide with the start in Broome of a horse ride relay around Australia.

62 Michael and Margaret Clancy and Fr Gerald Brennan, SJ, a school friend of Michael.

63 Ben Ward, Traditional Owner, adopted son of Jeff Chunuma Rainyerri, was recovering from a serious road accident. His mother-in-law, Sheba, was a young woman on Ivanhoe in the 1930s.

64 David Durack, physician, eldest son of Reg Durack based in the US for many years.

65 "The Adelaide trip" – to attend the Festival exhibition: *From Appreciation to Appropriation: Indigenous Influences and Images in Australian Visual Art* curated by Christine Nicholls of Flinders University.

66 This possibly refers to increased doses of morphine for pain.

67 Elizabeth Durack,"The Way It Was", a reminiscence of Wyndham published in *TorchSong* a supplement to *The Australian* for the Sydney Olympics, September, 2000.

68 Elizabeth's Anzac Day painting became *Crested Ibis landed at low tide on Karacumbi bar. The mission boat picked him up.* It echoes an incident from 60 years earlier when she sailed with Mary on *Maroubra* from Timber Creek to Darwin.

69 Christine Stevens, *Tin Mosques and Ghan Towns* (OUP, Melbourne, 1989).

70 *Finnegan's Wake*: "Is that the Poolbeg flasher beyant, pharphar. Or a fireboat coasting nyar the Kyshtna or a glow I behold within a hedge or *my Garry come back from the Indies*?"

Index

www.ingramcontent.com/pod-product-compliance
Lightning Source LLC
LaVergne TN
LVHW010053110826
845155LV00028B/325

* 9 7 8 1 9 2 5 5 0 1 0 9 4 *